Where do I go for answers to my travel questions?

What's the best and easiest way to plan and book my trip?

frommers.travelocity.com

Frommer's, the travel guide leader, has teamed up with **Travelocity.com,** the leader in online travel, to bring you an in-depth, easy-to-use resource designed to help you plan and book your trip online.

At **frommers.travelocity.com**, you'll find free online updates about your destination from the experts at Frommer's plus the outstanding travel planning and purchasing features of Travelocity.com. Travelocity.com provides reservations capabilities for 95 percent of all airline seats sold, more than 47,000 hotels, and over 50 car rental companies. In addition, Travelocity.com offers more than 2,000 exciting vacation and cruise packages. Travelocity.com puts you in complete control of your travel planning with these and other great features:

> **Expert travel guidance from Frommer's** - over 150 writers reporting from around the world!

> **Best Fare Finder** - an interactive calendar tells you when to travel to get the best airfare

> **Fare Watcher** - we'll track airfare changes to your favorite destinations

> **Dream Maps** - a mapping feature that suggests travel opportunities based on your budget

> **Shop Safe Guarantee** - 24 hours a day / 7 days a week live customer service, and more!

Whether traveling on a tight budget, looking for a quick weekend getaway, or planning the trip of a lifetime, Frommer's guides and Travelocity.com will make your travel dreams a reality. You've bought the book, now book the trip!

A New Star-Rating System
& Other Exciting News
from Frommer's!

In our continuing effort to publish the savviest, most up-to-date, and most appealing travel guides available, we've added some great new features.

Frommer's guides now include a new star-rating system. Every hotel, restaurant, and attraction is rated from 0 to 3 stars to help you set priorities and organize your time.

We've also added seven brand-new features that point you to the great deals, in-the-know advice, and unique experiences that separate travelers from tourists. Throughout the guide look for:

Finds	Special finds—those places only insiders know about
Fun Fact	Fun facts—details that make travelers more informed and their trips more fun
Kids	Best bets for kids—advice for the whole family
Moments	Special moments—those experiences that memories are made of
Overrated	Places or experiences not worth your time or money
Tips	Insider tips—some great ways to save time and money
Value	Great values—where to get the best deals

Frommer's®

PORTABLE

London

2002

by Darwin Porter and Danforth Prince

Hungry Minds™

Best-Selling Books • Digital Downloads • e-Books
Answer Networks • e-Newsletters • Branded Web Sites • e-Learning
New York, NY • Cleveland, OH • Indianapolis, IN

ABOUT THE AUTHORS

Authors **Darwin Porter** and **Danforth Prince** share their love of their favorite European city in this guide. Porter, a bureau chief for *The Miami Herald* at 21 who later worked in television advertising, wrote the first-ever book about London for Frommer's. He's joined by Prince, formerly of the Paris bureau of the *New York Times*. Together, they're the authors of several best-selling Frommer's guides, notably to England, France, the Caribbean, Italy and Germany.

Published by:

HUNGRY MINDS, INC.

909 Third Avenue
New York, NY 10022

ISBN: 0-7645-6474-9
ISSN: 1094-7663

Editor: Kathleen Warnock
Production Editor: Ian Skinnari
Photo Editor: Richard Fox
Cartographer: John Decamillis
Production by Hungry Minds Indianapolis Production Services

SPECIAL SALES

For general information on Hungry Minds' products and services, please contact our Customer Care department; within the U.S. at 800-762-2974, outside the U.S. at 317-572-3993, or fax 317-572-4002. For sales inquiries and reseller information, including discounts, bulk sales, customized editions, and premium sales, please contact our Customer Care department at 800-434-3422.

Manufactured in the United States of America

5   4   3   2   1

Contents

List of Maps

An Invitation to the Reader

In researching this book we have discovered many wonderful places—hotels, restaurants, shops, and more. We're sure you'll find others. Please tell us about them, so that we can share the information with your fellow travelers in upcoming editions. If you were disappointed with a recommendation, we'd love to know that, too. Please write to:

Frommer's Portable London 2002
Hungry Minds, Inc. • 909 Third Avenue • New York, NY 10022

An Additional Note

Please be advised that travel information is subject to change at any time, and this is especially true of prices. We therefore suggest that you write or call ahead for confirmation when making your travel plans. The authors, editors, and publishers cannot be held responsible for the experiences of readers while traveling. Your safety is important to us, however, so we encourage you to stay alert and be aware of your surroundings. Keep a close eye on cameras, purses, and wallets, all favorite targets of thieves and pickpockets.

What the Symbols Mean

The following abbreviations are used for credit cards:

AE	American Express	DISC	Discover	V	Visa
DC	Diners Club	MC	MasterCard		

FROMMERS.COM

Now that you have the guidebook to a great trip, visit our website at **www.frommers.com** for travel information on nearly 2,000 destinations. With features updated regularly, we give you instant access to the most current trip-planning information available. At Frommers.com, you'll also find the best prices on air fares, accommodations, and car rentals—and you can even book travel online through our travel booking partners. At Frommers.com, you'll also find the following:

- Daily Newsletter highlighting the best travel deals
- Hot Spot of the Month/Vacation Sweepstakes & Travel Photo Contest
- More than 200 Travel Message Boards
- Outspoken Newsletters and Feature Articles on travel bargains, vacation ideas, tips and resources, and more!

Here's what critics say about Frommer's:

"Amazingly easy to use. Very portable, very complete."

—*Booklist*

"The only mainstream guide to list specific prices. The Walter Cronkite of guidebooks—with all that implies."

—*Travel & Leisure*

"Complete, concise, and filled with useful information."

—*New York Daily News*

"Hotel information is close to encyclopedic."

—*Des Moines Sunday Register*

"Detailed, accurate, and easy-to-read information for all price ranges."

—*Glamour Magazine*

Planning Your Trip to London

This chapter tackles the hows of your trip to London—issues required to get your trip together and hit the road, whether you're a frequent traveler or a first-timer.

1 Visitor Information

The British Tourist Authority maintains a webpage at **www. visitbritain.com**. You can also get information from **British Tourist Authority** offices. There's one in the **United States,** at 551 Fifth Ave., Suite 701, New York, NY 10176-0799 (© **800/462-2748** or 212/986-2200). In **Canada,** it's at 5915 Airport Rd., Mississagua, Toronto, ON L4V 1T1 (© **888/VISITUK;** fax 905/405-1835). In **Australia,** the office is at Level 16, Gateway, 1 Macquarie Place, Sydney, NSW 2000 (© **02/9377-4400**). In **New Zealand,** go to the NZI House, 17th Floor, 151 Queen St., Auckland 1 (© **09/ 303-1446;** fax 09/377-6965).

For a full information pack on London, write to the **London Tourist Board,** Glen House, Stag Place, Victoria, SWIE 5LT (© **020/7932-2000**). You can also call the recorded-message service, **Visitorcall** (© **0839/123456**), 24 hours a day. This number cannot be dialed outside Britain. Various topics are listed; calls cost 60p ($1) per minute.

Time Out, the most up-to-date magazine for what's happening in London, is online at **www.timeout.co.uk**. You can pick up a print copy at any international newsstand.

London Guide (**www.cs.ucl.ac.uk**) is run by London's University College and has information on cheap dining and accommodations in the Bloomsbury area. There are also travelogues and tips for theatergoers.

To book rooms with a credit card (MasterCard or Visa), call the **London Tourist Board Booking Office** at © **020/7604-2890,** or fax them at 020/7372-2068. They're open Monday to Friday from 9am to 6pm (London time). There is a £5 ($7.50) fee for booking.

2 Entry Requirements & Customs Documents

Citizens of the United States, Canada, Australia, New Zealand, and South Africa require a passport to enter the United Kingdom, but no visa. Irish citizens and citizens of European Union countries need only an identity card. The maximum stay for visitors is 6 months. Some Customs officials request proof that you have the means to leave the country (usually a round-trip ticket) and means of support while you're in Britain. If you're planning to fly on from the United Kingdom to a country that requires a visa, it's wise to secure the visa before you leave home.

Your valid driver's license and at least 1 year's experience is required to drive personal or rented cars.

WHAT YOU CAN BRING INTO THE U.K.   Visitors (17 and older) from non-European Union (EU) countries bringing in goods bought tax-free within the EU may bring in 200 cigarettes (or 50 cigars or 250 grams of loose tobacco), 2 liters of wine, 1 liter of liquor (over 44 proof) or 2 liters of liquor (under 44 proof), and 2 fluid ounces of perfume. Visitors entering England from a European Union country may bring in goods bought tax-paid in the EU as follows: 800 cigarettes, 200 cigars, and 1 kilogram of loose tobacco; 90 liters of wine, 10 liters of alcohol (over 44 proof), and 110 liters of beer; plus unlimited amounts of perfume.

You can't bring your pet to England. Six months' quarantine is required. An illegally imported animal may be destroyed.

WHAT YOU CAN BRING HOME   Returning **U.S. citizens** who have been away for 48 hours or more are allowed to bring back, once every 30 days, $400 worth of merchandise duty free. You'll be charged a flat rate of 10% duty on the next $1,000 worth of purchases. Have your receipts handy. On gifts, the duty-free limit is $100. You cannot bring fresh foodstuffs into the United States; tinned foods, however, are allowed. For more information, contact the **U.S. Customs Service,** 1301 Constitution Ave. (P.O. Box 7407), Washington, DC 20044 (© **202/927-6724**), and request the free pamphlet *Know Before You Go.* It's also available on the Web at **www.customs.ustreas.gov**.

For a summary of **Canadian** rules, write for the booklet *I Declare,* issued by **Revenue Canada,** 2265 St. Laurent Blvd., Ottawa, Ontario K1G 4KE (© **506/636-5064;** www.ccra-adrc.gc.ca). Canada allows its citizens a Can$750 exemption, and you're allowed to bring back, duty free, 200 cigarettes, 200 grams of tobacco,

40 imperial ounces of liquor, and 50 cigars. You're also allowed to mail gifts to Canada from abroad at the rate of Can$60 a day, if they're unsolicited and don't contain alcohol or tobacco (write on the package "Unsolicited gift, under $60 value"). Valuables should be declared on the Y-38 form before departure, including serial numbers of valuables you already own, like foreign-made cameras. *Note:* The $750 exemption can be used only once a year and only after an absence of 7 days.

The duty-free allowance in **Australia** is A$400 or, for those under 18, A$200. Personal property mailed back from England should be marked "Australian goods returned" to avoid payment of duty. Upon returning to Australia, citizens can bring in 250 cigarettes or 250 grams of loose tobacco, and 1.125 liters of alcohol. If you're returning with valuable goods you already own, such as foreign-made cameras, you should file form B263. A helpful brochure, available from Australian consulates or Customs offices, is *Know Before You Go.* For more information, contact **Australian Customs Services,** GPO Box 8, Sydney, NSW 2001 (✆ **02/9213-2000;** www.customs.gov.au).

The duty-free allowance for **New Zealand** is NZ$700. Citizens over 17 can bring in 200 cigarettes, 50 cigars, or 250 grams of tobacco (or a mixture of all three if their combined weight doesn't exceed 250 grams); plus 4.5 liters of wine and beer, or 1.125 liters of liquor. New Zealand currency does not carry import or export restrictions. Fill out a certificate of export, listing the valuables you are taking out of the country; that way, you can bring them back without paying duty. Most questions are answered in a free pamphlet available at New Zealand consulates and Customs offices: *New Zealand Customs Guide for Travelers,* Notice no. 4. For more information, contact **New Zealand Customs,** 50 Anzac Ave., P.O. Box 29, Auckland (✆ **09/359-6655;** www.customs.govt.nz).

3 Money

POUNDS & PENCE   Britain's monetary system is based on the pound (£), which is made up of 100 pence (written as "p"). Britons also call pounds "quid." There are £1 and £2 coins, as well as coins of 50p, 20p, 10p, 5p, 2p, and 1p. Banknotes come in denominations of £5, £10, £20, and £50.

As a general guideline, the price conversions in this book have been computed at the rate of £1 = $1.50 (U.S.). Bear in mind, however, that exchange rates fluctuate daily.

ATMs   ATMs are easily found throughout London. ATMs are also connected to the major networks at airports such as Heathrow and Gatwick. You'll usually get a better exchange rate by withdrawing money at an ATM (currency exchange booths take a huge commission or give an unfavorable rate, or both), but your bank may charge a fee for using a foreign ATM. You may also need a different PIN to use overseas ATMs. Call your bank before you go.

The most popular ATM networks are **Cirrus** (℃ **800/424-7787;** www.mastercard.com) and **Plus** (℃ **800/843-7587;** www.visa. com), check the back of your ATM card to see which your bank belongs to. You can use the websites or the 800 numbers to locate ATMs in your destination or ask your bank for a list of overseas ATMs.

CURRENCY EXCHANGE   When exchanging money, you'll have to pay a service charge at both banks and ATMs. London banks are usually open Monday to Friday from 9:30am to 3:30pm. Many of the "high street" branches are now open until 5pm; a handful of central London branches are open until noon on Saturday, including **Barclays,** 208 Kensington High St., W8 (℃ **08457/ 555-555**). Money exchange is now also available at competitive rates at major London **post offices,** with a 1% service charge. Money can be exchanged during off-hours at change bureaus found at small shops and in hotels, railway stations (including the international terminal at Waterloo Station), travel agencies, and airports, but their rates are poor and they charge high service fees. Examine the prices and rates before handing over your dollars, as there's no consumer organization to regulate the activities of privately run change bureaus.

In a recent *Time Out* survey of exchange facilities, **American Express** came out on top, with the lowest commission on dollar transactions. They're at 30-31 Haymarket, SW1 (℃ **800/221-7282** or 020/7484-9600) and other locations throughout the city. They charge no commission when cashing traveler's checks. However, a flat rate of £2 ($3) is charged when exchanging the dollar to the pound. Most agencies tend to charge a percentage rate commission (usually 2%) with a £2 to £3 ($3 to $4.50) minimum charge. Other reputable firms are **Thomas Cook,** 6 Mount St., WI (℃ **800/ 223-7373** or 0800/622-101), which has branches at Victoria Station, Marble Arch, and other locations; and, for 24-hour foreign exchange, **Chequepoint,** at 548 Oxford St., W1N 9HJ (℃ **020/ 7723-1005**) and locations throughout London (hours vary). Try not to change money at your hotel; the rates tend to be horrendous.

CREDIT CARDS   Credit cards are a safe way to carry money and provide a convenient record of all your expenses. You can also withdraw cash advances from your credit cards at any bank (although you'll pay interest on the advance the moment you receive the cash, and you won't get frequent-flyer miles on an airline credit card). At most banks, you can get a cash advance at the ATM with your PIN. If you don't have a PIN, call your credit card company and ask for one. It usually takes 5 to 7 business days, but some banks provide the number over the phone if you pass a security clearance.

TRAVELER'S CHECKS   Traveler's checks are becoming something of an anachronism from the days before 24-hour ATMs. However, traveler's checks are as reliable as currency, unlike personal checks, and can be replaced if lost or stolen.

You can get traveler's checks at almost any bank. **American Express** offers denominations of $10, $20, $50, $100, $500, and $1,000. You'll pay a service charge ranging from 1% to 4%. You can also get American Express traveler's checks over the phone by calling ✆ **800/221-7282;** by using this number, Amex gold and platinum cardholders are exempt from the 1% fee. AAA members can get checks without a fee at most AAA offices.

Visa offers traveler's checks at Citibank locations nationwide, as well as several other banks. The service charge ranges between 1.5% and 2%; checks come in denominations of $20, $50, $100, $500, and $1,000. **MasterCard** also offers traveler's checks. Call ✆ **800/223-9920** for a location near you.

Keep a record of your traveler's checks' serial numbers—separate from the checks—so you're ensured a refund in an emergency.

Odds are that if your wallet is gone, the police won't recover it. However, it is still worth informing them; your credit card company or insurer might require a police report number.

4 When to Go

CLIMATE

Charles Dudley Warner said that the trouble with the weather is that everybody talks about it but nobody does anything about it. Well, Londoners talk about weather more than anyone, but have also done something about it: air pollution control has resulted in the virtual disappearance of the pea soup fogs that once blanketed the city.

A typical London-area weather forecast for a summer day predicts "scattered clouds with sunny periods and showers, possibly heavy at times." Summer temperatures seldom rise above 78°F, nor do they drop below 35°F in winter. London, being in one of the mildest parts of the country, can be very pleasant in the spring and fall. Yes, it rains, but you'll rarely get a true downpour. Rains are heaviest in November, when the city averages 2½ inches.

The British consider chilliness wholesome and usually try to keep room temperatures about 10°F below the American comfort level.

For weather conditions before you go, check out the Weather Channel's website: **www.weather.com**.

HOLIDAYS

In England, public holidays include New Year's Day, Good Friday, Easter Monday, May Day (first Monday in May), spring and summer bank holidays (last Monday in May and August), Christmas Day, and Boxing Day (December 26).

LONDON CALENDAR OF EVENTS

January

London Parade, from Parliament Square to Berkeley Square in Mayfair. Bands, floats, and carriages. January 1. Procession starts around 12pm.

January sales. Most shops offer good reductions. Many sales start in late December to beat the post-Christmas slump. The most voracious shoppers camp overnight outside Harrods to get in first.

February

Chinese New Year. The Lion Dancers in Soho. Free. Either in late January or early February (based on the lunar calendar).

Great Spitalfields Pancake Race. Teams of four run in relays, tossing pancakes. At Old Spitalfields Market, Brushfield Street, E1. To join in, call © **020/7375-0441.** At noon on Shrove Tuesday (last day before Lent).

March

Chelsea Antiques Fair, a twice-yearly gathering of England's best dealers, held at Old Town Hall, King's Road, SW3 (© **014/ 4448-2514**). Mid-March (and again in mid-September).

April

The Queen's Birthday is celebrated with 21-gun salutes in Hyde Park and on Tower Hill by troops in parade dress. April 21.

National Gardens Scheme. Over 100 private gardens in London are open to the public on set days, and tea is sometimes served.

Pick up the NGS guidebook for £5 ($7.50) from most book-stores, or contact the National Gardens Scheme Charitable Trust, Hatchlands Park, East Clandon, Guildford, Surrey GU4 7RT (© **01483/211-535**). Late April to early May.

May

The Royal Windsor Horse Show is at Home Park, Windsor Castle (© **01753/860-633**); you may even see a royal. Mid-May.

Chelsea Flower Show, Chelsea Royal Hospital. The best of British gardening, with displays of plants and flowers of all seasons. Tickets are available through TicketMaster (© **020/7344-4444**). The show runs from 8am to 8pm on May 24; tickets are £27 ($40.50). On May 28, the show runs from 8am to 5:30pm, and tickets are £25 ($37.50). Call © **020/7630-7422** for information. Tickets must be purchased in advance.

June

Royal Ascot Week. Ascot Racecourse is open year-round for guided tours, events, exhibitions, and conferences. There are 25 race days throughout the year with the feature race meetings being the Royal Meeting in June, Diamond Day in late July, and the Festival at Ascot in late September. For further information, contact **Ascot Racecourse,** Ascot, Berkshire, SL5 7JN (© **1344/622-211**).

Trooping the Colour, Horse Guards Parade, Whitehall. The official birthday of the queen (her actual birthday is April 21). Seated in a carriage, the monarch inspects her regiments and takes their salute as they parade their colors. It's a quintessential British event, with pageantry and pomp. Held on a designated day in June. Tickets for the parade and reviews, held on preceding Saturdays, are allocated by ballot. Those interested in attending must apply for tickets between January 1 and the end of February, enclosing a stamped, self-addressed envelope, or International Reply Coupon—dates and ticket prices are supplied later. The drawing is held in mid-March, and successful applicants are informed in April. Write to **HQ Household Division,** Horse Guards, Whitehall, London SW1X 6AA, enclosing a SASE and International Reply Coupon (available at any post office).

Lawn Tennis Championships, Wimbledon, Southwest London. There's still an excited hush at Centre Court and a thrill in being here. Savoring the strawberries and cream is part of the experience. Late June to early July. Tickets for Centre and Number One courts are handed out through a lottery; write to **All England**

Lawn Tennis Club, P.O. Box 98, Church Road, Wimbledon, London SW19 5AE (☎ 020/8946-2244), between August and December. A number of tickets are set aside for visitors from abroad, so you may be able to purchase some in spring for this year's games; call to inquire. Outside court tickets are available daily, but *be prepared to wait in line.*

July

Hampton Court Palace Flower Show, East Molesey, Surrey. This 5-day international show is eclipsing its sister show in Chelsea; here, you can purchase the exhibits on the last day. Call ☎ 020/7834-4333 for exact dates and details. Early July.

The Proms. "The Proms"—the Henry Wood Promenade Concerts at Royal Albert Hall—attract music aficionados from around the world. Staged daily (except for a few Sundays), the concerts were launched in 1895 and are the principal summer venue for the BBC Symphony Orchestra. Cheering, clapping, Union Jacks on parade, banners, and balloons create summer fun. Call ☎ 020/7589-3203 for more information. Mid-July to mid-September.

August

Notting Hill Carnival, Notting Hill. One of the largest street festivals in Europe, attracting more than a half-million people annually. Live reggae and soul music combine with great Caribbean food. Free. Call ☎ 020/8964-0544 for information. Two days in late August (usually the last Sunday and Monday).

September

Raising of the Thames Barrier, Unity Way, SE18. Once a year, a full test is done on this miracle of modern engineering; all 10 of the massive steel gates are raised against the high tide. Call ☎ 020/8854-1373 for exact date and time.

October

Opening of Parliament, House of Lords, Westminster. The monarch opens Parliament in the House of Lords, reading an official speech written by the government of the day. The monarch rides from Buckingham Palace to Westminster in a royal coach accompanied by the Yeoman of the Guard and the Household Cavalry. The Strangers' Gallery is open to spectators on a first-come, first-served basis. First Monday in October.

November

Guy Fawkes Night. Anniversary of the Gunpowder Plot, an attempt to blow up King James I. Huge bonfires are lit throughout the city, and Guy Fawkes, the most famous conspirator, is burned in effigy. Free. Check *Time Out* for locations. Early November.

Lord Mayor's Procession and Show, from the Guildhall to the Royal Courts of Justice, in the City of London. This annual event marks the inauguration of the new lord mayor of the City of London. You can watch the procession from the street; the banquet is by invitation only. Second week in November.

December

Watch Night, St. Paul's Cathedral, where a rather lovely New Year's Eve service takes place at 11:30pm; call © **020/7236-4128** for information. December 31.

5 Tips for Travelers with Special Needs

FOR FAMILIES

You can rent baby equipment from **Chelsea Baby Hire,** 20 Denmark Rd., SW19 4PG (© **020/8540-8830**). The **London black cab** is great for families; the roomy interior allows a stroller to be lifted right into the cab without unstrapping the baby. A recommended baby-sitting service is **Childminders** (© 020/7487-5040). Baby-sitters can also be found for you at most hotels.

To find out what's on for kids while you're in London, pick up the leaflet *Where to Take Children,* published by the London Tourist Board. If you have questions, ring **Kidsline** (© 020/7222-8070) Monday to Friday from 4 to 6pm and summer holidays from 9am to 4pm, or the **London Tourist Board**'s children's information lines (© **0839/123-425**) for listings of events and places to visit for children. The number is accessible in London at £.50 (85¢) per minute.

FOR TRAVELERS WITH DISABILITIES

Many London hotels, museums, restaurants, and sightseeing attractions have wheelchair ramps. Persons with disabilities are often granted special discounts at attractions and, in some cases, nightclubs. These are called "concessions" in Britain. It always pays to ask. Free information and advice is available from **Holiday Care Service,** Imperial Building, 2nd floor, Victoria Road, Horley, Surrey RH6 7PZ (© **01293/774-535;** fax 01293/784-647; www.holidaycare. org.uk).

Bookstores in London often carry *Access in London* (£8 or $13.20), a publication listing facilities for persons with disabilities, among other things.

The transport system, cinemas, and theaters are still pretty much off-limits, but **Transport for London** does publish a leaflet called *Access to the Underground,* which gives details of elevators and ramps at Underground stations; call ℭ **020/7918-3312.** The **London black cab** is perfectly suited for those in wheelchairs; the roomy interiors have plenty of room for maneuvering.

London's most visible organization for information about access to theaters, cinemas, galleries, museums, and restaurants is **Artsline,** 54 Chalton St., London NW1 1HS (ℭ **020/7388-2227;** fax 020/7383-2653). It offers free information about wheelchair access, theaters with hearing aids, tourist attractions, and cinemas. Artsline will mail information to North America, but it's more helpful to contact Artsline once you arrive in London; the line is staffed Monday to Friday from 9:30am to 5:30pm.

An organization that cooperates closely with Artsline is **Tripscope,** The Courtyard, 4 Evelyn Rd., London W4 5JL (ℭ **020/ 8580-7021**), which offers advice on travel in Britain and elsewhere for persons with disabilities.

FOR SENIORS

Many discounts are available to seniors. Be advised that in England you often have to be a member of an association to get discounts.

If you're over 60, you're eligible for special 10% discounts on **British Airways** through its Privileged Traveler program. You also qualify for reduced restrictions on APEX cancellations. Discounts are also granted for BA tours and for intra-Britain air tickets booked in North America. **British Rail** offers seniors discounted rates on first-class rail passes around Britain. See "Getting There by Train," below.

Members of the **American Association of Retired Persons (AARP),** 601 E St. NW, Washington, DC 20049 (ℭ **800/ 424-3410** or 202/434-AARP; www.aarp.org), get discounts not only on hotels but on airfares and car rentals, too. AARP offers members a wide range of special benefits, including *Modern Maturity* magazine and a monthly newsletter.

FOR GAY & LESBIAN TRAVELERS

London has one of the most active gay and lesbian scenes in the world; we recommend a number of the city's best gay clubs in chapter 7, "London After Dark." For up-to-the-minute information, we recommend the monthly *Gay Times* (London).

You can also pick up *Frommer's Gay & Lesbian Europe,* which covers London as one of the gay meccas of Europe.

Lesbian and Gay Switchboard (℡ 020/7837-7324) is open 24 hours a day, providing information about gay-related activities in London or advice in general. The **Bisexual Helpline** (℡ 020/8569-7500) offers useful information, but only on Tuesday and Wednesday from 7:30 to 9:30pm, and Saturday between 9:30am and noon. London's best gay-oriented bookstore is **Gay's the Word,** 66 Marchmont St., WC1 (℡ 020/7278-7654; Tube: Russell Square), the largest such store in Britain. The staff is friendly and helpful and will offer advice about the ever-changing scene in London. It's open Monday to Saturday from 10am to 6:30pm, and Sunday from 2 to 6pm. At Gay's the Word, as well as other gay-friendly venues, you can find a number of publications, many free, including the popular *Boyz.*

FOR STUDENTS

The best resource for students is the **Council on International Educational Exchange,** or CIEE (℡ 212/822-2700; www.ciie. org). They can set you up with an ID card (see below), and their travel branch, **Council Travel Service** (℡ 888/COUNCIL; www.counciltravel.com), the biggest student travel agency in the world. They can get you discounts on plane tickets, rail passes, and the like. Ask for a list of CTS offices in major cities so that you can keep the discounts flowing (and aid lines open) as you travel.

From CIEE you can get the student traveler's best friend, the $18 **International Student Identity Card (ISIC).** It's the only officially accepted form of student identification, good for cut rates on rail passes, plane tickets, and other discounts. It also offers basic health and life insurance and a 24-hour help line. If you're no longer a student but are still under 26, you can get a **GO 25** card from the same group, which gets you the insurance and some of the discounts (but not student admission prices in museums).

In Canada, **Travel CUTS,** 200 Ronson St., Suite 320, Etobicoke, Ontario M9W 5Z9 (℡ 800/667-2887 or 416/614-2887; www.travelcuts.com), offers similar services. **USIT Campus,** 52 Grosvenor Gardens, London SW1W 0AG (℡ 020/7730-3402 or 0870/240-1010; www.usitcampus.co.uk), opposite Victoria Station, is Britain's leading specialist in student and youth travel.

STA Travel, 86 Old Brompton Rd., SW7 3LQ (℡ 800/781-4040; www.statravel.com; Tube: South Kensington), is the only worldwide company specializing in student- and youth-discounted airfares. It's open Monday to Friday from 8:30am to 7pm, Saturday from 10am to 5pm, and Sunday from 10am to 2pm.

The International Student House, 229 Great Portland St., W1 (© 020/7631-8300; www.ish.org.uk), is at the foot of Regent's Park across from the Tube stop for Great Portland Street. It's a bee-hive of activity, with discos and film showings, and rents blandly furnished, institutional rooms for £31 ($46.50) single, £22.50 ($33.75) per person double, £20 ($30) per person triple, and £9.99 ($15) per person in a dorm. Laundry facilities are available, and a £10 ($15) key deposit is charged. Reserve way in advance.

University of London Student Union, 1 Malet St., WC1E 7HY (© 020/7664-2000; www.ulu.lon.ac.uk; Tube: Goodge Street or Russell Square), is the best place to learn about student activities in the Greater London area. The Union has a swimming pool, a fitness center, a gymnasium, a general store, a sports shop, a ticket agency, banks, bars, inexpensive restaurants, venues for live events, an office of STA Travel (see above), and many other facilities. It's open Monday to Thursday from 8:30am to 11pm, Friday from 8:30am to 1pm, Saturday from 9am to 2pm, and Sunday from 9:30am to 10:30pm. Bulletin boards at the Union provide a rundown on events, some of which you might be able to attend; others might be "closed door."

6 Getting There

BY PLANE

Heathrow is closer to central London than Gatwick, but both offer fast train service to the West End (see below).

FROM THE UNITED STATES   **American Airlines** (© 800/433-7300; www.aa.com) offers daily nonstops to London Heathrow Airport from five U.S. gateways: New York's JFK (six times daily), Chicago's O'Hare (three times daily), Boston's Logan (twice daily), and Miami International and Los Angeles International (once daily).

British Airways (© 800/247-9297; www.britishairways.com) offers mostly nonstop flights from 21 U.S. cities to Heathrow and Gatwick. With more add-on options than any other airline, British Airways can make a visit to Britain cheaper than you might expect. Of particular interest are the "Value Plus," "London on the Town," and "Europe Escorted" packages that include airfare and discounted accommodations throughout Britain.

Continental Airlines (© 800/231-0856; www.continental. com) flies daily to Gatwick Airport from Newark, Houston, and Cleveland.

Delta Air Lines (℡ 800/241-4141; www.delta.com) runs either one or two daily nonstop flights between Atlanta and Gatwick. Delta also offers nonstop daily service from Cincinnati.

Although **Air India** (℡ 800/223-7776 or 212/751-6200) doesn't immediately come to mind when you think of a flight from the U.S. to London, it's a viable option and competitively priced. Air India (www.airindia.com) offers daily flights from New York's JFK and three flights a week—Tuesday, Friday, and Sunday—from Chicago to London.

Northwest Airlines (℡ 800/225-2525; www.nwa.com) flies nonstop from Minneapolis and Detroit to Gatwick, with connections from cities such as Boston and New York.

United Airlines (℡ 800/538-2929; www.ual.com) flies nonstop from New York's JFK and Chicago's O'Hare to Heathrow two or three times a day, depending on the season. United also offers nonstop service 3 times a day from Dulles Airport, near Washington, D.C., plus once-a-day service to Heathrow from Newark, Los Angeles, San Francisco, and Boston.

Virgin Atlantic Airways (℡ 800/862-8621; www.virgin-atlantic.com) flies daily to either Gatwick or Heathrow from Boston, Newark, New York's JFK, Los Angeles, San Francisco, Washington, D.C.'s Dulles, Miami, Orlando, and Chicago.

FROM CANADA For travelers departing from Canada, **Air Canada** (℡ 888/247-2262; www.aircanada.ca) flies daily to London Heathrow nonstop from Vancouver, Montreal, and Toronto. There are also frequent direct flights from Calgary and Ottawa.

FROM AUSTRALIA **Qantas** (℡ 131313; www.qantas.com) flies from both Sydney and Melbourne daily. **British Airways** (℡ 800/227-4500; www.britishairways.com) has five to seven flights weekly from Sydney and Melbourne.

FROM SOUTH AFRICA **South African Airways** (℡ 011/978-1762; www.saa.co.za) schedules two daily flights from Johannesburg and two daily flights from Cape Town. From Johannesburg, both **British Airways** (℡ 0845/773-3377; www.britishairways.com) and **Virgin Atlantic Airways** (℡ 011/340-3400; www.virgin-atlantic.com) have daily flights to Heathrow. British Airways flies five times weekly from Cape Town.

FLYING FOR LESS: TIPS FOR GETTING THE BEST AIRFARES

Check your newspaper for advertised discounts or call the airlines directly and ask for **promotional rates** or special fares. Of course, you'll almost never see a sale during the peak summer months of July and August or during the winter holiday. If your schedule is flexible, ask if you can secure a cheaper fare by staying an extra day or by flying midweek. (Many airlines won't volunteer this.) If you hold a ticket when a sale breaks, it may pay to exchange your ticket, which usually incurs a $75 charge. *Note:* the lowest fares are often nonrefundable, require advance purchase of 1 to 3 weeks and a certain length of stay, and carry penalties for changing dates.

Consolidators, also known as "bucket shops," are a good place to find low fares. Consolidators buy seats in bulk from the airlines, and then sell them to the public at prices below even the airlines' discounted rates. Their ads usually run in the Sunday travel section of newspapers at the bottom of the page. Before you pay a consolidator, however, ask for a record locator number and confirm your seat with the airline itself. Be prepared to book your ticket with a different consolidator—there are many to choose from—if the airline can't confirm your reservation. Also be aware that bucket shop tickets are usually nonrefundable or have stiff cancellation fees, often as high as 50% to 75% of the ticket price.

Council Travel (© 888/COUNCIL; www.counciltravel.com) and **STA Travel** (© 800/781-4040; www.statravel.com) cater especially to young travelers, but their bargain-basement prices are available to people of all ages. **1-800/AIR-FARE** (www.1800airfare.com) was formerly owned by TWA, but now offers the deepest discounts on many other airlines, with a 4-day advance purchase. Other reliable consolidators include **1-800-FLY-CHEAP** (www.flycheap.com); **TFI Tours International** (© 800/745-8000 or 212/736-1140), which serves as a clearinghouse for unused seats; or "rebators" such as **Travel Avenue** (© 800/333-3335 or 312/876-1116).

BY TRAIN

VIA THE CHUNNEL FROM THE CONTINENT   Since 1994, when the Channel Tunnel opened, the *Eurostar Express* has been operating twice-daily passenger service between London and both Paris and Brussels. The $15-billion tunnel, one of the great engineering feats of all time, is the first link between Britain and the Continent since the Ice Age.

Rail Europe (✆ **800/361-RAIL;** www.raileurope.com) sells tickets on the *Eurostar* direct train service between Paris or Brussels and London. A round-trip between Paris and London, for example, costs $500 for first class, or $300 in second class. You can reduce that rate to $120, with a second-class, 14-day advance purchase (nonrefundable). In London, make reservations for *Eurostar* at ✆ **0990/300-003** or 800/EUROSTAR in the U.S. (www.eurostar. com). *Eurostar* trains arrive and depart from London's Waterloo Station, Paris's Gare du Nord, and Brussels's Central Station.

VIA BRITRAIL FROM OTHER PARTS OF EUROPE If you're traveling to London from elsewhere in the United Kingdom, consider buying a **BritRail Classic Pass,** which allows unlimited rail travel during a set time period (8 days, 15 days, 22 days, or 1 month). *Remember:* Eurailpasses aren't accepted in Britain, although they are in Ireland. For 8 days, a pass costs $400 in first class, and $265 in standard class; for 15 days, it's $600 and $400, respectively; for 22 days, it's $760 and $505; and for 1 month, it's $900 and $600. If a child age 5 to 15 is traveling with a full-fare adult, the fare is half the adult fare. Children under age 5 travel free if not occupying a seat. Senior citizens (60 and over) qualify for discounts on first-class travel: It's $340 for an 8-day pass, $510 for a 15-day pass, $645 for a 22-day pass, and $765 for a 1-month pass. Travelers between 16 and 25 can purchase a **BritRail Classic Youth Pass,** which allows unlimited second-class travel: $215 for 8 days, $280 for 15 days, $355 for 22 days, or $420 for 1 month.

New is the **BritRail Weekender Pass,** promoting 4 consecutive days of travel to be used either Friday through Monday or for any 4-day period, which includes a Saturday and Sunday. It's accepted on the Heathrow rail service between Heathrow Airport and Paddington Station, as well as the Gatwick rail service from the airport into Victoria Station. You can choose first- or standard-class train travel. The pass costs $130 in first class or $103 in standard. Children ages 5 to 15 pay half the adult fare.

Travelers who arrive from France by boat and pick up a British Rail train at Dover arrive at **Victoria Station.** Those journeying south by rail from Edinburgh arrive at **King's Cross Station.**

BY CAR

If you plan to take a rented car across or under the Channel, check with the company about license and insurance requirements before you leave.

FERRIES FROM THE CONTINENT   There are many "drive-on, drive-off" car-ferry services across the Channel. The most popular ports in France for Channel crossings are Boulogne and Calais, where you can board Stena ferries or hovercraft taking you to the English ports of Dover and Folkestone.

LE SHUTTLE   The Chunnel accommodates not only trains, but also passenger cars, charter buses, taxis, and motorcycles. Le Shuttle, a half-mile long train carrying motor vehicles under the English Channel (© **0990/353-535;** www.eurodrive.co.uk), connects Calais, France, with Folkestone, England, and vice versa. It operates 24 hours a day, 365 days a year, running every 15 minutes during peak travel times and at least once an hour at night.

With Le Shuttle, gone are weather-related delays, seasickness, and a need for reservations. Before boarding Le Shuttle, you stop at a tollbooth to pay, and then pass through Immigration for both countries at one time. During the ride, you travel in bright, air-conditioned carriages, remaining inside your car or stepping outside to stretch your legs. An hour later, when you reach England, you drive off toward London. The cost of Le Shuttle varies according to the season and the day of the week. Count on at least £239 ($358.50) for a return ticket.

Stores selling duty-free goods, restaurants, and service stations are available to travelers on both sides of the Channel. A bilingual staff is on hand to assist travelers at both the British and French terminals.

Hertz offers **Le Swap,** a service for passengers taking Le Shuttle. At Calais, you can switch cars for one with the steering wheel on the opposite side depending upon which country you're heading for.

2

Getting to Know London

England's largest city is like a great wheel, with Piccadilly Circus at its hub and dozens of communities branching out from it. First-time visitors might be intimidated until they get the hang of it.

This chapter will provide a brief orientation and preview of the city's neighborhoods and tell you about getting around London by public transport or on foot. In addition, the "Fast Facts" section covers everything from baby-sitters to shoe repair.

1 Orientation

ARRIVING
BY PLANE
LONDON HEATHROW AIRPORT   Located west of London in Hounslow (© **0870/000-0123** for flight information), Heathrow is one of the world's busiest airports. Terminal 4 handles the long haul and transatlantic operations of British Airways. Most transatlantic flights on U.S. based airlines arrive at Terminal 3. Terminals 1 and 2 receive the intra-European flights of several European airlines.

It takes 50 minutes by **Underground** and costs £3.50 ($5.25) to make the 15-mile trip from Heathrow to center city. If you prefer a bus for comfort and easier transfer of baggage, you can take a shuttle bus operated by **Berkeley's Hotel Connection** (© **014/4225-0400;** www.berkeleys.co.uk), costing £12 ($18) one way. The service uses 14-seat midi-buses. A taxi is likely to cost from £35 to £40 ($52.50–$60). For more information about train or bus connections, call © **020/7222-1234.**

The British Airport Authority operates **Heathrow Express** (© **0845/600-1515;** www.heathrowexpress.com), a 100-mph train service every 15 minutes daily from 5:10am until 11:40pm between Heathrow and Paddington Station in London. Trips cost £12 ($18) each way in economy class, rising to £20 ($30) in first class. Children under 15 go for free (with an adult). You can save £1 ($1.50) by booking online or by phone. The trip takes 15 minutes each way between Paddington and Terminals 1, 2, and 3, or 23 minutes from Terminal 4. The trains are wheelchair accessible. From Paddington, passengers can connect to other trains or hail a taxi. You can buy tickets on the train or at machines at Heathrow (and from travel agents). At Paddington, a bus link, **Hotel Express,** takes passengers to a number of hotels in central London. The cost is £2 ($3) for adults, £1.05 ($1.60) for children 5 to 15, and free for children under 5. This service has revolutionized travel to and from the airport, much to the regret of London cabbies. Catch the bus outside the station. There are frequent departures throughout the day.

GATWICK AIRPORT   While Heathrow still dominates, many scheduled flights land at Gatwick (© **0129/353-5353** for flight information), 25 miles south of London in West Sussex, a 30-minute train ride away. From Gatwick, the fastest way to London is the **Gatwick Express** train (**08705/301-530; www.gatwickexpress.com**), which leaves for Victoria Station in London every 15 minutes during the day and every hour at night. The one-way charge is £10.50 ($15.75) "Express Class" for adults, £17 ($25.50) for First Class, half price for children 5 to 15, free for children under 5. There are also Airbus **buses** from Gatwick to Victoria coach station operated by **National Express** (© **0870/580-8080;** www.gobycoach.com), approximately every hour from 4:15am to 9:15pm; the round-trip fare is £12.50 ($18.75) per person, and the trip takes approximately 1½ hours. A **taxi** from Gatwick to central London usually costs £55 to £65 ($82.50–$97.50). You must negotiate a fare before you enter the cab; the meter doesn't apply because Gatwick lies outside the Metropolitan Police District. For further transportation information, call © **020/7222-1234.**

BY TRAIN

Each of London's train stations is connected to the city's bus and Underground network, and each has phones, restaurants, luggage storage areas, and London Regional Transport Information Centres.

For one-stop travel, you can take the Chunnel train direct from Paris to Waterloo Station in London.

BY CAR

Once you arrive on the English side of the channel, the M20 takes you directly into London. *Remember to drive on the left.* Two roadways encircle London: the A406 and A205 form the inner beltway; the M25 rings the city farther out.

We suggest you confine driving in London to the bare minimum, which means arriving and parking. Because of parking problems and heavy traffic, getting around London by car is not a viable option. We suggest garaging the car and taking public transportation or taxis.

VISITOR INFORMATION

The **British Travel Centre,** Rex House, 4–12 Lower Regent St., London SW1 4PQ (Tube: Piccadilly Circus), caters to walk-in visitors who need information about all of Britain. There's no telephone service; you must go in person and wait in line. You'll also find a British Rail ticket office, travel and theater-ticket agencies, a hotel-booking service, a bookshop, and a souvenir shop. It's open Monday to Friday 9am to 6:30pm, Saturday and Sunday 10am to 4pm, with extended hours on Saturday from June to September.

London Tourist Board's **Tourist Information Centre,** Victoria Station Forecourt, SW1 (walk-ins only; no phone; Tube: Victoria Station), can help with almost anything. The center deals chiefly with accommodations in all price categories and can handle most travelers' questions. It also arranges tour-ticket sales and theater reservations, and offers a wide selection of books and souvenirs. From Easter to October, the center is open daily 8am to 7pm; November to Easter, it's open Monday to Saturday, 8am to 6pm and Sunday, 9am to 4pm.

The Tourist Board also has offices at **Heathrow** Terminals 1, 2, and 3, and on the Underground concourse at **Liverpool Street Railway Station.**

CITY LAYOUT
AN OVERVIEW OF THE CITY

While **Central London** doesn't formally define itself, most Londoners would probably accept the Underground's Circle Line as a fair boundary.

"The City" is where London began; it's the original square mile the Romans called *Londinium.* **The West End,** unofficially bounded by the Thames to the south, Farringdon Road/Street to the east, Marylebone Road/Euston Road to the north, and Hyde Park and Victoria Station to the West, is where most visitors will spend their time, whether at Buckingham Palace, the British Museum, or the shops and theaters in Soho. You'll also find the greatest concentration of hotels and restaurants in the West End.

Farther west are upscale Belgravia, Kensington, Knightsbridge, Chelsea, Paddington and Bayswater, Earl's Court, and Notting Hill. This is also prime hotel and restaurant territory. To the east of the City is the **East End,** which forms the eastern boundary of **Inner London** (Notting Hill and Earl's Court roughly form the western boundary).

FINDING YOUR WAY AROUND

It's not easy to find an address in London, as the city's streets—both names and house numbers—follow no pattern whatsoever. London is checkered with innumerable squares, mews, closes, and terraces that jut into, cross, overlap, or interrupt whatever street you're try-ing to follow. And house numbers run in odds and evens, clockwise and counterclockwise—when they exist at all. Many establishments, such as the Four Seasons Hotel and Langan's Brasserie, don't have numbers, even though the building right next door is numbered.

Throughout this book, street addresses are followed by designa-tions like SW1 and EC1, which are postal areas. The original post office was at St. Martin-le-Grand in the City, so the postal districts are related to where they lie geographically from there. Victoria is SW1 since it's the first area southwest of St. Martin-le-Grand; Covent Garden is west (west central), so its postal area is WC1 or WC2; Liverpool Street is east of there, so its postal area is EC1.

LONDON'S NEIGHBORHOODS IN BRIEF
The City & Environs
The City   When the Londoners speak of "the City" (EC2, EC3) they mean the original square mile that's now the British version of Wall Street. Despite its age, the City doesn't easily reveal its past. Although it retains some of its medieval character, much was swept away by the Great Fire of 1666, the Blitz, the IRA bombs of the 1990s, and modern developers. Landmarks include Sir Christopher Wren's masterpiece, **St. Paul's Cathedral,** which stood virtually alone in the rubble after the Blitz. Some 2,000 years of history unfold at the **Museum of London** and the **Barbican Centre.**

Following the Strand eastward from Trafalgar Square, you'll come to Fleet Street. In the 19th century, this corner of London became the most concentrated newspaper district in the world. William Caxton printed the first book in English here, and the *Daily Consort,* the first daily newspaper printed in England, was launched at Ludgate Circus in 1702. Most London tabloids have abandoned Fleet Street for the Docklands across the river.

The City of London still prefers to function on its own, separate from the rest of the city; it maintains its own **Information Centre** at St. Paul's Churchyard, EC4 (© **020/7332-1456**). It is open Monday to Friday, 9am to 5pm and Saturday, 9am to noon.

The East End   Traditionally, this was one of London's poorest districts, nearly bombed out of existence in World War II. The East End extends east from the City Walls, encompassing Stepney, Bow, Poplar, West Ham, Canning Town, and other districts. The East End is the home of the Cockney, London's most colorful character. To be a true Cockney, it's said that you must have been born within the sound of Bow Bells, a reference to a church, St. Mary-le-Bow, rebuilt by Sir Christopher Wren in 1670.

Docklands   In 1981, the London Docklands Development Corporation (LDDC) was formed to redevelop Wapping, the Isle of Dogs, the Royal Docks, and Surrey Docks. The area is bordered roughly by Tower Bridge to the west and London City Airport and the Royal Docks to the east. Many businesses have moved here; Thames-side warehouses have been converted to lofts; and museums, shops, and an ever-growing list of restaurants have popped up at this 21st-century river city in the making.

Canary Wharf, on the Isle of Dogs, is the heart of Docklands; this 71-acre site is dominated by an 800-foot-high tower, designed by Cesar Pelli. The Piazza is lined with shops and restaurants. On the south side of the river at Surrey Docks is Butler's Wharf, home to the **Design Museum.**

To get to Docklands, take the Underground to Tower Hill and pick up the **Docklands Light Railway** (© **020/7363-9696**), which operates Monday to Friday from 5:30am to 12:30am, with selected routes offering weekend service from 6am to 12:30am Saturday and 7:30am to 11:30pm Sunday.

South Bank   Here you'll find the **South Bank Arts Centre,** the largest in Western Europe and still growing. Reached by Waterloo Bridge (or on foot by Hungerford Bridge), it lies across the Thames from the Victoria Embankment. Culture buffs flock to its galleries and halls, including the **National Theatre, Queen Elizabeth Hall, Royal Festival Hall,** and the **Hayward Gallery.** It's also the setting of the National Film Theatre and the Museum of the Moving Image (MOMI).

The South Bank is known more for its cultural attractions in the evening, and restaurants. Nearby are such neighborhoods as

London's Neighborhoods

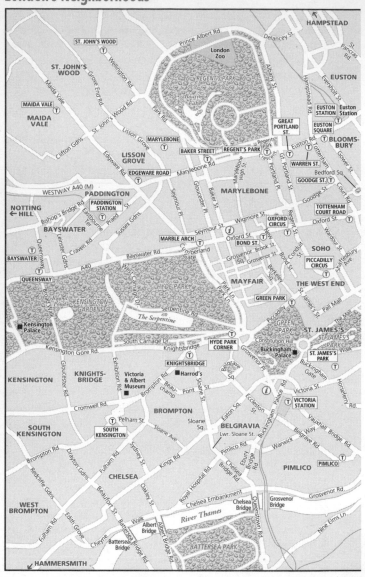

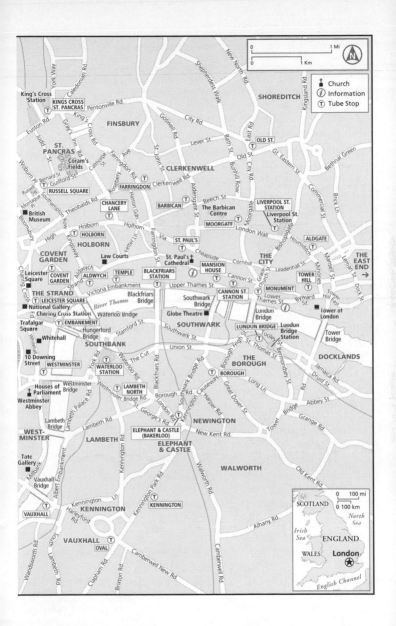

23

Elephant and Castle and Southwark, home to **Southwark Cathedral.** To get here, take the Tube to Waterloo Station.

Clerkenwell   This neighborhood, north and a bit west of the City, was the site of London's first hospital and the home of several early churches. **St. Bartholomew-the-Great,** built in 1123, still stands as London's oldest church and the best piece of large-scale Norman building in the city. In the 18th century, Clerkenwell declined into a muck-filled cattle yard. During a 19th-century revival, John Stuart Mill's London Patriotic Club moved and William Morris's socialist press of the 1890s called Clerkenwell home; Lenin worked here editing *Iskra.* The neighborhood has recently been reinvented by the moneyed and groovy. A handful of hot restaurants and clubs have sprung up, and art galleries line St. John's Square and the border of Clerkenwell Green. Farringdon is the central Tube stop.

West End Neighborhoods

Bloomsbury   This district is bounded roughly by Euston Road to the north, Gower Street to the west, and Clerkenwell to the east. It is, among other things, the academic heart of London; you'll find the **University of London,** other colleges, and many **bookstores.** Despite its student population, it is a fairly staid neighborhood. Writers like Virginia Woolf, who lived within its bounds, have fanned its reputation.

The heart of Bloomsbury is **Russell Square,** whose outlying streets are lined with moderately priced to expensive hotels and B&Bs. It's a noisy but central place to stay. Most visitors come to visit the **British Museum,** one of the world's greatest repositories of treasures. The **British Telecom Tower** (1964) on Cleveland Street is a familiar landmark.

The western edge of Bloomsbury is **Fitzrovia,** bounded by Great Portland, Oxford, and Gower streets, and reached by the Goodge Street Tube. Goodge Street, with its many shops and pubs, forms the heart of the "village." Fitzrovia was once the stamping ground for writers and artists like Ezra Pound, Wyndham Lewis, and George Orwell, among others.

Holborn   The old borough of Holborn (*Ho*-burn), which abuts the City southeast of Bloomsbury, takes in the heart of legal London—the city's barristers, solicitors, and law clerks call it home. Still Dickensian in spirit, the area preserves the Victorian author's footsteps in the two Inns of Court and the Bleeding Heart Yard of *Little Dorrit* fame. **The Old Bailey,** where judges and lawyers still wear old-fashioned wigs, has stood for English justice through the years. Even as you're downing a half-pint of bitter at the **Viaduct Tavern,** 126 Newgate St. (Tube: St. Paul's), you learn the pub was built over the notorious Newgate Prison.

Covent Garden & The Strand   The flower, fruit, and "veg" market is long gone, but memories of Professor Higgins and his "squashed cabbage leaf," Eliza Doolittle, linger on. **Covent Garden** contains the city's liveliest group of restaurants, pubs, and cafes outside Soho, as well as some of the city's hippest shops. The restored marketplace, with its glass and iron roofs, is a magnificent example of urban recycling. London's **theater district** begins in Covent Garden and spills over into Leicester Square and Soho. Inigo Jones's **St. Paul's Covent Garden** is known as the actors' church; over the years, it has attracted everybody from Ellen Terry to Vivien Leigh. The **Theatre Royal Drury Lane** was where Charles II's mistress Nell Gwynne made her debut. The place is not packed with hotel beds, but there are a few choice ones.

The **Strand** forms the southern border of Covent Garden. It's flanked with theaters, shops, first-class hotels, and restaurants. **Ye Olde Cheshire Cheese** pub, **Dr. Johnson's House,** and rooms fragrant with brewing Twinings English tea—all these evoke memories of the rich heyday of this district. The Strand runs parallel to the River Thames, and to walk it is to follow in the footsteps of Charles Lamb, Mark Twain, Henry Fielding, James Boswell, William Thackeray, and Sir Walter Raleigh. The **Savoy Theatre** helped make Gilbert and Sullivan household names.

Piccadilly Circus & Leicester Square   Piccadilly Circus, with its statue of Eros, is the heart and soul of London. Its traffic, neon, and jostling crowds indeed make "circus" an apt word here. Piccadilly, traditionally the western road out of town, was named for the "picadil," a ruffled collar created by Robert Baker, a 17th-century tailor. If you want a little more grandeur, retreat to the Regency promenade of exclusive shops, the **Burlington Arcade,** designed in 1819. The 35 shops house a treasure trove of expensive goodies. A bit more tawdry is **Leicester Square,** a center of theaters, restaurants, movie palaces, and nightlife.

Soho   A nightclubber's paradise, Soho is a confusing grid of streets and restaurants. It's a great place to visit, but you probably won't want to stay there. These densely packed streets in the heart of the West End are famous for their cosmopolitan mix of people and trades. A decade ago, much was heard about the decline of Soho with the influx of sex shops. Since then, non-sex-oriented businesses have returned, and fashionable restaurants and shops prosper; it's now the heart of London's expanding gay scene.

Soho starts at Piccadilly Circus and is more or less bordered by Regent Street to the west, Oxford Street to the north, and Charing Cross Road to the east, and the **theaters along Shaftesbury Avenue.** Across Shaftesbury Avenue is London's **Chinatown,** centered on Gerrard Street. It's small, authentic, and packed with good restaurants. But **Soho's heart**—with delicatessens, butchers, fish stores, and wine merchants—is farther north, on Brewer, Old Compton, and Berwick streets; Berwick is also a wonderful open-air food market. To the north of Old Compton Street, Dean, Frith, and Greek streets have fine restaurants, pubs, and clubs. The British movie industry is centered in Wardour Street.

Marylebone   West of Bloomsbury and Fitzrovia, Marylebone extends the eastern edge of Hyde Park. Visitors head here to explore **Madame Tussaud's** or walk along **Baker Street** in the footsteps of Sherlock Holmes. The streets form a near-perfect grid, with the major ones running north-south between Regent's Park and Oxford Street. Robert Adam laid out **Portland Place,** one of the most characteristic squares, from 1776 to 1780, and at **Cavendish Square** Mrs. Horatio Nelson waited for the return of the admiral. Marylebone Lane and High Street retain some village atmosphere. Dickens wrote nearly a dozen books when he resided here. At **Regent's Park,** you can visit Queen Mary's Gardens or, in summer, see Shakespeare performed in an open-air theater.

Mayfair   Bounded by Piccadilly, Hyde Park, and Oxford and Regent streets, this is the most elegant, fashionable section of London, filled with luxury hotels, Georgian town houses, and swank shops. **Grosvenor Square** (*Grov*-nor) is nicknamed "Little America" because it's home to the American Embassy and a statue of Franklin D. Roosevelt; **Berkeley Square** (*Bark*-ley) was made famous by the song, whose nightingale sang here. One of the curiosities of Mayfair is **Shepherd Market,** a village of pubs, two-story inns, restaurants, and book and food stalls, sandwiched within Mayfair's grandness. If you're seeking sophisticated, albeit expensive, accommodations, close to the **Bond Street** shopping, boutiques, and art galleries, then Mayfair is for you.

St. James's   Often called "Royal London," St. James's basks in its associations with everybody from the "merrie monarch" Charles II to Elizabeth II, who calls **Buckingham Palace** home. The neighborhood begins at **Piccadilly Circus** and moves southwest, incorporating **Pall Mall, The Mall, St. James's Park,** and **Green Park.** Within its confines are American Express and many of London's leading department stores. This is where the English gentleman seeks haven at that male-only bastion of English tradition, the gentlemen's club. Stop in at **Fortnum & Mason,** 181 Piccadilly, the world's most luxurious grocery store. Launched in 1788, the store sent hams to the duke of Wellington's army and baskets of tinned goodies to Florence Nightingale in the Crimea. Hotels in this neighborhood tend to be almost as expensive as the royal addresses surrounding them.

Westminster   Westminster has been the seat of the British government since the days of Edward the Confessor (1042 to 1066). Dominated by the **Houses of Parliament** and **Westminster Abbey,** the area runs along the Thames to the east of St. James's Park. **Trafalgar Square,** at the area's northern end and one of the city's major landmarks, remains a testament to England's victory over Napoleon in 1805, and the paintings in its landmark National Gallery will restore your soul. Whitehall links Trafalgar Square with **Parliament Square.** You can visit Churchill's Cabinet War Rooms and walk down **Downing Street** to see **Number 10,** home to Britain's prime minister. No visit is complete without a call at **Westminster Abbey,** one of the great Gothic churches in the world. It has witnessed a parade of history, beginning when William the Conqueror was crowned here on Christmas Day, 1066.

Westminster also encompasses **Victoria,** an area that takes its name from bustling Victoria Station, "the gateway to the Continent." Because of its location, many B&Bs and hotels have sprouted up. It's not a tiny neighborhood, but it is cheap and convenient, if you don't mind the noise and crowds.

Beyond the West End
Knightsbridge   One of London's most fashionable neighborhoods, Knightsbridge is a top residential, hotel, and shopping district, just south of Hyde Park. **Harrods** on Brompton Road is its chief attraction. Founded in 1901, it's been called "the Notre Dame of department stores." Right nearby, **Beauchamp Place** (*Bee*-cham) is one of London's most fashionable shopping streets, a Regency-era boutique-lined street with a scattering of restaurants. Most hotels here are deluxe or first class.

Belgravia   South of Knightsbridge, this area has long been the aristocratic quarter of London, rivaling Mayfair in grandness. It's a haven for chic hotels; the duke and duchess of Westminster still live at **Eaton Square.** The area's centerpiece is **Belgrave Square.** When town houses were built in 1825 to 1835, aristocrats followed—the duke of Connaught, the earl of Essex, even Queen Victoria's mother.

Chelsea   This stylish Thames-side district lies south and to the west of Belgravia. It begins at **Sloane Square,** with **Gilbert Ledward's Venus fountain** playing watery music. The area has always been a favorite of writers and artists, including Oscar Wilde (who was arrested here), George Eliot, James Whistler, J.M.W. Turner, Henry James, and Thomas Carlyle (whose former home can be visited). Mick Jagger and Margaret Thatcher (not together) have been more recent residents. There are some swank hotels here and a scattering of modestly priced ones. The main drawback to Chelsea is inaccessibility. Except for Sloane Square, there's a dearth of Tube stops, and unless you like to take a lot of buses or expensive taxis, you may find getting around a chore.

Its major boulevard is **King's Road,** where Mary Quant launched the miniskirt in the 1960s and where the English punk look began. King's Road runs the length of Chelsea; it's at its liveliest on Saturday. The hip-hop of King's Road isn't typical of otherwise upmarket Chelsea, an elegant village filled with town houses and little mews dwellings that only successful stockbrokers and solicitors can afford to occupy.

On the Chelsea/Fulham border is **Chelsea Harbour,** a luxury development of apartments and restaurants with a marina. You can spot its tall tower from far away; the golden ball on top moves up and down to indicate the tide level.

Kensington   This Royal Borough (W8) lies west of Kensington Gardens and Hyde Park and is traversed by two of London's major shopping streets, **Kensington High Street** and **Kensington Church Street.** Since 1689, when asthmatic William III fled Whitehall Palace for Nottingham House (where the air was fresher), the district has enjoyed royal associations. Nottingham House became Kensington Palace, and the royals grabbed a chunk of Hyde Park to plant their roses. Queen Victoria was born here. "KP," as the royals say, is still home to Princess Margaret, Prince and Princess Michael of Kent, and the duke and duchess of Gloucester. Kensington Gardens is open to the public, ever since George II decreed that "respectably dressed" people would be permitted in on

Saturday—providing that no servants, soldiers, or sailors came. In the footsteps of William III, Kensington Square developed, attracting artists and writers. Thackeray wrote *Vanity Fair* while living here. Kensington is a fashionable neighborhood. If you're a frugal traveler, head for South Kensington (see below) for moderately priced hotels and B&Bs.

Southeast of Kensington Gardens and Earl's Court, primarily residential **South Kensington** is often called "museumland" because it's dominated by a complex of museums and colleges, including the **Natural History Museum,** the **Victoria and Albert Museum,** and the **Science Museum;** nearby is **Royal Albert Hall.** South Kensington hosts some fashionable restaurants and town-house hotels. One of its curiosities is the **Albert Memorial,** completed in 1872 by Sir George Gilbert Scott; for sheer excess, this Victorian monument is unequaled in the world.

Earl's Court   Earl's Court lies below Kensington, bordering the western half of Chelsea. For decades a staid residential district, Earl's Court now attracts a new and younger crowd (often gay) to its pubs, wine bars, and coffeehouses. It's a popular base for budget travelers thanks to its wealth of B&Bs and budget hotels and convenient access to central London: A 15-minute Tube ride takes you into the heart of Piccadilly.

Once regarded as the "boondocks," **West Brompton** is seen today as an extension of central London. It lies south of Earl's Court (take the Tube to West Brompton) and southeast of West Kensington. Its focal point is the **Brompton Cemetery,** a flower-filled "green lung" and burial place of such names as Frederick Leyland, the Pre-Raphaelite patron who died in 1892. It also has good restaurants, pubs, and taverns, and some budget hotels.

Paddington & Bayswater   The **Paddington** section radiates out from Paddington Station, north of Hyde Park and Kensington Gardens. It attracts budget travelers who fill the B&Bs in Sussex Gardens and Norfolk Square. After the first railway was introduced in London in 1836, it was followed by a circle of sprawling railway terminals, including Paddington Station in 1838, which spurred the growth of this middle-class area.

Just south of Paddington, north of Hyde Park, and abutting more fashionable Notting Hill to the west is **Bayswater,** also filled with a large number of B&Bs attracting budget travelers. Inspired by Marylebone and elegant Mayfair, a relatively prosperous set of Victorian merchants built terrace houses around spacious squares.

On the other (north) side of Westway/Marylebone Road arc **Maida Vale** and **St. John's Wood,** two villages that have been absorbed by central London. Maida Vale lies west of **Regent's Park,** north of Paddington, and next to St. John's Wood (home to the Beatles' Abbey Road Studios). The area is very sports oriented; if you take the Tube to Maida Vale, you'll find Paddington Recreation Ground, plus Paddington Bowling and Sports Club. It's also home to some of the BBC studios.

Notting Hill   Increasingly fashionable Notting Hill is bounded on the east by Bayswater and on the south by Kensington. Hemmed in on the north by Westway and on the west by the Shepherd's Bush ramp leading to the M40, it has many turn-of-the-century mansions and small houses on quiet, leafy streets, and a growing number of restaurants and clubs. Gentrified in recent years, it's becoming an extension of central London. Hotels are few, but increasingly chic.

More remote than Paddington and Bayswater, Notting Hill lies another 10 minutes west from those districts. In spite of that, many young professional visitors to London wouldn't stay anywhere else.

The northern half of Notting Hill is the hip neighborhood known as **Notting Hill Gate.** Portobello Road is home to one of London's most famous street markets. The area Tube stops are Notting Hill Gate, Holland Park, or Ladbroke Grove.

Nearby **Holland Park,** an expensive neighborhood, promotes itself as "10 minutes by Tube from practically anywhere," a bit of an exaggeration.

2 Getting Around

BY PUBLIC TRANSPORTATION

The London Underground and the city's buses operate on a common system of six fare zones. They radiate out in rings from the central zone 1, which is where most visitors spend the majority of their time. It covers an area from Liverpool Street in the east to Notting Hill in the west, and from Waterloo in the south to Baker Street, Euston, and King's Cross in the north. To travel beyond zone 1, you need a two-zone ticket. Note that all one-way, round-trip, and 1-day pass tickets are valid only on the day of purchase.

Tube and bus maps should be available at any Underground station. You can also download them from the excellent **London Transport (LT)** website: www.londontransport.co.uk. (You can also send away for a map by writing to **London Transport,** Travel

Information Service, 55 Broadway, London SW1H 0BD.) There are also **LT Information Centres** at several major Tube stations: Euston, King's Cross, Oxford Circus, St. James's Park, Liverpool Street Station, and Piccadilly Circus; in the British Rail stations at Euston and Victoria; and in each of the terminals at Heathrow Airport. Most are open daily (some close Sunday) from at least 9am to 5pm. **A 24-hour information service** is also available (© **020/7222-1234**).

TRAVEL DISCOUNTS   If you plan to use public transportation a lot, investigate the fare discounts available. **Travelcards** offer unlimited use of buses, Underground, and British Rail services in Greater London for any period ranging from a day to a year. Travelcards are available from Underground ticket offices, Travel Information Centres, main post offices, and some newsstands. You need to bring a passport-size photo to purchase a Travelcard; there are instant photo booths in many London train stations. Children under age 5 generally travel free on the Tube and buses.

The **One-Day Travelcard** allows you to go anywhere throughout Greater London. For zones 1 and 2, the cost is £4.50 ($6.75) for adults or £2.80 ($4.20) for children 5 to 15. The **Off-Peak One-Day Travelcard,** which isn't valid until after 9:30am on weekdays (or on night buses), is even cheaper. For two zones, the cost is £3.80 ($5.70) for adults and £1.90 ($2.85) for children 5 to 15.

Weekend Travelcards are valid for 1 weekend, plus the Monday if it's a national holiday. They're not valid on night buses; travel anywhere within zones 1 and 2 all weekend costs £5.70 ($8.55) for adults or £2.80 ($4.20) for children 5 to 15.

One-Week Travelcards cost adults £18.20 ($27.30) and children £7.50 ($11.25) for travel in zones 1 and 2.

The 1-day **Family Travelcard** allows unlimited travel on the Tube, buses (excluding night buses) displaying the London Transport bus sign, and the Docklands Light Railway or any rail service within the travel zones designated on your ticket. The family card is valid Monday to Friday after 9:30am, all day weekends and public holidays. It's available for families as small as two (one adult and one child) to as large as six (two adults and four children). The cost is £3 to £3.20 ($4.50 to $4.80) per adult 60p (90¢) per child.

You can also buy **Carnet** tickets, a booklet of 10 single Underground tickets valid for 12 months from the issue date. These are valid for travel only in zone 1 (Central London), and cost £10

Value **Don't Leave Home Without It!**

If you plan to use public transportation a lot in London, buy a **London Visitor Travelcard** before you leave (it isn't available in the U.K.). The card allows unlimited transport within all six zones of Greater London's Underground (as far as Heathrow) and bus network, as well as some discounts on London attractions. A pass for 3 consecutive days of travel is $31 for adults $14 for children 5 to 15; for 4 consecutive days of travel, it's $41 for adults $16 for children; and for 7 consecutive days of travel, it's $61 for adults $26 for children. Contact **BritRail Travel International**, 500 Mamaroneck Ave., Suite 314, Harrison, NY 10528 (© **800/677-8585;** 800/555-2748 in Canada; www.raileurope.com).

($15) for adults and £5 ($7.50) for children (up to 15). A book of Carnet tickets gives you a savings of £2 ($3) over the cost of 10 separate single tickets.

THE UNDERGROUND

The Underground, or Tube, is the fastest and easiest way to get around. All Tube stations are clearly marked with a red circle and blue crossbar. Routes are conveniently color-coded.

With British coins, you can get your ticket at a vending machine. Otherwise, buy it at the ticket office. You can transfer as many times as you like as long as you stay in the Underground. The flat fare for one trip within the central zone is £1.50 ($2.25). Trips from the central zone to destinations in the suburbs range from £1.40 to £3.50 ($2.10–$5.25) in most cases. You can also purchase weekly passes for £7.50 ($11.25) for adults or £4 ($6) for children in the central zone, £11.50 ($17.25) adults or £4 ($6) children for all four zones.

Slide your ticket into the slot at the gate, and pick it up as it comes through on the other side and *hold on to it*—it must be presented when you exit the station at your destination. If you're caught without a valid ticket, you'll be fined £10 ($15) on the spot. If you owe extra money, you'll be asked to pay the difference by the attendant at the exit. The Tube runs roughly from 5am to 11:30pm. After that you must take a taxi or night bus. For information on the London Tube system, call the **London Underground** at © **020/7222-1234,** but expect to stay on hold for a while before a live person comes on the line.

The long-running saga known as the Jubilee Line Extension is beginning to reach completion. This line, which once ended at Charing Cross, has been extended eastward to serve the growing suburbs of the southeast and the Docklands area. This east-west axis helps ease traffic on some of London's most hard-pressed Underground lines.

BY BUS

The first thing you learn about London buses is that nobody just boards them. You "queue up"— form a single-file line at the bus stop.

The comparably priced bus system is almost as good as the Underground and gives you better views of the city. For specific routes, pick up a free bus map at one of London Transport's Travel Information Centres, listed above. The map is not available by mail.

London still has some old-style Routemaster buses, with both driver and conductor: After you board, a conductor comes to your seat; you pay a fare based on your destination and receive a ticket. This type of bus is being replaced with buses that have only a driver; you pay as you enter and you exit via a rear door. As with the Underground, the fares vary according to distance traveled. Generally, bus fares are 70p to £1 ($1.05–$1.50), slightly less than Tube fares. If you travel for two or three stops, the cost is £1.50 ($2.25). If you want your stop called out, simply ask the conductor or driver.

Buses generally run between about 5am and 11:30pm. There are a few night buses on special routes, running once an hour or so; most pass through Trafalgar Square. Note that night buses are often so crowded (especially on weekends) that they are unable to pick up passengers after a few stops. You might find yourself waiting a long time. Consider taking a taxi. Call the 24-hour **hotline** (✆ **020/ 7222-1234**) for schedule and fare information.

BY TAXI

London cabs are among the most comfortable and best designed in the world. You can pick one up either by heading for a cab rank or by hailing one in the street (the taxi is available if the yellow taxi sign on the roof is lit); once they have stopped for you, taxis are obliged to take you anywhere you want to go within 6 miles of the pickup point, provided it's within the metropolitan area. To **call a cab,** phone ✆ **020/7272-0272** or ✆ 020/7253-5000.

The minimum fare is £3.80 ($5.70). The meter starts at £3.60 ($5.40), with increments of 20p (35¢) thereafter, based on distance or time. Each additional passenger is charged 40p (70¢). Passengers pay 10p (15¢) for each piece of luggage in the driver's compartment and any other item more than 2 feet long. Surcharges are imposed after 8pm and on weekends and public holidays. All these tariffs include VAT. Fares usually increase annually. It's recommended that you tip 10% to 15% of the fare.

If you call for a cab, the meter starts running when the taxi receives instructions from the dispatcher, so you could find that the meter already reads a few pounds more than the initial drop of £3.60 when you step inside.

Minicabs are also available, and they're often useful when the regular taxis become scarce or when the Tube stops running. These cabs are meterless, so the fare must be negotiated in advance. Unlike regular cabs, minicabs are forbidden to cruise for fares. They operate from sidewalk kiosks, such as those around Leicester Square. If you need to call one, try **Brunswick Chauffeurs/Abbey Cars** (© 020/8969-2555) in west London; **Greater London Hire** (© 020/8340-2450) in north London; **London Cabs, Ltd.** (© 020/8778-3000) in east London; or **Newname Minicars** (© 020/8472-1400) in south London. Minicab kiosks can be found near many Tube or BritRail stops, especially in outlying areas.

If you have a complaint about taxi service, or if you leave something in a cab, contact the **Public Carriage Office,** 15 Penton St., N1 9PU (Tube: Angel Station). If it's a complaint, you must have the cab number, which is displayed in the passenger compartment. Call © 020/7230-1631 with complaints.

Cab sharing is permitted in London, with cabbies permitted to carry two to five persons. Taxis accepting such riders display a notice with the words "Shared Taxi." Each of two riders sharing is charged 65% of the fare a lone passenger would be charged. Three persons pay 55%, four pay 45%, and five (the seating capacity of all new London cabs) pay 40% of the single-passenger fare.

 FAST FACTS: London

American Express The main office is at 30–31 Haymarket, SW1 (© 020/7484-9600; Tube: Piccadilly Circus). Full services are available Monday to Saturday, 9am to 5:30pm. On

Sundays, from 10am to 5pm, only the foreign-exchange bureau is open.

Business Hours Banks are usually open Monday to Friday, 9:30am to 3:30pm. Business offices are open Monday to Friday, 9am to 5pm; the lunch break lasts an hour, but most places stay open during that time. Pubs and bars stay open from 11am to 11pm on Monday to Saturday and from noon to 10:30pm on Sunday. Stores generally open at 9am and close at 5:30pm, staying open until 7pm on Wednesday or Thursday. Most central shops close on Saturday around 1pm. By law, most stores are closed on Sunday. Some service stores, such as small groceries, might remain open.

Dentists For emergencies, call **Eastman Dental Hospital** (© 020/7915-1000; Tube: King's Cross or Chancery Lane).

Doctors In an emergency, some hotels have physicians on call. Also try **Medical Express,** 117A Harley St., W1 (© 020/7499-1991; Tube: Regent's Park), a private clinic; it's not part of the free British medical establishment. For filling the British equivalent of a U.S. prescription, there's sometimes a surcharge of £20 ($30) above the cost of the medicine. The clinic is open Monday to Friday, 9am to 6pm and Saturday, 9:30am to 2:30pm.

Drugstores In Britain they're called chemist shops. Every police station has a list of emergency chemists (dial 0 and ask for the local police). One of the most centrally located, keeping long hours, is **Bliss the Chemist,** 5 Marble Arch, W1 (© 020/7723-6116; Tube: Marble Arch), open daily, 9am to midnight. Every London neighborhood has a branch of **Boots,** Britain's leading pharmacy.

Electricity British current is 240 volts, AC, so you'll need a converter or transformer for U.S.-made appliances, as well as an adapter that allows the plug to match British outlets. Some (but not all) hotels supply them for guests. If you've forgotten one, you can buy a transformer/adapter at most branches of **Boots the Chemist.**

Embassies & High Commissions If you lose your passport or experience some other emergency, here's a list of addresses and phone numbers: **Australia** The high commission is at Australia House, Strand, WC2 (© 020/7379-4334; Tube: Charing Cross or Aldwych); it's open Monday to Friday from 10am to 4pm. **Canada** The high commission is located at

MacDonald House, 38 Grosvenor Sq., W1 (© 020/7258-6600; Tube: Bond Street); it's open Monday to Friday from 8am to 4pm. **Ireland** The embassy is at 17 Grosvenor Place, SW1 (© 020/7235-2171; Tube: Hyde Park Corner); it's open Monday to Friday from 9:30am to 1pm and 2:15 to 5pm. **New Zealand** The high commission is at New Zealand House, 80 Haymarket at Pall Mall, SW1 (© 020/7930-8422; Tube: Charing Cross or Piccadilly Circus); it's open Monday to Friday from 9am to 5pm, but hours vary by department. **The United States** The embassy is at 24 Grosvenor Sq., W1 (© 020/7499-9000; Tube: Bond Street). For passport and visa information, go to the U.S. Passport & Citizenship Unit, 55–56 Upper Brook St., W1 (© 020/7499-9000, ext. 2563 or 2564; Tube: Marble Arch or Bond Street). Hours are Monday to Friday from 8:30am to 5:30pm. Passport and Citizenship unit hours are Monday to Friday, 8:30am to 11:30am and Monday, Wednesday, and Friday, 2 to 4pm.

Emergencies For police, fire, or an ambulance, dial © **999.**

Hospitals The following offer emergency care in London 24 hours a day, with the first treatment free: **Royal Free Hospital,** Pond Street, NW3 (© 020/7794-0500; Tube: Belsize Park), and **University College Hospital,** Grafton Way, WC1 (© 020/7387-9300; Tube: Warren Street or Euston Square). Many other London hospitals also have accident and emergency departments.

Hotlines For police or medical emergencies, dial © **999** (no coins required). If you're in some sort of **legal emergency,** call **Release** at © 020/7729-9904, 24 hours a day. **The Rape Crisis Line** is © 020/7837-1600, accepting calls after 6pm. **Samaritans,** 46 Marshall St., W1 (© 020/7734-2800; Tube: Oxford Circus or Piccadilly Circus), maintains a crisis hotline that helps with all kinds of trouble, even threatened suicides. Doors are open from 9am to 9pm daily, but phones are open 24 hours. **Alcoholics Anonymous** (© 020/7833-0022) answers its hotline daily from 10am to 10pm. The **AIDS** 24-hour hotline is © **0800/567-123.**

Liquor Laws No alcohol is served to anyone under 18. Children under 16 aren't allowed in pubs, except in certain rooms, and only when accompanied by a parent or guardian. Pubs are open Monday to Saturday from 11am to 11pm and Sunday noon to 10:30pm. Restaurants are allowed to serve liquor during the same hours as pubs; only people eating a meal on the premises can be served. You can buy beer, wine, and liquor in supermarkets, liquor stores (called off-licenses), and local grocery stores during any hour that pubs are open. In hotels, liquor may be served from 11am to 11pm to residents and nonresidents; after 11pm, only residents may be served. Any nightclub that charges admission is allowed to serve alcohol until 3am or so. Don't drink and drive; penalties are stiff.

Newspapers/Magazines *The Times, Daily Telegraph, Daily Mail,* and *Guardian* are dailies carrying the latest news. The *International Herald Tribune,* published in Paris, and an international edition of *USA Today* are available daily. *Time* and *Newsweek* are sold at most newsstands. *Time Out, City Limits,* and *Where* are magazines containing useful information about the latest happenings in London.

Police In an emergency, dial ✆ **999** (no coins required). You can also go to a local police station in central London, including New Scotland Yard, Broadway, SW1 (✆ **020/7230-1212;** Tube: St. James's Park).

Post Offices The **main post office** is at 24–25 William IV St. (✆ **020/7484-9307;** Tube: Charing Cross). Inland and international postal service and banking are available Monday to Friday, 8am to 8pm and Saturday, 9am to 8pm; philatelic postage stamp sales Monday to Saturday, 8am to 8pm; and the post shop, selling greeting cards and stationery, Monday to Saturday, 8am to 8pm. Other post offices are open Monday to Friday, 9am to 5:30pm and on Saturday, 9am to 12:30pm. Many sub-post offices and some main post offices close for an hour at lunchtime.

Rest Rooms They're marked by PUBLIC TOILETS signs in streets, parks, and Tube stations; many are sterilized after each use. The English often call toilets "loos." You'll find well-maintained lavatories in all larger public buildings, such as museums and art galleries, large department stores, and railway stations. It's not really acceptable to use the lavatories in hotels, restaurants, and pubs if you're not a customer, but we can't say that we always stick to this rule. Public lavatories are usually free, but you may need a small coin to get in or to use a proper washroom.

Smoking   Most U.S. cigarette brands are available in London. Smoking is forbidden in the Underground and on buses, and it's increasingly frowned upon in many other places. Most restaurants have nonsmoking tables, but they're usually separated from the smoking section by a little bit of space. Nonsmoking rooms are available in the bigger hotels. Some of the smaller hotels claim to have nonsmoking rooms, but we've often found that this means the room is smoke-free only during our visit; if you're bothered by the odor, ask to be shown another room.

Taxes   There is a 17.5% national **value-added tax (VAT)** added to all hotel and restaurant bills and included in the price of many items you purchase. It can be refunded if you shop at stores that participate in the Retail Export Scheme (signs are posted in the window). See the "How to Get Your VAT Refund" box in chapter 6, "Shopping."

You also pay a departure tax of £10 ($15) for flights within Britain and the European Union; it's £20 ($30) for flights to the U.S. and other countries. Your airline ticket may or may not include this tax. Ask in advance to avoid a surprise at the gate.

To encourage energy conservation, the British government levies a 25% tax on gasoline ("petrol").

Telephone   For directory assistance in London, dial ℂ **142;** for the rest of Britain, ℂ **192.**

To call London from the United States, dial 011 (international code), **44** (Britain's country code), **020** (the area code for anywhere in London), and the eight-digit local number. To make an international call from London, dial the international access code (00), the country code, the area code, and finally the local number. Or use one of the following long-distance access codes: **AT&T USA Direct** (ℂ **0800/890011**), **Canada Direct** (ℂ **0800/890016**), **Australia** (ℂ **0800/890061**), and **New Zealand** (ℂ **0800/890064**). Country codes: **U.S. and Canada,** 1; **Australia,** 61; **New Zealand,** 64; **South Africa,** 27.

To call within London, dial the local seven- or eight-digit number. Phone numbers outside the major cities consist of an exchange name plus telephone number. To dial the number, you need to dial the exchange code first. Information sheets on call-box walls give the codes in most instances. If your code isn't there, call the operator at **100.**

There are three types of public pay phones: those taking only coins, those accepting only phonecards (called Cardphones), and those that take both. At coin-operated phones, insert your coins before dialing. The minimum charge is 10p (15¢).

Phonecards are available in four values—£2 ($3), £5 ($7.50), £10 ($15), and £20 ($30)—and are reusable until the total value has expired. Cards can be purchased from newsstands and post offices. You can also use credit cards—Access (MasterCard), Visa, American Express, and Diners Club—at credit-call pay phones, commonly found at airports and large railway stations.

Time England follows Greenwich Mean Time (5 hours ahead of Eastern Standard Time). Most of the year Britain is 5 hours ahead of the East Coast of the United States. When it's noon in New York, it's 5pm in London. Because the U.S. and Britain observe Daylight Saving Time at slightly different times of year, there's a brief period (about a week) in spring when it's 6 hours ahead of New York.

Tipping In restaurants, service charges in the 15% to 20% range are usually added to the bill. Sometimes this is clearly marked; at other times, it isn't. When in doubt, ask. If service isn't included, it's customary to add 15% to the bill. Sommeliers get about £1 ($1.50) per bottle of wine served. There's no tipping in pubs. In cocktail bars, the server usually gets about 75p ($1.15) per round of drinks.

Hotels, like restaurants, often add a service charge of 10% to 15% to most bills. In smaller B&Bs, the tip isn't likely to be included. Therefore, tip for special service, such as for the person who served you breakfast. If several persons have served you in a B&B, many guests ask that 10% or 15% be added to the bill and divided among the staff. Tip chambermaids $1 per day for cleaning up (more if you've made their job extra difficult).

It's standard to tip taxi drivers 10% to 15% of the fare, although a tip for a taxi driver should never be less than 30p (45¢). Barbers and hairdressers expect 10% to 15%. Tour guides expect £2 ($3), although it's not mandatory. Theater ushers don't expect tips.

3

Accommodations

Worried that it would not have enough room for all the people coming to visit the city, the London Tourist Board campaigned to secure another 10,000 hotel rooms by 2000. The city met that target, but the new hotels are mostly in districts far from the center and are of the no-frills, budget chain variety.

With all the improvements and upgrades at the turn of the 21st century, chances are you'll like your room. What you won't like is the price. Even if a hotel remains scruffy, hoteliers will still jack up the price. Hotels in all categories remain overpriced.

The following services will arrange a B&B room for you: **Bed & Breakfast** (© **800/367-4668** or 423/690-8484), **London Bed & Breakfast Association** (© **800/852-2632** in the United States, or 020/7842-9123 for homes in inner and downtown London; fax 020/8749-7084; fax from U.S. 619/531-1686), and **The London Bed and Breakfast Agency Limited** (© **020/7586-2768;** fax 020/7586-6567), another reputable agency that can provide inexpensive accommodations in selected private homes. Prices range from £20 to £42 ($30 to $63) per person per night, based on double occupancy, although some will cost a lot more. **US/European B&B** (© **800/872-2632** in the U.S. or 619/531-1179; fax 619/531-1686; www.londonbandb.com) offers B&B accommodations in private family residences or unhosted apartments. They are inspected for quality and comfort, amenities, and convenience.

1 The West End

BLOOMSBURY

EXPENSIVE

Academy Hotel 🅰 The Academy is in the heart of London's publishing district. Many original architectural details were preserved when these three 1776 Georgian rowhouses were joined. The hotel was substantially upgraded in the 1990s, with a bathroom added to every bedroom (whether there was space or not). Fourteen have a tub-shower combination; the rest have showers only. The beds, so they say, were built to "American specifications." True or not, they assure you of a restful night's sleep. Grace notes include the glass panels, colonnades, and plasterwork on the facade. With their overstuffed armchairs and half-canopied beds, rooms here evoke English country-house living, but with poorer relations. *Warning:* If you can't do stairs, this may not be the place for you—there are no elevators rising to the four floors. Return guests request rooms opening on the garden in back, not those in front with ducted fresh air, although the front units have double-glazing to cut down on the noise. The theater district and Covent Garden are within walking distance. The in-house, award-winning restaurant, Alchemy, has been refurbished and offers a reasonably priced menu of modern European food.

17–21 Gower St., London WC1E 6HG. (©) **800/678-3096** in the U.S., or 020/7631-4115. Fax 020/7636-3442. E-mail: academy@aol.com. 48 units. £125–£145 ($187.50–$217.50) double; £185 ($277.50) suite. AE, DC, MC, V. Tube: Tottenham Court Rd., Goodge St., or Russell Sq. **Amenities:** restaurant; bar; library; patio garden; room service; laundry/dry cleaning. *In room:* A/C, TV.

Myhotel *(Finds* Creating shock waves among staid Bloomsbury hoteliers, Myhotel is a London rowhouse on the outside with Asian *moderne* in its interior. It is designed according to *feng shui* principles—the ancient Chinese art of placement that analyzes the flow of energy in a space. Tipping is discouraged, and each guest is assigned a personal assistant responsible for one's happiness. Aimed at today's young, hip traveler, Myhotel lies within a short walk of Covent Garden and the British Museum. Rooms are pockets of comfort and taste. Excellent sleep-producing beds are found in all rooms, plus a small bathroom with shower stall.

11–13 Bayley St., Bedford Sq., London WC1B 3HD. (©) **020/7667-6000.** Fax 020/7667-6044. www.holidaycity.com/myhotel-london/. 76 units. £195–£225 ($292.50–$337.50) double; from £315 ($472.50) family room. AE, DC, MC, V. Tube: Tottenham Court Rd. **Amenities:** breakfast cafe; restaurant; bar; 24-hour room service. *In room:* A/C, TV, minibar, hair dryer.

MODERATE

Harlingford Hotel   This hotel is comprised of three townhouses built in the 1820s, joined around 1900 via a bewildering array of staircases and hallways. Set in the heart of Bloomsbury, it's run by a management that seems concerned about the welfare of their guests, unlike many of their neighboring rivals. (They distribute little mincemeat pies to their guests during the Christmas holidays.) Double-glazed windows cut down on the noise, and all the bedrooms are comfortable, especially because of the firm mattresses.

Hotels of London

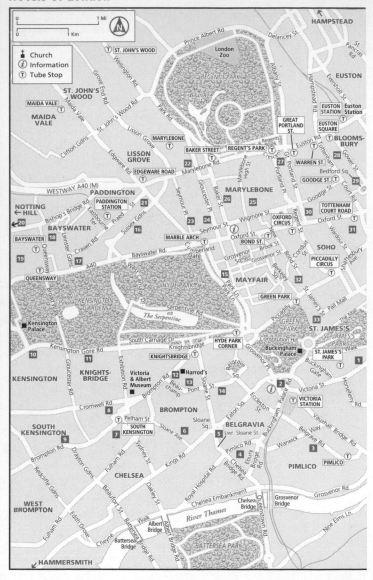

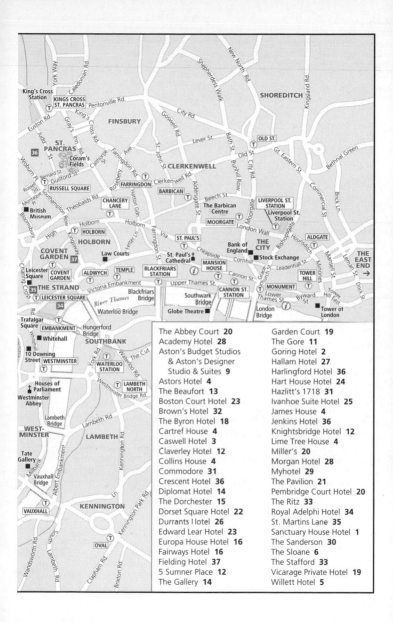

The Abbey Court **20**
Academy Hotel **28**
Aston's Budget Studios
  & Aston's Designer
  Studio & Suites **9**
Astors Hotel **4**
The Beaufort **13**
Boston Court Hotel **23**
Brown's Hotel **32**
The Byron Hotel **18**
Cartref House **4**
Caswell Hotel **3**
Claverley Hotel **12**
Collins House **4**
Commodore **31**
Crescent Hotel **36**
Diplomat Hotel **14**
The Dorchester **15**
Dorset Square Hotel **22**
Durrants Hotel **26**
Edward Lear Hotel **23**
Europa House Hotel **16**
Fairways Hotel **16**
Fielding Hotel **37**
5 Sumner Place **12**
The Gallery **14**

Garden Court **19**
The Gore **11**
Goring Hotel **2**
Hallam Hotel **27**
Harlingford Hotel **36**
Hart House Hotel **24**
Hazlitt's 1718 **31**
Ivanhoe Suite Hotel **25**
James House **4**
Jenkins Hotel **36**
Knightsbridge Hotel **12**
Lime Tree House **4**
Miller's **20**
Morgan Hotel **28**
Myhotel **29**
The Pavilion **21**
Pembridge Court Hotel **20**
The Ritz **33**
Royal Adelphi Hotel **34**
St. Martins Lane **35**
Sanctuary House Hotel **1**
The Sanderson **30**
The Sloane **6**
The Stafford **33**
Vicarage Private Hotel **19**
Willett Hotel **5**

Shower-only bathrooms are small, since the house wasn't originally designed for them. The most comfortable rooms are on the second and third levels; otherwise, expect to climb some steep English stairs (there's no elevator). Rooms on ground level are darker and have less security. You'll have use of the tennis courts in Cartwright Gardens.

61–63 Cartwright Gardens, London WC1H 9EL. ℂ 020/7387-1551. Fax 020/7387-4616. 44 units. £88 ($132) double; £98 ($147) triple; £108 ($162) quad. Rates include English breakfast. AE, DC, MC, V. Tube: Russell Sq., King's Cross, or Euston. **Amenities:** Use of tennis courts in Cartwright Gardens. *In room:* TV, coffeemaker, hair dryer.

INEXPENSIVE

Crescent Hotel   Although Ruskin and Shelley no longer pass by, the Crescent still stands in the heart of academic London. The private square is owned by the City Guild of Skinners and guarded by the University of London. You have access to the gardens and tennis courts belonging to the Skinners. Mrs. Bessolo and Mrs. Cockle, the managers, are the kindest hosts along the street; they view Crescent as an extension of their home and welcome you to its comfortably elegant Georgian surroundings, which date from 1810. Some guests have been returning for 4 decades. Bedrooms range from small singles with shared bathrooms to more spacious twin and double rooms with private showers. All have good mattresses, plus extras such as alarm clocks. Twins and doubles have private plumbing, with tiny bathrooms. Many rooms are singles, however, ranging in price from £43 to £70 ($64.50 to $105), depending on the plumbing. The ladies will even let you do your ironing, so that you'll look sharp when you go out on the town.

49–50 Cartwright Gardens, London WC1H 9EL. ℂ 020/7387-1515. Fax 020/7383-2054. www.crescenthoteloflondon.com. 27 units, 18 with bathroom (some with shower only, some with tub only). £85 ($127.50) double with bathroom. Rates include English breakfast. MC, V. Tube: Russell Sq., King's Cross, or Euston. **Amenities:** Use of tennis courts in Cartwright Gardens. *In room:* TV, coffeemaker, hair dryer.

Jenkins Hotel 🅡 *(Value*   Followers of the Agatha Christie TV series "Poirot" recognize this Cartwright Gardens residence—it was featured in the series. The antiques are gone and the rooms are small, but some of the original charm of the Georgian house remains— enough so that the London *Mail on Sunday* proclaimed it one of the "ten best hotel values" in the city. All the rooms have been redecorated and many completely refurbished, with firm mattresses added to all the beds. Only a few have private shower-only bathrooms, and they're quite small, but the corridor bathrooms are well maintained.

The location is great, near the British Museum, London University, theaters, and antiquarian bookshops. There are some drawbacks: no lift and no reception or sitting room. But this is a place where you can settle in and feel at home.

45 Cartwright Gardens, London WC1H 9EH. ℂ 020/7387-2067. Fax 020/7383-3139. www.jenkinshotel.demon.co.uk. 15 units, 6 with bathroom. £68 ($102) double without bathroom, £90 ($153) double with bathroom; £115 ($195.50) triple with bathroom. Rates include English breakfast. MC, V. Tube: Russell Sq., King's Cross, or Euston. *In room:* TV, minibar, fridge, coffeemaker, hair dryer, iron/ironing board, safe.

Morgan Hotel   In a row of Georgian houses, each built in the 1790s, this much-restored hotel is distinguished by its gold-tipped iron fence railings. The flower boxes outside preview the warmth and hospitality inside. The family managers do all the work themselves, and have such a devoted following that it's hard to get a reservation in summer. Several rooms, each individually designed, overlook the British Museum. Even if things are a bit cramped and the stairs steep, the rooms are pleasant and the atmosphere congenial. The carpeted bedrooms have big beds (by British standards), dressing tables with mirrors, ample wardrobe space, and batik bedspreads; about 11 of the rooms have air-conditioning. The suites are worth the extra money if you can afford it. They're furnished tastefully with polished dark English pieces, framed English prints, and decorator fabrics, all with spacious bathrooms. Suites also have irons and kitchenettes.

24 Bloomsbury St., London WC1B 3QJ. ℂ 020/7636-3735. Fax 020/7636-3045. 21 units. £80 ($120) double; £120 ($180) triple; £110 ($165) suite. Rates include English breakfast. MC, V. Tube: Russell Sq. or Tottenham Court Rd. *In room:* TV, hair dryer, safe.

COVENT GARDEN & THE STRAND
VERY EXPENSIVE

The Savoy 𝄢𝄢𝄢   Although not as swank as the Dorchester, this London landmark is the premier hotel in the Strand/Covent Garden area. Richard D'Oyly Carte built it in 1889 as an annex to his Savoy Theatre, where many Gilbert and Sullivan operettas were staged. Each room is individually decorated with color-coordinated accessories, comfortable furniture, large closets, and an eclectic blend of antiques, such as gilt mirrors, Queen Anne chairs, and Victorian sofas; 48 units have their own sitting rooms. The handmade beds have top-of-the-line crisp linen clothing and luxury mattresses. Some bathrooms have shower stalls, but most have a combination shower and tub. Bathrooms are spacious, with deluxe toiletries. The riverview suites are the most sought after, and for good reason—the vistas are the best in London. *Tip:* You can ask for one of the newer rooms in what was formerly a riverview storage space. They are among the best in the hotel, with views of the Thames and Parliament.

The Strand, London WC2R 0EU. ☎ **800/63-SAVOY** or 020/7836-4343. Fax 020/7240-6040. www.savoy-group.co.uk. 207 units. £330–£370 ($495–$555) double; from £455 ($682.50) suite. AE, DC, MC, V. Parking £25 ($37.50). Tube: Charing Cross or Covent Garden. **Amenities:** Celebrated Savoy Grill; River Restaurant overlooking Thames; bistro; city's best health club; valet; hairdresser; business center; 24-hour room service; laundry/dry cleaning. *In room:* A/C, TV, minibar, fridge, hair dryer, safe.

St. Martins Lane 🏵🏵🏵   "Eccentric and irreverent, with a sense of humor," is how Ian Schrager describes his cutting-edge Covent Garden hotel, transformed from a 1960s office building into a chic enclave. This was Schrager's first hotel outside the U.S., after a string of successes from New York to West Hollywood. The hip mix of design and a sense of cool have made it across the pond. Whimsical touches abound: a string of daisies replaces DO NOT DISTURB signs. Rooms are all white, but you can use the full-spectrum lighting to make them any color. Floor-to-ceiling glass windows in every room offer a panoramic view of London, and down comforters and soft pillows ensure a good night's sleep. Some rooms are nonsmoking, and bathrooms are spacious with deluxe toiletries and full plumbing.

45 St. Martins Lane, London WC2N 4HX. ☎ 020/7300-5500. Fax 020/7300-5501. www.ianschragerhotels.com. 204 units. £275–£500 ($412.50–$750) double; from £700 ($1,050) suite. AE, DC, MC, V. Tube: Covent Garden or Leicester Sq. **Amenities:** restaurant, Asia de Cuba; outdoor garden restaurant; 24-hour brasserie; bar; play area for kids; business center; 24-hour room service; laundry/dry cleaning. *In room:* A/C, TV, minibar, hair dryer, safe.

MODERATE

Fielding Hotel 🏵 *Finds*   One of London's more eccentric hotels, the Fielding is quirky and quaint, but an enduring favorite. Luring media types, the hotel is named after novelist Henry Fielding of *Tom Jones* fame, who lived in Broad Court. It lies on a pedestrian street lined with 19th-century gas lamps; the Royal Opera House is across the street; and the pubs, shops, and restaurants of Covent Garden are just beyond the front door. Rooms are small, but old-fashioned and traditional. Some units are redecorated or at least "touched up" every year, and the mattresses are renewed frequently.

Bathrooms with tubs are minuscule, and few rooms have anything approaching a view. Floors dip and sway, and the furnishings and fabrics have known better times. The bathrooms, some with antiquated plumbing, have a set of good-size towels. If you want a hair dryer, request one from the front desk. But with a location like this, guests keep coming back; many love the hotel's rickety charm. There's no room service or restaurant, but breakfast is served.

4 Broad Ct., Bow St., London WC2B 5QZ. © 020/7836-8305. Fax 020/7497-0064. www.the-fielding-hotel.co.uk. 24 units. £88–£98 ($132–$147) double; £140 ($210) triple; £185 ($277.50) suite. AE, DC, MC, V. Tube: Covent Garden. **Amenities:** breakfast room; small bar. *In room:* TV, coffeemaker.

INEXPENSIVE

Royal Adelphi Hotel   If you care most about location, consider the Royal Adelphi. Close to Covent Garden, the theater district, and Trafalgar Square, it's an unorthodox choice but it's away from the typical B&B stamping grounds. Villiers Street, on which the hotel sits, was named for George Villiers, Duke of Buckingham and 17th-century courtier. The hotel is above an Italian restaurant. Although the bedrooms call to mind London's swinging 1960s heyday, accommodations are decently maintained and comfortable, with good beds. The plumbing is a bit creaky. The lack of air-conditioning can make London seem like summer in the Australian outback during the few hot days. London has better B&Bs, but not in this part of town.

21 Villiers St., London WC2N 6ND. © 020/7930-8764. Fax 020/7930-8735. www.royaladelphi.co.uk. 47 units, 34 with bathroom. £68 ($102) double without bathroom; £90 ($135) double with bathroom; £120 ($180) triple with bathroom. Extra bed £15 ($22.50). AE, DC, MC, V. Tube: Charing Cross or Embankment. *In room:* TV, coffeemaker, hair dryer.

SOHO
VERY EXPENSIVE

The Sanderson ☆☆☆   Ian Schrager strikes again. For his latest London hotel, celebrity hotelier Schrager secured the help of talented partners, Philippe Starck and Andra Andrei, to create an "ethereal, transparent urban spa," in which walls are replaced by glass and layers of curtains. The location is near Oxford Street, north of Soho. The hotel comes with a lush bamboo-filled roof garden, a large courtyard, and spa. Its two restaurants are directed by Alain Ducasse, one of the world's great chefs. How does Schrager explain this hotel? Enigmatically he says, "the envelope is minimalist, but the contents are baroque, which gives rise to a certain tension." A former corporate headquarters, the transformation into a hotel has been remarkable, although the dreary grid facade in aluminum squares and glass remains. Your bed is likely to be an Italian silver leaf sleigh attended by spidery polished steel night tables and draped with a fringed pashmina shawl the color of dried lemon verbena.

50 Berners St., London W1P 3AD. ℂ **020/7300-1400.** Fax 020/7300-1401. www.hotels-london.co.uk/fivestar-sandersons/. 150 units. £317.25–£552.25 ($475.90–$828.40) double. Ask about weekend specials. AE, DC, MC, V. Tube: Leicester Sq. or Covent Garden. **Amenities:** 2 restaurants; 3 bars; health bar; yoga and fitness studio; children's area; 24-hour room service. *In room:* A/C, TV, minibar, hair dryer.

EXPENSIVE

Hazlitt's 1718 🤿🤿 *Finds*   This gem, housed in three historic homes on Soho Square, is one of London's best small hotels. Built in 1718, it is named for William Hazlitt, who founded the Unitarian church in Boston and wrote four volumes on the life of his hero, Napoleon.

It's eclectic, filled with odds and ends picked up around the country at estate auctions. Some find the Georgian decor a bit spartan, but the 2,000 original prints hanging on the walls brighten it considerably. Many bedrooms have four-poster beds, and some bathrooms have original claw-footed tubs (only one unit has a shower). If you can afford it, opt for the Baron Willoughby suite, with its giant four-poster bed and wood-burning fireplace. Some of the floors dip and sway and there's no elevator, but it's all part of the charm. It has just as much character as the quirky Fielding Hotel (above) but is a lot more comfortable. Some rooms are a bit small, but most are spacious, and all have state-of-the-art mattresses. Most of the bathrooms have 19th-century styling but up-to-date plumbing with oversize tubs and old brass fittings; the showers, however, are mostly hand-held. Accommodations in the back are quieter but perhaps too dark, and only those on the top floor have air-conditioning. Soho is at your doorstep; the young, hip staff will direct you to the local hot spots.

6 Frith St., London W1V 5TZ. ℂ **020/7434-1771.** Fax 020/7439-1524. www.hazlittshotel.com. 23 units. £195 ($331.50) double; £300 ($450) suite. AE, DC, MC, V. Tube: Leicester Sq. or Tottenham Court Rd. **Amenities:** video rentals; 24-hour room service; baby-sitting; laundry/dry cleaning. *In room:* TV, minibar, hair dryer, safe.

MAYFAIR
VERY EXPENSIVE

Brown's Hotel ✦✦✦   Almost every year a hotel sprouts up trying to evoke an English country house ambience with Chippendale and chintz; Brown's always comes out on top. It was founded by James Brown, former manservant to Lord Byron, who wanted to create a dignified, clublike place for them. He opened its doors in 1837, the same year Queen Victoria took the throne.

Brown's, which occupies 14 historic houses off Berkeley Square, is still true to its founder's vision. The guest rooms vary in decor, but all show restrained taste; even the washbasins are antiques. Accommodations, which range from small to spacious, have such extras as voicemail, dual-phone lines, and dataports. Beds may be antiques, but the luxurious mattresses are of more recent vintage. Bathrooms come in a variety of sizes, with robes, cosmetics, tubs, and showers. The lounges include the Roosevelt Room (TR honeymooned here in 1886), the Rudyard Kipling Room (he was a frequent visitor), and the paneled St. George's Bar.

Albemarle St., London W1X 4BP. ✆ **020/7493-6020.** Fax 020/7493-9381. www.brownshotel.com. 118 units. £290–£400 ($493–$680) double; from £435 ($652.50) suite. AE, DC, MC, V. Off-site parking £40 ($68). Tube: Green Park. **Amenities:** restaurant; bar; health club nearby; business center; 24-hour room service. *In room:* A/C, TV, minibar, hair dryer, safe.

The Dorchester ✦✦✦   This is one of London's best hotels. Few hotels have the time-honored experience of "The Dorch," which has maintained a tradition of fine comfort and cuisine since 1931.

Breaking from the neoclassical tradition, the architects designed a building of reinforced concrete clothed in terrazzo slabs. Within, you'll find a 1930s take on Regency motifs: monumental arrangements of flowers and the elegance of the promenade, appropriate for a diplomatic reception, yet with a comfort in which guests from all over the world feel at ease.

The Dorchester boasts guest rooms outfitted with Irish linen on deluxe mattresses, plus all the gadgetry you'd expect, and double- and triple-glazed windows, armchairs, cherrywood furnishings, and, in many cases, four-poster beds. The large bathrooms are equally stylish, with Carrara marble and Lalique-style sconces, makeup mirrors and toiletries, and deep tubs. The best rooms have views of Hyde Park.

The hotel's restaurant, **The Grill Room,** is among the finest establishments in London, and the **Dorchester Bar** is a legendary meeting place. The promenade, with its lush sofas, is the ideal setting to enjoy afternoon tea and watch the world go by. The hotel also offers Cantonese cuisine at **The Oriental,** London's most exclusive—and expensive—Chinese restaurant.

53 Park Lane, London W1A 2HJ. ℭ **800/727-9820** or 020/7629-8888. Fax 020/7409-0114. www.dorchester.hotel.com. 248 units. £320–£350 ($480–$525) double; from £475 ($712.50) suite. AE, DC, MC, V. Parking £32 ($48). Tube: Hyde Park Corner or Marble Arch. **Amenities:** 3 restaurants; bar; 24-hour room service; laundry/dry cleaning; health club; car rental desk; spa; hair salons; business services; baby-sitting. *In room:* A/C, TV, minibar, hair dryer, iron/ironing board, safe.

ST. JAMES'S
VERY EXPENSIVE

The Ritz 𝕽𝕽𝕽   Built in the French-Renaissance style by César Ritz in 1906, this hotel overlooking Green Park is synonymous with luxury: Gold-leaf molding, marble columns, and potted palms abound. After a major restoration, the hotel is better than ever: New carpeting and air-conditioning have been installed, and an overall polishing has recaptured much of the Ritz's original splendor. The Belle Epoque guest rooms, each with its own character, are spacious and comfortable. Many have marble fireplaces, gilded plasterwork, and a decor of soft pastel hues. A few rooms have their original brass beds and marble fireplaces. Beds are deluxe with luxury mattresses, and the bathrooms are elegantly appointed in either tile or marble and filled with deep tubs with showers, robes, phones, and deluxe toiletries. Corner rooms are grander and more spacious.

The Ritz is the most fashionable place in London for tea at the **Ritz Palm Court** (see "Teatime," in chapter 4, "Dining"). The **Ritz Restaurant,** one of the loveliest dining rooms in the world, has been restored to its original splendor.

150 Piccadilly, London W1J 9BR. ℭ **877/748-9536** or 020/7493-8181. Fax 020/7493-2687. www.theritzlondon.co.uk. 133 units. £295–£415 ($442.50–$622.50) double; from £485 ($727.50) suite. Children under 12 stay free in parents' room. AE, DC, MC, V. Parking £50 ($75). Tube: Green Park. **Amenities:** restaurant; palm court; fitness center; business services; 24-hour room service; massage; laundry/dry cleaning. *In room:* A/C, TV, minibar, hair dryer.

The Stafford 𝕽𝕽𝕽   Famous for its American Bar, its discretion, and the warmth of its Edwardian decor, the Stafford is in a cul-de-sac off one of London's most centrally located neighborhoods. It's reached via St. James's Place or by a cobble-covered courtyard known today as the Blue Ball Yard. The recently refurbished 19th-century hotel has retained a country-house atmosphere, with antique charm and modern amenities.

All the guest rooms are individually decorated, reflecting the hotel's origins as a private home. Many singles contain queen-size beds. Most of the units have king-size or twin beds, and all contain quality mattresses. Some of the deluxe units also offer four-poster beds to make you feel like Henry VIII. Nearly all the bathrooms are clad in marble with tubs and stall showers, toiletries, and chrome fixtures. A few of the hotel's newest accommodations in the restored stable mews require a walk across the yard. These rooms are superior in some ways to those in the main building, and much has been saved to preserve their original style, including A-beams on the upper floors—but no 18th-century horse ever slept like this. Units come with electronic safes, stereo systems, and quality furnishings, mostly antique reproductions. Rooms on the top floor are smaller than you may want.

16–18 St. James's Place, London SW1A 1NJ. ✆ **800/525-4800** or 020/7493-0111. Fax 020/7493-7121. www.thestaffordhotel.co.uk. 81 units. £230–£350 ($345–$525) double; from £345 ($517.50) suite. AE, DC, MC, V. Tube: Green Park. **Amenities:** restaurant; famous American bar; health club privileges nearby; secretarial services; 24-hour room service; baby-sitting; laundry/dry cleaning. *In room:* A/C, TV, hair dryer.

2 Westminster & Victoria

VERY EXPENSIVE

Goring Hotel 🏨🏨🏨   For tradition and location, the Goring is our premier choice in Westminster. Just behind Buckingham Palace, it lies close to the royal parks, Victoria Station, Westminster Abbey, and the Houses of Parliament. It also offers the finest personal service of its nearby competitors.

Built in 1910 by O. R. Goring, this was the first hotel in the world to have central heating and a private bathroom in every room. Today's rooms still offer all the comforts, including luxurious bathrooms with extra-long tubs, red marble walls, dual pedestal basins, bidets, deluxe toiletries, and power showerheads. There is an ongoing refurbishment of all bedrooms, including frequent replacement of mattresses. The beds are among the most comfortable in London. Preferred is one of the rooms overlooking the garden. Queen Anne and Chippendale are usually the decor style. The maintenance is of the highest order. The charm of a traditional English country hotel is evoked in the paneled drawing room, where fires crackle in the ornate fireplaces on nippy evenings. The adjoining bar overlooks the rear gardens.

15 Beeston Place, Grosvenor Gardens, London SW1W 0JW. ℂ **020/7396-9000**. Fax 020/7834-4393. www.goringhotel.co.uk. 75 units. £205–£275 ($348.50–$467.50) double; from £275 ($467.50) suite. AE, DC, MC, V. Parking £25 ($37.50). Tube: Victoria. **Amenities:** Grand afternoon tea in the drawing room (a London highlight); classic restaurant; bar; free use of nearby health club; 24-hour room service; baby-sitting. *In room:* A/C, TV, hair dryer.

MODERATE

Lime Tree Hotel   The Wales-born Davies family, longtime veterans of London's B&B business, have transformed a rundown guesthouse into a cost-conscious but cozy hotel for budget travelers. The simply furnished bedrooms are scattered over four floors of a brick townhouse; each has been refitted with new curtains, cupboards, firm mattresses, and upholstery. The front rooms have small balconies overlooking Ebury Street; units in the back don't have balconies, but are quieter and have views of the hotel's rose garden. The rooms tend to be larger than many at similar prices, and breakfasts are generous. Six rooms come with a tub and shower combo, the rest with shower only. Buckingham Palace, Westminster Abbey, and the Houses of Parliament are close, as is Harrods.

135–137 Ebury St., London SW1W 9RA. ℂ **020/7730-8191**. Fax 020/7730-7865. www.limetreehotel.co.uk. 26 units. £105–£115 ($157.50–$172.50) double. Rates include English breakfast. AE, CB, DC, MC, V. Tube: Victoria. *In room:* TV, coffeemaker, hair dryer, safe.

The Sanctuary House Hotel ✿   Only in the new London, where hotels are bursting into bloom like daffodils, would you find a hotel so close to Westminster Abbey. And a pub hotel, no less, with rooms above the tavern. Rooms have a rustic feel, but first-rate beds and mattresses, and newly restored bathrooms with state-of-the-art plumbing. The building was converted by Fuller Smith and Turner, a traditional brewery in Britain. Downstairs, a pub/restaurant, part of The Sanctuary, offers old-style British meals. "We like tradition," one of the staff members told us. "Why must everything be trendy? Some people come to England nostalgic for the old." The food is excellent if you like the roast beef, Welsh lamb, and Dover sole known to Churchill's palate. Naturally, there's always plenty of brew on tap.

33 Tothill St., London SW1H 9LA. ℂ **020/7799-4044**. Fax 020/7799-3657. www.fullers.co.uk. 34 units. £79–£109 ($118.50–$163.50) double. AE, DC, MC, V. Parking £20 ($30). Tube: St. James's Park. **Amenities:** restaurant; pub. *In room:* A/C, TV, coffeemaker, hair dryer.

INEXPENSIVE

Astors Hotel   This well-located choice is a stone's throw from Buckingham Palace and a short walk from Victoria Station. It was once home to Victorian novelist Margaret Oliphant (1828–1897); Noel Coward was a neighbor; and H. G. Wells, Yeats, Bennett, and Shaw called down the street at no. 153 when poet, novelist, and autobiographer George Moore (1852–1933) was at home. Guests today are travelers looking for a decent, affordable address in pricey London. Although more functional than glamorous, the rooms are satisfactory in every way. Much of the hotel, including the shower-only bathrooms, was renovated in 1998. Each unit is fitted with a comfortable mattress, and bathrooms are well maintained. Because space and furnishings vary, ask to take a peek before committing to a room.

110–112 Ebury St., London SW1W 9QD. 𝒞 020/7730-3811. Fax 020/7823-6728. www.astors.uk.com. 35 units, 12 with bathroom. £60 ($90) double without bathroom, £72 ($108) double with bathroom; from £140 ($210) family unit with bathroom. Rates include English breakfast. MC, V. Parking £30 ($45) nearby. Tube: Victoria. *In room:* TV, coffeemaker. No phone.

Caswell Hotel   Run with consideration and thoughtfulness by Mr. and Mrs. Hare, Caswell is on a cul-de-sac, a calm oasis in a busy area. Mozart lived nearby while he completed his first symphony, as did that "notorious couple," Harold Nicholson and Victoria Sackville-West of the literati. Beyond the chintz-filled lobby, the decor is understated. There are four floors of well-furnished but not spectacular bedrooms. Mattresses are acceptable, but could use replacement soon. Private bathrooms are small units with a shower stall; however, corridor bathrooms are well maintained. How do they explain their success? One staff member said, "This year's guest is next year's business."

25 Gloucester St., London SW1V 2DB. 𝒞 020/7834-6345. www.hotellondon. co.uk. 18 units, 7 with bathroom. £60 ($90) double without bathroom, £80 ($120) double with bathroom. Rates include English breakfast. MC, V. Tube: Victoria. *In room:* TV, minibar, coffeemaker, hair dryer, safe.

Collin House   This B&B emerges as a winner on a street that is lined with the finest Victoria Station–area B&Bs. Queen Victoria was halfway through her reign when this house was built. Private, shower-only bathrooms have been installed in areas not designed for plumbing, but everything works efficiently. For rooms without a bathroom, there are hallway facilities, some of which are shared by no more than two rooms. Traffic in this area of London is heavy, and the front windows are not soundproof, so be warned. Each year, the owners make improvements in the furnishings and carpets. All bedrooms, which vary in size, are comfortably furnished and well maintained. Two rooms are large enough for families. A generous breakfast awaits you each morning in this nonsmoking facility.

104 Ebury St., London SW1W 9QD. ℂ and fax **020/7730-8031**. www.milford. co.uk/england/accom/h-l-3229.html. 13 units, 8 with bathroom (shower only). £68 ($102) double without bathroom, £82 ($123) double with bathroom; £95 ($142.50) triple without bathroom. Rates include English breakfast. No credit cards. Tube: Victoria. **Amenities:** Breakfast room. *In room:* safe. No phone.

James House/Cartref House *(Kids)* Hailed by many publications, including the *Los Angeles Times,* as one of the top 10 B&B choices in London, James House and Cartref House (across the street from each other) deserve their accolades. Each room is individually designed; some of the large ones have bunk beds that make them suitable for families, although these mattresses are a bit thin (mattresses on the other beds are reliably firm). Clients in rooms with a private bathroom will find somewhat cramped quarters, but each room is tidily arranged. Corridor bathrooms are adequate and frequently refurbished. *Warning:* Whether or not you like this hotel will depend on your room assignment. Some rooms are fine, but several (often when the other units are full) are quite small. That is especially true of some third-floor units. Some "bathrooms" evoke those found on small ocean-going freighters. The English breakfast is so generous that you might end up skipping lunch. There's no elevator, but the guests don't seem to mind. Both hotels are nonsmoking. You're a stone's throw from Buckingham Palace should the Queen invite you over for tea.

108 and 129 Ebury St., London SW1W 9QD. James House ℂ **020/7730-7338**; Cartref House ℂ **020/7730-6176**. Fax 020/7730-7338. www.jamesandcartref. co.uk. 21 units, 11 with bathroom. £70 ($119) double without bathroom, £85 ($144.50) double with bathroom; £136 ($231.20) quad with bathroom. Rates include English breakfast. AE, MC, V. Tube: Victoria. *In room:* TV, coffeemaker, hair dryer. No phone.

3 Hotels from Knightsbridge to South Kensington

KNIGHTSBRIDGE
VERY EXPENSIVE

The Beaufort *(🌟🌟)* If you'd like to stay at one of London's finest boutique hotels, offering personal service in an elegant, tranquil atmosphere, head here. The Beaufort, only 200 yards from Harrods, sits on a cul-de-sac behind two Victorian porticoes and an iron fence. Owner Diana Wallis combined a pair of adjacent houses from the 1870s, ripped out the old decor, and created a stylish hotel that has the feeling of a private house. You register at a small desk extending off a bay-windowed parlor, and then climb the stairway used by the queen of Sweden during her stay. Each guest room is bright and individually decorated in a modern color scheme, adorned with well-chosen paintings by London artists; they come with earphone radios, flowers, and a selection of books. Bedrooms are small, but tasteful and efficiently organized with luxurious mattresses. The most deluxe and spacious rooms are in the front. Those in the back are smaller and darker. Included in the rates are a 24-hour free bar, continental breakfast and light meals from room service, English cream tea each afternoon, brandy, chocolates, and shortbread in each room. Bathrooms are adequate, but have tidy maintenance, plus a hair dryer. The all-female staff is exceedingly helpful—a definite plus.

33 Beaufort Gardens, London SW3 1PP. © 800/888-1199 in the U.S. or Canada or 020/7584-5252. Fax 020/7589-2834. www.thebeaufort.co.uk. 28 units. £180–£260 ($306–$442) double; £295 ($501.50) junior suite. Rates include continental breakfast, bar, and afternoon tea. AE, DC, MC, V. Tube: Knightsbridge. **Amenities:** access to nearby health club; room service; bar; baby-sitting, junior suites include complimentary limo to or from the airport or aromatherapy massage. *In room:* TV, VCR, CD player, A/C, trouser press.

EXPENSIVE

Claverley Hotel ⓖ   On a quiet cul-de-sac, this hotel, one of the neighborhood's very best (winner of the Spencer Trophy for the Best Bed & Breakfast Hotel in Central London), is a few blocks from Harrods. It's a cozy place accented with Georgian-era accessories. The Lounge evokes a country house, and complimentary tea, coffee, and biscuits are served all day in the Reading Room. Most rooms have wall-to-wall carpeting and comfortably upholstered armchairs, each coming with a tidy bathroom with a shower stall. Recently refurbished rooms have a marble bathroom and "power shower." Rooms are individually decorated, some with four-poster beds.

13–14 Beaufort Gardens, London SW3 1PS. © 800/747-0398 in the U.S., or 020/7589-8541. Fax 020/7584-3410. www.claverleyhotel.co.uk. 29 units, 27 with bathroom. £120–£190 ($180–$285) double; £160–£200 ($240–$300) junior suite. Rates include English breakfast. AE, DC, MC, V. Tube: Knightsbridge. **Amenities:** breakfast room; same-day valet service; free parking on weekends *In room:* TV, safe, hair dryer.

Knightsbridge Hotel ⭐   The Knightsbridge Hotel attracts visitors from all over the world seeking a small hotel in a high-rent district. It's fabulously located, sandwiched between Beauchamp Place and Harrods, with many of the city's top theaters and museums close by. Built in the 1800s as a private townhouse, this family-run place sits on a tree-lined square, free from traffic. Small and unpretentious, with a Victorian ambience, it's recently been renovated to a high standard. All the well-furnished rooms have shower-only private bathrooms. Most bedrooms are spacious and furnished with traditional English fabrics. The best are numbers 311 and 312 at the rear, each with a pitched ceiling and a small sitting area. Bathrooms are clad in marble or tile.

12 Beaufort Gardens, London SW3 1PT. ℂ 020/7589-9271. Fax 020/7823-9692. www.knightsbridgehotel.co.uk. 40 units. £150–£195 ($225–$292.50) double; from £165 ($247.50) suite. Rates include English or continental breakfast. AE, MC, V. Free parking on street from 6pm to 8am. Tube: Knightsbridge. **Amenities:** small fitness center; room service; laundry/dry cleaning. *In room:* TV, minibar, hair dryer.

BELGRAVIA
EXPENSIVE

Diplomat Hotel ⭐   Part of the Diplomat's charm is that it is small and reasonably priced in an extremely expensive neighborhood. Minutes from Harrods, it was built in 1882 as a private residence by the architect Thomas Cubbitt. It's very well appointed: The registration desk is framed by the sweep of a circular staircase; above it, cherubs gaze down from a Regency-era chandelier. The staff is helpful, well mannered, and discreet. The high-ceilinged guest rooms are tastefully done in Victorian style. You get good— not grand—comfort here. Rooms are a bit small and usually furnished with twin beds with exceedingly good mattresses. Bathrooms are also small but well maintained; they have shower stalls.

2 Chesham St., London SW1X 8DT. ℂ 020/7235-1544. Fax 020/7259-6153. www.btinternet.com/~diplomat.hotel. 27 units. £127–£170 ($195–$255) double. Rates include English buffet breakfast. AE, CB, DC, MC, V. Tube: Sloane Sq. or Knightsbridge. **Amenities:** snack bar; nearby health club; business services; back-and-neck shiatsu massage to arriving guests. *In room:* TV, coffeemaker, hair dryer.

CHELSEA
EXPENSIVE

The Sloane ⭐⭐   This toff address, a redbrick Victorian-era townhouse, tastefully renovated during recent years, is located in Chelsea near Sloane Square. It combines 19th-century antiques with modern comforts—if you happen to admire a piece of furniture, the staff at the front desk will probably quote you a price that could be attractive enough for you to actually buy it. Our favorite spot is the rooftop terrace with its views opening onto Chelsea, ideal for breakfast or a drink. Bedrooms come in varying sizes, ranging from small to spacious, but are opulently furnished with flouncy draperies, tasteful fabrics, and sumptuous beds. Many rooms have draped four-poster beds or canopied beds and, of course, those antiques. The deluxe bathrooms have combination tub and shower, chrome power showers, mostly wall-width mirrors, and luxurious toiletries.

29 Draycott Place, London SW3 2SH. © 800/324-9960 in the U.S., or 020/7581-5757. Fax 020/7584-1348. www.premierhotels.com. 12 units. £140 ($210) double; £225 ($337.50) suite. AE, DC, MC, V. Tube: Sloane Sq. **Amenities:** light meals 24 hours a day; room service; laundry/dry cleaning. *In room:* A/C, TV.

MODERATE

Willett Hotel ✦ *Value*   On a tree-lined street, leading off Sloane Square, this Victorian townhouse lies in the heart of Chelsea. Named for the famous London architect, William Willett, it evokes the days when King Edward was on the throne; stained glass and chandeliers reflect the opulence of that age. Under a mansard roof, with bay windows projecting, the hotel is a 5-minute walk from the shopping mecca of King's Road. Individually decorated bedrooms come in a wide range of sizes. Some are first class with swagged draperies, matching armchairs, and canopied beds. But a few of the twins are best left for Tiny Tim and his mate.

32 Sloane Gardens, London SW1 8DJ. © 020/7824-8415. Fax 020/7730-4830. www.eeh.co.uk. 19 units. £105–£170 ($157.50–$255). Rates include English or continental breakfast. AE, DC, MC, V. Tube: Sloane Sq. *In room:* TV, fridge, coffeemaker, hair dryer, trouser press.

SOUTH KENSINGTON
EXPENSIVE

5 Sumner Place ✦   This little charmer is frequently cited as one of the best B&Bs in the Kensington area, and we agree. Restored in an elegant, classically English style that captures the flavor of its bygone era, this Victorian terrace house (ca. 1848) enjoys landmark status. You'll feel the ambience as soon as you enter the reception hall and are welcomed by the staff. After you register, you're given your own front-door key, and London is yours. An elevator takes you up to the guest floors, where the well-maintained rooms are done in period furnishings; a few have refrigerators. Bedrooms are medium size with comfortable, soft beds where you may want to linger. Bathrooms are small but tidily kept and supplied with a tub and shower.

5 Sumner Place, London SW7 3EE. ℂ **020/7584-7586.** Fax 020/7823-9962. 14 units. £130–£140 ($195–$210) double. Rates include English breakfast. AE, MC, V. Parking £20 ($30). Tube: South Kensington. **Amenities:** room service; laundry/dry cleaning. *In room:* TV, hair dryer, iron, refrigerator.

The Gore 🐿🐿   Once owned by the Marquess of Queensberry's family, the Gore has been a hotel since 1892, and it's one of our favorites. Victorians would feel at home here among the walnut and mahogany, Oriental carpets, and walls covered in antique photos and the hotel's collection of some 4,000 English prints. The Gore has always been known for eccentricity. Each room is different, so try to find one that suits your personality. The Venus Room has a bed once owned by Judy Garland. The dark-paneled Tudor Room is the most fascinating, with its gallery and fireplace. Rooms no longer go for the 1892 price of 50p, but are still a good value (even at $300 a night). Although most are small, there is still room for a sitting area. Well-maintained bathrooms have custom brass taps. Some units have a shower stall but no tub, although most have a tub and shower combination. Some of the plumbing wares would be familiar to Queen Victoria, but everything works smoothly. Many rooms have four-poster beds or half testers, each with a good, firm mattress.

189 Queen's Gate, London SW7 5EX. ℂ **800/637-7200** or 020/7584-6601. Fax 020/7589-8127. 53 units. £194 ($291) double; £331–£338 ($496.50–$507) suite. AE, DC, MC, V. Tube: Gloucester Rd. **Amenities:** restaurant; bar; access to health club next door; secretarial services; room service; baby-sitting; laundry/dry cleaning. *In room:* TV, minibar, hair dryer.

MODERATE

The Gallery 🐿 *Finds*   This is the place if you want to stay in an exclusive townhouse hotel, but don't want to pay £300 a night for the privilege. Two Georgian residences have been restored and converted into this remarkable hotel (which remains relatively unknown). The location is ideal, near the V&A Museum, Royal Albert Hall, Harrods, Knightsbridge, and King's Road. Bedrooms are individually designed and decorated in Laura Ashley style, with half-canopied beds with firm mattresses, plus marble-tiled bathrooms with brass fittings and tub-and-shower combos. The junior suites have private roof terraces, minibars, Jacuzzis, and air-conditioning. A team of butlers takes care of everything. The lounge, with its paneling and moldings, has the ambience of a private club. The drawing room beckons you to a quiet corner. The

Gallery Room displays works for sale by known and unknown artists.

8–10 Queensberry Place, London SW7 2EA. ℂ **020/7915-0000.** Fax 020/7915-4400. www.eeh.co/uk/gallery.html. 36 units. £120–£145 ($180–$217.50) double; from £200 ($300) junior suite. Extra bed £35 ($52.50). Rates include buffet English breakfast. AE, DC, MC, V. Tube: South Kensington. **Amenities:** access to nearby health club; 24-hour butler service; baby-sitting; laundry/dry cleaning. *In room:* TV, coffeemaker, hair dryer, safe.

INEXPENSIVE

Aston's Budget Studios & Aston's Designer Studios and Suites ✦ *Value*   This carefully restored row of Victorian town-houses offers comfortable studios and suites that are among London's best values. Heavy oak doors and 18th-century hunting pictures give the foyer a traditional atmosphere. Accommodations range in size and style from budget to designer; every one has a compact but complete kitchenette. The designer studios and two-room designer suites are decorated with rich fabrics and furnishings, and each has a marble bathroom with a shower. Mattresses are good.

39 Rosary Gardens, London SW7 4NQ. ℂ **800/525-2810** in the U.S., or 020/7590-6000. Fax 020/7590-6060. www.astons-apartments.com. 54 units. Standard studios £85 ($127.50) double; £120 ($180) triple; £160 ($240) quad. Designer studios £130 ($195) double. AE, MC, V. Tube: South Kensington. **Amenities:** business center; laundry, dry cleaning. *In room:* TV, coffeemaker, hair dryer, iron/ironing board.

Vicarage Private Hotel ✦ *Finds*   Eileen and Martin Diviney enjoy a host of admirers. Their hotel is tops for old-fashioned English charm, affordable prices, and hospitality. Situated on a residential square close to Kensington High Street, not far from Portobello Road Market, this Victorian townhouse retains many original features. Individually furnished in a country-house style, the bedrooms can accommodate up to four. If you want a nest to hide away in, opt for the top-floor aerie (no. 19). Guests find the corridor bathrooms adequate, and well maintained. Each year a few rooms are refurbished, and beds have decent mattresses. Guests meet in a cozy sitting room for conversation and to watch the telly. As a thoughtful extra, hot drinks are available 24 hours a day. In the morning, a hearty English breakfast awaits.

10 Vicarage Gate, London W8 4AG. ℂ **020/7229-4030.** Fax 020/7792-5989. www.londonvicaragehotel.com. 18 units, 2 with bathroom. £98 ($147) double with bathroom, £74 ($111) double without bathroom; £90 ($135) triple without bathroom; £98 ($147) family room for 4 without bathroom. Rates include English breakfast. No credit cards. Tube: High St. Kensington or Notting Hill Gate. *In room:* coffeemaker, hair dryer (upon request). No phone.

4 Hotels from Marylebone to Holland Park

MARYLEBONE
EXPENSIVE

Dorset Square Hotel 🏵🏵🏵   Steps away from Regent's Park, this is one of London's best and most stylish "house hotels," overlooking Thomas Lord's first cricket pitch. Hoteliers Tim and Kit Kemp have furnished the interior of two Georgian townhouses in a comfy mix of antiques, reproductions, and chintz that makes you feel as though you're in an elegant private home. The rooms come with full marble bathrooms; about half are air-conditioned. All are decorated in a personal yet beautiful style—the owners are interior decorators known for their taste, which is often bold and daring. Eight rooms offer crown-canopied beds, all have high-quality mattresses. The bathrooms are exquisite, with robes and deluxe toiletries.

39–40 Dorset Sq., London NW1 6QN. 📞 020/7723-7874. Fax 020/7724-3328. www.firmdale.com. 38 units. £140–£240 ($210–$360) double; from £240 ($360) suite. AE, MC, V. Parking £25 ($37.50). Tube: Baker St. or Marylebone. **Amenities:** restaurant; bar; business center; 24-hour room service; massage; baby-sitting; laundry/dry cleaning; rides in owner's chauffeured vintage Bentley. *In room:* TV, minibar, hair dryer.

Durrants Hotel 🏵   This historic hotel off Manchester Square (established in 1789) with its Georgian facade is snug, cozy, and traditional. We find it one of the most quintessentially English of all London hotels. Hazlitt's and Fielding (see above) compete for the same crowds who prefer vintage English charm in their hotels. You could invite the queen of England to Durrants for tea. Over the 100 years they have owned the hotel, the Miller family has incorporated several neighboring houses into the original structure. A walk through the pine-and-mahogany paneled public rooms is like stepping back in time: You'll even find an 18th-century letter-writing room. The rooms are bland except for elaborate cove moldings and comfortable furnishings, including good beds. Some are air-conditioned, and some are small. Bathrooms are also tiny. Nearly all have both tubs and showers, but few other amenities except a bidet.

The in-house restaurant serves full afternoon tea and satisfying French or traditional English cuisine in one of the most beautiful Georgian rooms in the neighborhood. The less formal breakfast room is ringed with 19th-century political cartoons by a noted Victorian artist. The pub, a neighborhood favorite, has Windsor chairs, a fireplace, and decor that hasn't changed much in 2 centuries.

George St., London W1H 6BJ. ⓒ 020/7935-8131. Fax 020/7487-3510. 92 units. £140–£180 ($238–$306) double; £175 ($262.50) family room for 3; from £275 ($412.50) suite. AE, CB, MC, V. Tube: Bond St. or Baker St. **Amenities:** restaurant; pub; 24-hour room service; baby-sitting; laundry. In room: TV.

MODERATE

Hallam Hotel This heavily ornamented stone-and-brick Victorian—one of the few on the street to escape the Blitz—is a 10-minute stroll from Oxford Circus. It's the property of brothers Grant and David Baker, who maintain it well. The guest rooms, which were redone in 1991, are comfortably furnished with good beds. Some of the singles are so small they're called "cabinettes." Several of the twin-bedded rooms are quite spacious and have adequate closet space. Bathrooms are a bit cramped, and come with shower stalls.

12 Hallam St., Portland Place, London W1N 5LJ. ⓒ **020/7580-1166.** Fax 020/7323-4527. 25 units. £95 ($142.50) double. Rates include English breakfast. AE, DC, MC, V. Tube: Oxford Circus. In room: TV, minibar, coffeemaker, hair dryer, iron/ironing board.

Hart House Hotel 🐾 *Kids* Hart House is a long-enduring favorite with Frommer's readers. In the heart of Marylebone, this well-preserved building (one of a group of Georgian mansions occupied by exiled French nobles during the French Revolution) lies within walking distance of many theaters, as well as some of the most popular shopping areas in London. Cozy and convenient, it's run by Andrew Bowden, one of Marylebone's best B&B hosts. The rooms—done in a combination of furnishings ranging from Portobello antique to modern—are spic-and-span, each with a different character. Favorites include no. 7, a triple with a big bathroom and shower. Ask for no. 11, on the top floor, for a brightly lit aerie. Housekeeping rates high marks here, and the bedrooms are comfortably appointed with chairs, an armoire, a desk, a chest of drawers, and a good bed with a firm mattress. Bathrooms, although small, are efficiently organized and boast a shower. Hart House has long been known as a good, safe place for traveling families. Many rooms are triples. Larger families can avail themselves of family accommodations with connecting rooms. Literary buffs, take note: Poet Elizabeth Barrett resided at no. 99 with her family for many years.

51 Gloucester Place, Portman Sq., London W1U 8JF. ⓒ **020/7935-2288.** Fax 020/7935-8516. www.harthouse.co.uk. 16 units. £100 ($150) double; £120 ($180) triple; £140 ($210) quad. Rates include English breakfast. AE, MC, V. Tube: Marble Arch or Baker St. **Amenities:** baby sitting; laundry/dry cleaning. In room: TV, coffeemaker, hair dryer, iron/ironing board, safe.

Ivanhoe Suite Hotel *(Value*   Born-to-shop buffs flock to this discovery located in a part of town off Oxford Street not known for its
hotels. "It's like having my own little flatlet every time I come to
London," one guest told us. Above a restaurant on a pedestrian
street of boutiques and restaurants, close to the shop-flanked New
and Old Bond streets, this townhouse hotel has attractively furnished small and medium singles and doubles, each with a sitting
area. Each room has its own entry and security video. Bedrooms
were redecorated in 1998, with new mattresses. The newly tiled
bathrooms are small—half have showers only. Breakfast is served in
a small area at the top of the first flight of stairs, and you can stop
off for a nightcap at the corner pub, a real neighborhood locale.
Note: The four-floor hotel has no elevator.

1 St. Christopher's Place, Barrett St. Piazza, London W1M 5HB. ℭ 020/7935-1047.
Fax 020/7224-0563. www.scoot.co.uk/ivanhoe_suite_hotel/. 8 units. £88–£98
($132–$147) double; £120 ($180) triple. Rates include continental breakfast.
AE, DC, MC, V. Tube: Bond St. **Amenities:** secretarial service; room service; baby-
sitting; laundry. *In room:* TV, minibar, iron/ironing board, kitchenette, refrigerator,
coffeemaker, hair dryer.

INEXPENSIVE

Boston Court Hotel   Upper Berkeley is a classic street of B&Bs;
in days of yore, it was home to Elizabeth Montagu (1720–1800),
"queen of the bluestockings," who defended Shakespeare against
attacks by Voltaire. Today, it's a good, safe retreat at an affordable
price. This unfrilly hotel offers accommodations in a centrally
located Victorian-era building within walking distance of Oxford
Street shopping and Hyde Park. The small, basic rooms have been
refurbished and redecorated with a no-nonsense decor, but with
good mattresses; now all have private showers and tubs combined.

26 Upper Berkeley St., Marble Arch, London W1H 7PF. ℭ 020/7723-1445. Fax
020/7262-8823. www.boston-court-hotel.com. 15 units (7 with shower only). £65
($97.50) double with shower only, £75 ($112.50) double with bathroom; £70–£80
($105–$120) triple with bathroom. Rates include continental breakfast. MC, V.
Tube: Marble Arch. **Amenities:** video rentals; laundry. *In room:* TV fridge,
coffeemaker, hair dryer.

Edward Lear Hotel   This hotel 1 block from Marble Arch is
made all the more desirable by the bouquets of fresh flowers in the
public rooms. It occupies a pair of townhouses dating from 1780.
The western house was the London home of the 19th-century artist
and poet Edward Lear; his illustrated limericks adorn the walls of
one of the sitting rooms. Steep stairs lead up to the cozy rooms

which range from spacious to broom-closet size. Things are a bit tattered here and there, but with this location and price, few can complain as it's an area of £400 ($600) a night mammoths. The bacon on your plate came from the same butcher as used by the queen. One drawback: This is a very noisy part of town. Rear rooms are quieter. Bathrooms are tidy and well maintained, each with a shower unit.

28–30 Seymour St., London W1H 5WD. ℂ 020/7402-5401. Fax 020/7706-3766. www.edlear.com. 31 units, 12 with bathroom. £64.50 ($96.75) double without bathroom, £79.50–£89.50 ($119.25–$134.25) double with bathroom; from £105 ($157.50) suite. Rates include English breakfast. MC, V. Tube: Marble Arch. **Amenities:** breakfast room. *In room:* TV.

PADDINGTON & BAYSWATER
EXPENSIVE

Commodore 𝒢 Although it's been here for nearly 3 decades, the public has rediscovered the charm of this hotel, with its eclectically shaped rooms and eccentric layout. About a quarter of the rooms are split-level, with a sleeping gallery at the top of a short flight of stairs; many of the others have some quirky touch: stained glass, an unexpectedly large closet, or a layout that only Edwardians could have devised. The decor is comfortable and cozy. All bedrooms have been newly refurbished and have excellent mattresses; renewed bathrooms contain tubs and showers.

50 Lancaster Gate, London W2 3NA. ℂ 020/7402-5291. Fax 020/7262-1088. www.commodore-hotel.com. 90 units. £129–£150 ($193.50–$225) double; £150–£180 ($225–$270) triple; £180 ($270) family room. Rates include buffet breakfast. AE, DC, MC, V. Tube: Lancaster Gate. **Amenities:** restaurant; 24-hour room service; baby-sitting; laundry/dry cleaning. *In room:* TV, minibar, coffeemaker, hair dryer.

Miller's 𝒢 *(Finds)* A stay here is like a night spent in the Old Curiosity Shop of Charles Dickens. Others claim the little hotel looks like a set of *La Traviata*. Miller's calls itself an 18th-century rooming house. Regardless, there's nothing quite like this in London. A roaring log fire blazes in the large book-lined drawing room in winter. The individually designed rooms are named after romantic poets. They vary in shape and size, but all are luxuriously furnished with cushy mattresses and a small bathroom with a shower stall.

111A Westbourne Grove, London W2 4UW. ℂ 020/7243-1024. Fax 020/7243-1064. www.millersuk.com. 8 units. £160 ($240) double; £180 ($270) suite. Rates include continental breakfast. AE, DISC, MC, V. Tube: Bayswater or Notting Hill Gate. **Amenities:** breakfast room; baby-sitting; laundry *In room:* TV.

MODERATE

The Byron Hotel *Value* A mostly American clientele appreciates this family-run hotel, just north of Kensington Gardens, for its country-house atmosphere, its helpful staff (who spend extra time with guests to make their stay in London special), and the good value it offers. This is one of the best examples of a Victorian house conversion we've seen; it was modernized without ruining its appeal. The interior was recently redesigned and refurbished, and the rooms are better than ever, with ample closets, fine mattresses, and tile bathrooms with good showers. An elevator services all floors, and breakfast is served in a bright and cheery room.

36–38 Queensborough Terrace, London W2 3SH. © **020/7243-0987.** Fax 020/7792-1957. www.capricornhotels.co.uk. 45 units. £105–£120 ($178.50–$204) double; £135 ($202.50) triple; from £145 ($246.50) suite. Rates include English/continental breakfast. AE, DC, MC, V. Tube: Bayswater or Queensway. **Amenities:** room service; laundry/dry cleaning. *In room:* A/C, TV, coffeemaker, hair dryer, iron/ironing board, trouser press, safe.

The Pavilion *Finds* Until the early 1990s, this was a rather ordinary-looking B&B. Then, a team of entrepreneurs with ties to the fashion industry took over and redecorated the rooms with some-times wacky themes, turning it into an idiosyncratic little hotel. The result is a theatrical and often outrageous decor that's appreciated by the fashion models and music-industry buffs that make this their temporary home in London. Behind a blackened 1830s Victorian facade of bricks and stucco, the hotel offers rooms without any particular frills, that are rather small, but each has a distinctive style. Examples include a "kitsch 1970s" room ("Honky-Tonk Afro"), an Oriental bordello theme ("Enter the Dragon"), and even some with 19th-century ancestral themes. One Edwardian-style room, a gem of emerald brocade and velvet, is called "Green with Envy." Each contains tea-making facilities and a firm mattress. Bathrooms are also small, but efficiently organized, with excellent showers.

34–36 Sussex Gardens, London W2 1UL. © **020/7262-0905.** Fax 020/7262-1324. www.msi.com.mt/pavilion. 27 units. £90 ($135) double. Rates include continental breakfast. AE, DC, MC, V. Parking £5 ($7.50). Tube: Edgware Rd. **Amenities:** breakfast room. *In room:* TV, coffeemaker.

INEXPENSIVE

Europa House Hotel Another budget find along Sussex Gardens, this family-run hotel attracts those who want a room with a private bathroom, but at shared-bathroom prices. Like most along Sussex Gardens, the bedrooms are a bit cramped, but they're well maintained; each has color-coordinated decor, and most have been recently refurbished. Some units are custom built for groups, with three, four, or five beds per unit. Some of the multiple rooms have rather thin mattresses, but most are firm and comfortable. A hearty English breakfast awaits you in the bright dining room every morning.

151 Sussex Gardens, London W2 2RY. 🕐 **020/7723-7343.** Fax 020/7224-9331. www.visitus.co.uk/london/europa.htm. 20 units. £56–£65 ($84–$97.50) double; from £20 ($30) per person family room. Rates include English breakfast. AE, DC, MC, V. Parking £10 ($15). Tube: Paddington. *In room:* TV, coffeemaker.

Fairways Hotel   Jenny and Steve Adams welcome you into one of the finest B&Bs along Sussex Gardens. Even though it doesn't enjoy the pedigree it used to, this place near Hyde Park is still a favorite of bargain hunters. The black-and-white townhouse is recognizable: Look for its colonnaded front entrance with a wrought-iron balustrade stretching across the second floor. The Adams family opts for traditional charm and character. They call their breakfast room "homely" (Americans might say homey); it's decorated with photographs of the family and a collection of china. Bedrooms are attractive and comfortably furnished, with hot and cold running water and intercom. Beds are fitted with firm mattresses, and units with shower bathrooms are small but tidy. Those who share the corridor bathrooms will find them clean and well maintained. The home-cooked breakfast is plenty of fortification for a full day of sightseeing.

186 Sussex Gardens, London W2 1TU. 🕐 and fax **020/7723-4871.** www. fairways-hotel.co.uk. 17 units, 10 with bathroom. £68 ($102) double without bathroom, £74 ($111) double with bathroom. Rates include English breakfast. MC, V. Tube: Paddington or Lancaster Gate. *In room:* TV, coffeemaker, hair dryer (on request), safe.

Garden Court   This hotel was constructed in 1870 on this Victorian garden square in the heart of the city. Two private houses were combined to form one hotel near such attractions as Kensington Palace, Hyde Park, and the Portobello Antiques Market. Each year new rooms are redecorated and refurbished, although there would seem to be a lack of an overall plan. Most accommodations are spacious, with good lighting, generous shelf and closet space, and comfortable furnishings. If you're in a room without a bathroom, you'll generally have to share with the occupants of only one other room. Throughout are many homey touches, including ancestral portraits and silky flowers. Each room is individually decorated, and "comfy." Rooms open onto the square in front of the gardens in the rear. Bathrooms were installed in areas not intended as such and tend to be very cramped. There is no elevator.

30–31 Kensington Gardens Sq., London W2 4BG. ☎ **020/7229-2553.** Fax 020/7727-2749. www.gardencourthotel.co.uk. 32 units, 16 with bathroom. £56 ($84) double without bathroom, £86 ($129) double with bathroom; £72 ($108) triple without bathroom, £93 ($139.50) triple with bathroom. Rates include English breakfast. MC, V. Tube: Bayswater or Queensway. *In room:* TV, hair dryer.

NOTTING HILL GATE
EXPENSIVE
The Abbey Court ✦   This first-rate hotel is a white-fronted mid-Victorian townhouse with a flower-filled patio in front and a conservatory in back. Its recently renovated lobby has a sunny bay window, floral draperies, and a comfortable sofa and chairs. You'll find fresh flowers in the reception area and the hallways. Each room, though small, has coordinated fabrics and fine furnishings (mostly 18th- and 19th-century country antiques) plus excellent mattresses. Done in Italian marble, bathrooms are equipped with a Jacuzzi bath, shower, and heated towel racks. Light snacks and drinks are available from room service 24 hours a day and breakfast is served in the conservatory. Kensington Gardens is a short walk away, as are the antiques stores along Portobello Road and Kensington Church Street. *Note:* There is more than one Abbey Court Hotel in London, but this is the one we like best.

20 Pembridge Gardens, London W2 4DU. ☎ **020/7221-7518.** Fax 020/7792-0858. www.abbeycourthotel.co.uk. 22 units. £140–£160 ($210–$240) double; £180 ($270) suite with four-poster bed. AE, DC, MC, V. Tube: Notting Hill Gate. **Amenities:** access to nearby health club; Jacuzzi; 24-hour room service; tour desk; business services; baby-sitting; laundry/dry cleaning. *In room:* TV, robes, hair dryer, safe, iron/ironing board, fax, dataport.

Pembridge Court Hotel ✦   This hotel presents an elegant cream-colored neoclassical facade in the increasingly fashionable Notting Hill Gate neighborhood. Antiques hunters like its proximity to Portobello Road. Most rooms contain at least one antique, as well as 19th-century engravings and plenty of warm-toned floral fabrics, plus first-rate mattresses. Some of the largest and most stylish rooms are on the top floor. Bathrooms are tiled in Italian marble and feature showers. Three air-conditioned deluxe rooms, all with VCRs, overlook Portobello Road: The Spencer and Churchill Rooms are decorated in blues and yellows, and the Windsor Room has a contrasting array of tartans.

34 Pembridge Gardens, London W2 4DX. ☎ **020/7229-9977.** Fax 020/7727-4982. www.pemct.co.uk. 20 units. £180–£190 ($270–$285) double. Rates include English breakfast. AE, DC, MC, V. Tube: Notting Hill Gate. **Amenities:** restaurant; 24-hour room service; laundry/dry cleaning; nearby health club; secretarial services; baby-sitting. *In room:* A/C, TV, iron/ironing board, safe.

5 Near the Airports

NEAR HEATHROW

The reason for staying at one of the hotels below is obvious: You either want to catch an early plane or are arriving too late to search for a hotel in central London. The hotels below provide transportation to and from the airport.

VERY EXPENSIVE

Radisson Edwardian Heathrow ☆ The poshest digs at Heathrow, this hotel lies about 5 minutes east of the tunnel that leads to Terminals 1, 2, and 3. Since 1991 it has housed tired air travelers from all over the world. Its grand spa has a swimming pool and two whirlpools. You enter a courtyard with trees and a koi pond. Persian rugs, a brass-railed staircase, and chandeliers live up to the "Edwardian" in the hotel's name. Rooms are medium in size but adorned with hand-painted hardwood furnishings. Extras include deluxe mattresses and flight information broadcast on the TV. The bathrooms are in tile and marble, with robes, a shower, and a tub.

140 Bath Rd., Hayes UB3 5AW. ℂ **800/333-3333** from U.S. or 020/8759-6311. Fax 020/8759-4559. www.radisson.com. 459 units. £190–£235 ($285–$352.50) double; from £383 ($574.50) suite. AE, DC, MC, V. Parking £7 ($10.50). Heathrow Hopper bus service. **Amenities:** restaurant; brasserie; bar; plunge pool; health club; steam room; spa; sauna; 24-hour room service; laundry/dry cleaning. *In room:* A/C, TV, minibar, hair dryer.

EXPENSIVE

Hilton London Heathrow ☆ This first-class hotel with its five-story atrium evoking the feel of a hangar is linked to Heathrow's Terminal 4 by a covered walkway. A glass wall faces the runways, so you can see planes land and take off. You can take buses to Terminals 1, 2, or 3. Medium-size bedrooms are standard, but comfortable, with built-in wood furniture, sofas, and first-class mattresses. Bathrooms are tiled and trimmed in marble, with a phone, tub, and shower. The best accommodations are on the fifth floor; they have better amenities (such as bathrobes) as well as a private lounge with airport vistas.

Terminal 4, Hounslow TW6 3AF. ℂ **020/8759-7755.** Fax 020/8759-7579. www.hilton.com. 395 units. £110–£260 ($165–$390) double; £430 ($645) suite. AE, CB, DC, MC, V. Parking from £6.50 ($9.75). Tube: Piccadilly. **Amenities:** 3 restaurants; 2 bars; business services 24-hour room service; baby-sitting; laundry/dry cleaning; TV with flight information. *In room:* A/C, TV, coffeemaker, hair dryer.

MODERATE

Stanwell Hall   This sunny Victorian house was purchased in 1951 by the Parke family, who converted it into a comfortable hotel. The cheery house with its side garden is located in a village minutes from Heathrow; it's perfect for people tired of standard airport hotels. About half the rooms have been fully renovated; they are comfortably furnished, papered in warm shades, with chintz curtains covering the windows—a dramatic improvement over the washed-out, prerenovation rooms. All rooms have shower-only bathrooms and good mattresses. Bathrooms are efficiently organized and tidy.

   St. Anne's Restaurant, located on the ground floor, is small but inviting and serves modern British cuisine.

Town Lane, Stanwell, Staines, Middlesex TW19 7PW. ℂ **01784/252292.** Fax 01784/245250. www.stanwell-hall.co.uk. 19 units, 18 with bathroom. £100–£110 ($170–$187) double; £145 ($217.50) suite. Rates include continental breakfast. AE, DC, MC, V. Free parking. No bus or Tube service. **Amenities:** restaurant; bar; limited room service; laundry/dry cleaning. *In room:* TV, coffeemaker, hair dryer.

INEXPENSIVE

The Swan   Dating from the days of Samuel Pepys, the Swan is on the south bank of the Thames, beside Staines Bridge and within a 15-minute drive of Heathrow. Bedrooms were refurbished in 1999, with new mattresses added. The shower-only bathrooms are small, but the corridor bathrooms are adequate. The inn also has a reputation for good food ranging from bar snacks to traditional English fare. The food is served in a gazebo-style dining room.

The Hythe, Staines, Middlesex TW18 3JB. ℂ **0178/445-2494.** Fax 0178/446-1593. 13 units, 5 with bathroom. £65–£79 ($97.50–$118.50) double without bathroom, £79–£100 ($118.50–$150) double with bathroom; £100–£125 ($150–$187.50) suite. Rates include English breakfast. AE, DC, MC, V. Tube: Heathrow (you must take a taxi from there). **Amenities:** restaurant; laundry/dry cleaning. *In room:* TV.

NEAR GATWICK

EXPENSIVE

Hilton London Gatwick Airport 𝒞   This five-floor hotel—Gatwick's most convenient—is linked to the airport with a covered walkway; an electric buggy service transports people between hotel and airport. The most impressive part is the first floor lobby. Its glass-covered portico rises four floors and contains a replica of the de Havilland Gypsy Moth airplane *Jason,* used by Amy Johnson on her solo flight from England to Australia in 1930. The reception area has a lobby bar and greenery. The well-furnished, soundproofed rooms have triple-glazed windows and firm mattresses. Bathrooms are tidy and equipped with tub and shower. Recently, most of the rooms were refurbished, in addition to the executive floor and all their junior suites. Now 300 of the rooms have minibars.

South Terminal, Gatwick Airport, West Sussex RH6 OLL. ℂ 800/HILTONS or 01293/518080. Fax 01293/528980. www.hilton.com. 550 units. £160–£240 ($240–$360) double; from £260 ($390) suite. AE, MC, V. Parking £11.50 ($17.25). **Amenities:** 2 restaurants; health club; business center; bank; 2 bars; 24-hour room service; baby-sitting; laundry/dry cleaning. *In room:* A/C, TV, hair dryer.

INEXPENSIVE

The Manor House   Owners Steve and Joanne Jeffries include transportation from Gatwick as part of the price of their lodgings. Their home is a sprawling neo-Tudor affair on two acres of land, amid fields, which surround it on all sides. It was built in 1894 as a supplemental home for the Lord of Ifield, who occupied a larger house nearby and never actually moved in. Two of the rooms share a bathroom, the others have bathrooms with shower. Regardless of its plumbing, each accommodation has flowered wallpaper, and simple, traditional accessories. Breakfast is the only meal served.

Bonnetts Lane, Ifield, Crawley, Sussex RH11 ONY. ℂ 01293/510000. Fax 01293/518046. www.manorhouse-gatwick.co.uk. 6 units, 4 with private bathroom. £45 ($67.50) double with bathroom; £55 ($82.50) family unit. Rates include English breakfast. MC, V. **Amenities:** Free parking. *In room:* TV, tea/coffee maker.

4

Dining

London has emerged as one of the food capitals of the world. Both its veteran and upstart chefs have fanned out around the globe for inspiration and returned with innovative dishes, flavors, and ideas that London diners have never seen before. These chefs are pioneering a style called "Modern British," which is forever changing and innovative, yet familiar in many ways.

Traditional British cooking has made a comeback, too. The dishes that British mums have been forever feeding their families are fashionable again. Yes, we're talking British soul food: bangers and mash, Norfolk dumplings, nursery puddings, cottage pie. This may be a rebellion against the minimalism of the nouvelle cuisine of the 1980s, but maybe it's just plain nostalgia. Pig's nose with parsley-and-onion sauce may not be your idea of cutting-edge cuisine, but Simpson's-in-the-Strand is serving it for breakfast.

1 In & Around the City

THE CITY
EXPENSIVE

Prism ⭒⭒ MODERN BRITISH/CONTINENTAL   In the financial district this restaurant attracts London's movers and shakers with demanding palates. In the former Bank of New York, Harvey Nichols—known for his chic department store in Knightsbridge—took this 1920s neo-Grecian hall and installed Mies van der Rohe chairs in chrome and lipstick red leather. Traditional English dishes are given a light touch—try the tempura of Whitby cod or cream of Jerusalem artichoke soup with roasted scallops and truffle oil. For a first course, you might opt for a seared calf's liver with a mushroom risotto, or a salad composed of flecks of Parmesan cheese seasoning a savoy cabbage salad and Parma ham. The menu reveals the chef has traveled a bit—note such dishes as Moroccan spiced chicken livers, lemon and parsley couscous, and a zesty chili sauce. Unusual for a restaurant, the staff will compose a set menu for each individual table.

147 Leadenhall St., EC3. © 020/7256-3888. Reservations required. Main courses £16–£20 ($24–$30). Set menus £35–£45 ($52.50–$67.50). AE, DISC, DC, MC, V. Mon–Fri noon–3pm and 6–10pm. Tube: Bank.

MODERATE

Cafe Spice Namaste ✿ INDIAN   This is our favorite Indian restaurant in London. It's housed in a landmark Victorian hall near Tower Bridge, east of the Tower of London. The chef, Cyrus Todiwala, is Parsi and a former resident of Goa, where he learned many of his culinary secrets. He concentrates on Indian dishes with a strong Portuguese influence. Chicken and lamb are prepared a number of ways, from mild to spicy-hot. Todiwala occasionally even offers a menu of emu dishes; when marinated, the meat is rich and spicy and evocative of lamb. Emu is not the only dining oddity here. Ever have ostrich gizzard kebab, alligator tikka, or minced moose, bison, and blue boar? Many patrons journey here for the complex chicken curry known as *xacutti*. Lambs' livers and kidneys are also cooked in the tandoor. A weekly specialty menu complements the long list of regional dishes. The homemade chutneys alone are worth the trip; our favorite is made with kiwi. All dishes come with fresh vegetables and Indian bread. With the exotic ingredients, the often time-consuming preparation, the impeccable service, the warm hospitality, and the spicy but subtle flavors, this is no Indian dive.

16 Prescot St., E1. © 020/7488-9242. Reservations required. Main courses £12–£15 ($18–$22.50). AE, DC, MC, V. Mon–Fri noon–3pm and 6:15–10:30pm; Sat 6:30–10:15pm. Tube: Tower Hill.

Ye Olde Cheshire Cheese *Kids* TRADITIONAL BRITISH The foundation of this building was laid in the 13th century, and it holds the most famous of the old City chophouses and pubs. Established in 1667, it claims to be the spot where Dr. Samuel Johnson entertained with his acerbic wit. Charles Dickens and other literary lions also patronized the place. Later, many of the journalists of 19th- and early 20th-century Fleet Street made it their watering hole. You'll find six bars and two dining rooms here. The house specialties include "Ye Famous Pudding" (steak, kidney, mushrooms, and game) and Scottish roast beef with Yorkshire pudding and horseradish sauce. Sandwiches, salads, and favorites such as steak-and-kidney pie are also available, as are dishes such as Dover sole. When your kid says, "Mommy, what's an English pub?" the

Restaurants of London

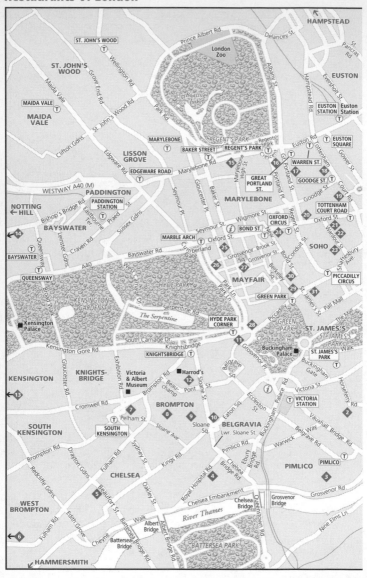

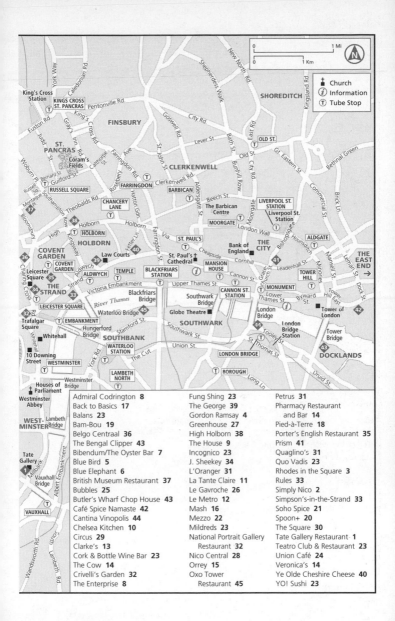

Admiral Codrington **8**	Fung Shing **23**	Petrus **31**
Back to Basics **17**	The George **39**	Pharmacy Restaurant
Balans **23**	Gordon Ramsay **4**	and Bar **14**
Bam-Bou **19**	Greenhouse **27**	Pied-à-Terre **18**
Belgo Centraal **36**	High Holborn **38**	Porter's English Restaurant **35**
The Bengal Clipper **43**	The House **9**	Prism **41**
Bibendum/The Oyster Bar **7**	Incognico **23**	Quaglino's **31**
Blue Bird **5**	J. Sheekey **34**	Quo Vadis **23**
Blue Elephant **6**	L'Oranger **31**	Rhodes in the Square **3**
British Museum Restaurant **37**	La Tante Claire **11**	Rules **33**
Bubbles **25**	Le Gavroche **26**	Simply Nico **2**
Butler's Wharf Chop House **43**	Le Metro **12**	Simpson's-in-the-Strand **33**
Café Spice Namaste **42**	Mash **16**	Soho Spice **21**
Cantina Vinopolis **44**	Mezzo **22**	Spoon+ **20**
Chelsea Kitchen **10**	Mildreds **23**	The Square **30**
Circus **29**	National Portrait Gallery	Tate Gallery Restaurant **1**
Clarke's **13**	Restaurant **32**	Teatro Club & Restaurant **23**
Cork & Bottle Wine Bar **23**	Nico Central **28**	Union Café **24**
The Cow **14**	Orrey **15**	Veronica's **14**
Crivelli's Garden **32**	Oxo Tower	Ye Olde Cheshire Cheese **40**
The Enterprise **8**	Restaurant **45**	YO! Sushi **23**

Cheshire is the best and safest venue to take him (or her) to see this type of British institution.

Wine Office Court, 145 Fleet St., EC4. © **020/7353-6170.** Main courses £8.95–£13.95 ($13.40–$20.90). AE, DC, MC, V. Mon–Fri 11:30am–11pm; Sat noon–3pm and 5:30–11pm; Sun noon–3pm. Drinks and bar snacks daily 11:30am–11pm. Tube: St. Paul's or Blackfriars.

DOCKLANDS
EXPENSIVE

Butler's Wharf Chop House ✶ TRADITIONAL BRITISH   Of the restaurants in Butler's Wharf, this one maintains its commitment to moderate prices, and although there's an even cheaper restaurant, La Cantina del Ponte, most diners consider that merely a place for pastas. The Chop House was modeled after a large boathouse, with banquettes, lots of exposed wood, flowers, candles, and windows overlooking Tower Bridge and the Thames. Lunchtime crowds include workers from the city's financial district; evening crowds are made up of friends dining together more leisurely.

Dishes are adaptations of British recipes: fish-and-chips with mushy peas; steak and kidney pudding with oysters; stewed rabbit leg with bitter leaves and mustard; roast rump of lamb, garlic mash, and rosemary; and grilled pork fillet, apples, chestnuts, and cider sauce. After, there might be a dark-chocolate tart with whiskey cream or toffee pudding. The bar offers such choices as Theakston's best bitter, several English wines, and a half-dozen French clarets by the jug.

36E Shad Thames, SE1. © **020/7403-3403.** Reservations recommended. Fixed-price 2-course lunch£19.75 ($29.65); fixed-price 3-course lunch £23.75 ($35.65); dinner main courses £12–£29.50 ($18–$44.25). AE, DC, MC, V. Sun–Fri noon–3pm (last order); Mon–Sat 6–11pm. Tube: Tower Hill.

MODERATE

The Bengal Clipper ✶ INDIAN   A former spice warehouse by the Thames serves what it calls "India's most remarkable dishes." This likable restaurant is outfitted with cream-colored walls, tall columns, and artwork inspired by the Moghul Dynasty's replicas of royal figures, soaring trees, and well-trained elephants. Seven windows afford views over the Thames-side neighborhood. You can enjoy a cuisine that includes vegetarian choices derived from the formerly Portuguese colony of Goa and the once English colony of Bengal. There is a zestiness and spice to the cuisine, but never overpowering. The chefs keep the menu fairly short so that all ingredients can be purchased fresh every day.

A tasty specialty is stuffed *murgh masala,* breast of chicken with potato, onion, apricots, and almonds cooked with yogurt and served with a delectable curry sauce. The perfectly cooked duckling (off the bone) comes in a tangy sauce with a citrus bite. One of the finest dishes we've tasted in North India is served here: marinated lamb simmered in cream with cashew nuts and seasoned with fresh ginger. One of the best offerings is the karkra chop, a spicy patty of minced crab blended with mashed potatoes and peppered with Goan spices.

Shad Thames, Butler's Wharf, SE1. © 020/7357-9001. Reservations recommended. Main courses £8–£25 ($12–$37.50); set menu from £12 ($18); Sunday buffet £8 ($12). AE, DC, MC, V. Daily noon–2:30pm and 6–11:30pm. Tube: Tower Hill.

SOUTH BANK
EXPENSIVE
Oxo Tower Restaurant *&* MODERN BRITISH/EUROPEAN
In the South Bank complex, on the eighth floor of the Art Deco Oxo Tower Wharf, is this dining sensation. Down the street from the Globe Theater, this 140-seat restaurant has a great view, as well as stellar cuisine. You'll enjoy a sweeping view of St. Paul's Cathedral and the City, all the way to the House of Parliament. The decor is a chic 1930s style, and the cuisine under Chef Simon Arkless offers a finesse and richness.

Menu items change based on the season and the market. Count on a modern interpretation of British cookery. The fish is incredibly fresh, and you can order the English classics. The whole sea bass for two is delectable, as is the cannon of lamb with creamed garlic. The grilled escalopes of salmon with smoked chili and mango salsa adds an exotic touch, and the pan-fried fillet of John Dory with scallops is delicately flavored with a *fines herbes* risotto and a champagne sauce.

Barge House St., South Bank, SE1. © 020/7803-3888. Main courses £15–£30 ($22.50–$45); fixed-price lunch £27.50 ($41.25). AE, DC, MC, V. Mon–Fri noon–3pm; Mon–Sat 6–11:30pm; Sun 6–10:30pm. Tube: Blackfriars or Waterloo.

MODERATE
Cantina Vinopolis *&* *Finds* MEDITERRANEAN Not far from the Globe Theatre, this place is a "Walk-Through Wine Atlas." From abandoned Victorian railway arches, this brick walled, high-vaulted brasserie was created in what was once the entertainment center of London. Inside, you can visit both the Vinopolis Wine Gallery and the Cantina Restaurant. Although many come here to

drink the wine, the food is prepared with quality ingredients (very fresh), and the menu is sensibly priced. Start with some bit of heaven like a pumpkin and parmesan soup with a lime-flavored crème fraîche or chargrilled asparagus with artichoke hearts and rocket. Dishes are flavorful and never overcooked. Squid fried in a crispy batter won us over along with its side dish, wasabi slaw. A rump of lamb was tender and perfectly flavored, served with a polenta cake. Seared blue tuna arrived with sliced warm new potatoes and a tomato confit and chorizo salad. Many dishes have the country taste of a trattoria in southern Italy. Naturally, the wine list is the biggest in the U.K.

1 Bank End, London Bridge, SE1. © 020/7940-8333. Reservations required. Main courses £8.50–£13.50 ($12.75–$20.25). Daily noon–3pm; Mon–Sat 6–10:30pm. Tube: London Bridge.

2 The West End

HOLBORN
EXPENSIVE
High Holborn ⚜ MODERN BRITISH/CONTINENTAL   At last a worthy restaurant appears in Holborn. David Cavalier attracts a lot of business clients during the day but more couples in the evening. The decor is light, colorful, and ultra-modern with artwork on the walls (it's all for sale). We would come across town to sample his veal sweetbreads bourguignonne or his lusty halibut *pot-au-feu*. Begin with the wild mushroom ravioli (it doesn't get much better than this), and follow with perhaps the best two items among the main courses—pork in a splendid truffle sauce and the classic filet of beef Rossini. Cavalier offers such carnivore favorites as pig's trotters in a creamy *gribiche* sauce. Smoked squab slices and minced squab arrive with an artichoke velouté that is clearly the chef's pièce-de-rèsistance. Desserts are classics given modern touches by the additions of such ingredients as lemongrass or rose petals.

95–96 High Holborn. © 020/7404-3338. Reservations needed 3 days in advance. Main courses £15–£25 ($22.50–$37.50). AE MC, V. Mon–Fri noon–2:30pm and 6:30–10:30pm. Tube: Holborn.

BLOOMSBURY
VERY EXPENSIVE
Pied-à-Terre ⚜ MODERN FRENCH   This foodie heaven understates its decor for a more intense focus on its subtle, sophisticated cuisine. You'll dine in a minimalist room, where gray and

pale pink walls alternate with metal furniture and focused lighting that highlights a collection of modern art. France is the inspiration for the impressive wine list and some cuisine. The menu might include braised snails with celeriac, garlic, and morille-creamed sauce; roasted scallops with apple and puréed ginger; halibut fillets with queen scallops and caramelized endive; roasted partridge with pear; and the house specialty, ballotine of duck confit. If you're not dining with a vegetarian, braised pig's head is another specialty. The smoothest item on the menu? Sea bass with vichyssoise and caviar sauce. The food is beautifully presented on hand-painted plates with lush patterns.

34 Charlotte St., W1. © **020/7636-1178**. Reservations recommended. Fixed-price 3-course lunch £25–£35 ($37.50–$52.50); fixed-price 3-course dinner £45–£60 ($67.50–$90); 8-course tasting menu £65 ($97.50). AE, DC, MC, V. Mon–Fri noon–2:30pm (last order); Mon–Sat 7–11pm. Closed last week of Dec and first week of Jan. Tube: Goodge St.

MODERATE

Back to Basics ⭐ SEAFOOD   Stefan Plaumer's Fitzrovia bistro draws discerning palates for some of the freshest seafood in London. When the weather's fair, you can dine outside. Otherwise, retreat inside to a vaguely Parisian setting with a blackboard menu and checked tablecloths. The fish is served in large portions, and you may forgo an appetizer unless you're ravenous. More than a dozen seafood dishes are offered; the fish can be broiled, grilled, baked, or poached, but frying is not permitted. In other words, this is no fish-and-chippie. Start with a bowl of tasty, plump mussels or sea bass flavored with fresh basil and chili oil. Brill appears with green peppercorn butter, and plaice is jazzed up with fresh ginger and soy sauce. For the meat eater, there is Scotch rib eye or perhaps lamb steak. Freshly made salads accompany most meals, and an excellent fish soup is offered daily. For dessert, try the bread pudding or freshly made apple pie.

21A Foley St., W1. © **020/7436-2181**. Reservations recommended. Main courses £10–£15 ($15–$22.50). AE, DC, MC, V. Mon–Fri noon–3pm and 6–10pm. Tube: Oxford Circus or Goodge St.

INEXPENSIVE

British Museum Restaurant TRADITIONAL BRITISH   This is the best place for lunch if you're exploring the world-renowned museum. It's on the lobby level of the West Wing and decorated with full-size copies of the bas-reliefs from a temple in the town of

Nereid in ancient Greece (you'll find the originals in nearby galleries). The format is self-service. A few hot specials (including a vegetarian selection) and crisp salads are made fresh every day, and there's a good selection of fish and cold meat dishes. Try the soup and baguette special, changed daily. Desserts include pastries and cakes. There's also a cafe offering coffee, sandwiches, pastries, and soup.

Great Russell St., WC1. ✆ **020/7323-8256.** Main courses £6.75 ($10.15); £5.75 ($8.65) soup and baguette special. MC, V. Cold food Mon–Wed 10am–5pm, Thurs–Fri 10am–7:45pm, Sat–Sun 10am–5pm. All days, hot food 11am–3pm. Tube: Russell Sq., Holborn, or Tottenham Court Rd.

COVENT GARDEN & THE STRAND

The restaurants in and around Covent Garden and the Strand are the most convenient choices for attending theaters in the West End.

EXPENSIVE

Rules ✪ TRADITIONAL BRITISH   If you're looking for a quintessentially British restaurant, come here. London's oldest restaurant was established in 1798 as an oyster bar; today, the antler-encrusted Edwardian dining rooms exude nostalgia. You can order such classic dishes as Irish or Scottish oysters, jugged hare, and mussels. Game dishes are offered from mid-August to February or March: wild Scottish salmon or wild sea trout; wild Highland red deer; and game birds like grouse, snipe, partridge, pheasant, and woodcock. As a finale, the "great puddings" continue to impress.

35 Maiden Lane, WC2. ✆ **020/7836-5314.** Reservations recommended. Main courses £16.95–£19.95 ($28.80–$33.90). AE, DC, MC, V. Daily noon–11:30pm. Tube: Covent Garden.

Simpson's-in-the-Strand ✪ *(Kids)* TRADITIONAL AND MODERN BRITISH   Simpson's is more of an institution than a restaurant. It's been in business since 1828, and as a result of a recent £2 million renovation, it's now two separate restaurants. **The Grande Divan,** with its Adam paneling, crystal, and army of formal waiters serves traditional British fare. Simpson's serves the best roasts in London, an array including roast sirloin of beef, saddle of mutton with red-currant jelly, Aylesbury duckling, and steak, kidney, and mushroom pie. (Remember to tip the tail-coated carver.) For a pudding, try the treacle roll and custard or Stilton with vintage port.

Simpson's also serves traditional breakfasts. The most popular, despite the £15.95 ($23.90) price, is "The Ten Deadly Sins": sausage, fried egg, streaky and back bacon, black pudding, lamb's kidneys, bubble-and-squeak, baked beans, lamb's liver, and fried bread, mushrooms, and tomatoes. That will fortify you for the day!

Chequers, the new restaurant, specializes in modern British cuisine. Appetizers include tartare of Cornish crab with spiced avocado relish, dill dressed cucumber, and Avruga caviar. For a main course, try the thyme-infused Gressingham breast of duck with parsnip purée and red-wine blackcurrant jus. You can finish with desserts that include orange crème brûlée and pear marinated in spiced red wine syrup with gingerbread ice cream. Chequers is open Monday through Saturday noon to 7pm. Main dish prices range from £9 to £15.75 ($13.50–$23.65).

Jacket and tie are not essential; we recommend smart casual attire.

100 The Strand (next to the Savoy Hotel), WC2. ℰ 020/7836-9112. Reservations required. Main courses £22–£30 ($33–$45); fixed-price pre-theater dinner £15.50–£18.75 ($23.25–$28.15); breakfast from £14.50 ($21.75). AE, DC, MC, V. Mon–Fri 7:15am–10am; Mon–Sat 12:15–2:15pm and 5:30–10:30pm; Sun noon–2pm and 6–9pm. Tube: Charing Cross or Embankment.

MODERATE

Porter's English Restaurant ℛ (Kids) TRADITIONAL BRITISH

The 7th Earl of Bradford serves "real English food at affordable prices." He succeeds notably, and not just because Lady Bradford turned over her recipe for banana-and-ginger pudding. This comfortable, two-story restaurant is family friendly, informal, and lively. Porter's specializes in classic English pies, including Old English fish pie; lamb and apricot; ham, leek, and cheese; and, of course, bangers and mash. Main courses are so generous—and accompanied by vegetables and side dishes—that you hardly need appetizers. They have also added grilled English fare to the menu, with sirloin and lamb steaks and pork chops. The puddings, including bread-and-butter pudding or steamed syrup sponge, are served hot or cold, with whipped cream or custard. The bar does exotic cocktails, as well as beers, wine, or English mead. A traditional English tea is also served from 2:30 to 5:30pm for £3.50 ($5.25) per person.

17 Henrietta St., WC2. ℰ 020/7836-6466. Reservations recommended. Main courses £8.95–£12.95 ($13.45–$19.45); fixed-price menu £17.75 ($26.65). AE, DC, MC, V. Mon–Sat noon–11:30pm; Sun noon–10:30pm. Tube: Covent Garden or Leicester Sq.

INEXPENSIVE

The George TRADITIONAL BRITISH   Go here for the atmosphere of old England. Although its half-timbered facade would have

you believe it's older than it is, this pub has been around *only* since 1723. Set on the Strand at the lower end of Fleet Street opposite the Royal Courts of Justice, the George is a favorite of barristers, their clients, and the journalists who haven't moved to other parts of London. The pub's illustrious history saw Samuel Johnson having his mail delivered here and Oliver Goldsmith enjoying tankards of what eventually became draught Bass. Today, the setting seems only slightly changed; much of the original architecture is still intact. Hot and cold platters, including bangers and mash, fish-and-chips, steak-and-kidney pie, and lasagna, are served from a food counter at the back of the pub. Additional seating is available in the basement, where a headless cavalier is said to haunt the same premises where he enjoyed his liquor in an earlier day.

213 The Strand, WC2. ℂ **020/7427-0941**. Main courses £5–£7.95 ($7.50–$11.95). AE, MC, V. Mon–Fri 11am–11pm; Sat noon–3pm. Tube: Temple.

PICCADILLY CIRCUS & LEICESTER SQUARE

Both Piccadilly Circus & Leicester Square lie at the doorstep of West End theaters. All the choices below would make candidates for dining in this district.

EXPENSIVE

Fung Shing ⋒ CANTONESE   In a city where the competition is stiff, Fung Shing emerges as London's finest Cantonese restaurant. It dazzles with classic and nouvelle Cantonese dishes. Look for the seasonal specials. Some of the dishes may be experimental, notably stir-fried fresh milk with scrambled egg white, but you'll feel at home with the soft-shell crab sautéed in a light batter and served with tiny rings of red-hot chili and deep-fried garlic. Chinese gourmets go here for the fried intestines, but you may prefer the hotpot of stewed duck with yam or the tender ostrich with yellow bean sauce. The spicy sea bass and the stir-fried crispy chicken are worthy choices—there are some 150 dishes from which to choose. Most are moderate in price.

15 Lisle St., WC2. ℂ **020/7437-1539**. Reservations required. Main courses £10–£17 ($15–$25.50); fixed-price menus £25–£35 ($37.50–$52.50). AE, DC, MC, V. Daily noon–11:30pm. Tube: Leicester Sq.

J. Sheekey ⋒ SEAFOOD   British culinary tradition lives on in this fish joint, a favorite of West End actors. The jellied eels that delighted Laurence Olivier and Vivien Leigh are still here, along with fresh oysters from the coasts of Ireland and Brittany, plus that Victorian favorite, fried whitebait. Sheekey's fish pie is still on the menu, as is Dover sole, even a Cornish fish stew that's quite savory. The "mushy" vegetables still appear but the chefs also offer the likes of steamed organic sea beet. The double chocolate pudding soufflé is a delight, and many favorite puddings remain. Look for something daring now and then—fried plum ravioli with yogurt ice cream?

28–32 St. Martin's Court, WC2. ℂ 020/7240-2565. Reservations recommended. Main courses £10.50–£28 ($15.75–$42). AE, DC, DISC, MC, V. Daily noon–3pm and 7:30pm–midnight. Tube: Charing Cross.

MODERATE

Belgo Centraal BELGIAN   Chaos reigns supreme in this cavernous basement, where mussels mariniére with frites and 100 Belgian beers are the *raison d'être*. Take a freight elevator past the busy kitchen into a converted cellar, divided into two large eating areas. One is a beer hall seating about 250; the menu here is the same as in the restaurant, but you don't need reservations. The restaurant side has three nightly seatings: 5:30, 7:30, and 10pm. Between 5:30 and 8pm you can choose one of three fixed-price menus, and you pay based on the time: the earlier you order, the less you pay. Although heaps of fresh mussels are the attraction, you can opt for fresh Scottish salmon, roast chicken, a perfectly done steak, or one of the vegetarian specialties. Gargantuan plates of wild boar sausages arrive with *stoemp,* Belgian mashed spuds and cabbage. Belgian stews called *waterzooï* are also served. With waiters in monk's habits with black aprons, barking orders into headset microphones, it's all a bit bizarre.

50 Earlham St., WC2. ℂ 020/7813-2233. Reservations required for the restaurant. Main courses £8.95–£20.95 ($13.40–$31.40); fixed-price menus £6–£25.50 ($10.20–$43.35). AE, DC, MC, V. Mon–Sat noon–11:30pm; Sun noon–10:30pm. Closed Christmas. Tube: Covent Garden.

Incognico ⟨☆☆⟩ FRENCH/ECLECTIC   Michelin's three-star chef, Nico Ladenis, is firmly entrenched in Theaterland. It's ideal for a pre-theater meal. A modern brasserie with dark-wood paneling and leather banquettes, Incognico offers better food than the traditional area favorite, Ivy. Some items on the menu evoke the more famous Chez Nico, but most of the food is straightforward though not simplistic. The cuisine makes for a superlative dining experience, especially if you opt for such delights as fillet of salmon with ginger accompanied by a delicate plum sauce. The chef isn't afraid of the oldies like the marvelous veal kidneys in a mustard sauce. Our favorites are the seared fillet of cod and the breast of guinea fowl with lentils. Here is Theaterland's best osso bucco, and you might enjoy the artichokes with mushrooms and a sensuous hollandaise. One of the most contemporary dishes is open ravioli with goat's cheese.

117 Shaftesbury Ave., WC2. ☏ 020/7836-8866. Reservations required. Lunch or pre-theater menu £12.50 ($18.75). Main courses £9.50–£16 ($14.25–$24). AE, MC, V. Mon–Sat noon–3pm and 5:30pm–midnight. Tube: Leicester Square.

The Ivy ☆ MODERN BRITISH/INTERNATIONAL   Effervescent and sophisticated, The Ivy is the choice of the theatrical luminaries. It has been associated with the theater district since it opened in 1911. With its ersatz 1930s look and tiny bar near the entrance, this place is fun, and hums with the energy of London's glamour scene. The menu may seem simple, but the kitchen has a solid appreciation for fresh ingredients and a talent for preparation. Favorite dishes include white asparagus with sea kale and truffle butter; seared scallops with spinach, sorrel, and bacon; and salmon fishcakes. There's also Thai-spiced chicken soup with coconut cream, a great mixed grill, and such English desserts as sticky toffee and caramelized bread-and-butter pudding. Meals are served late to accommodate the post-theater crowd.

1–5 West St., WC2. ☏ 020/7836-4751. Reservations required. Main courses £8.75–£35 ($13.15–$52.50); Sat–Sun fixed-price 3-course lunch £16.50 ($28.05). AE, DC, MC, V. Daily noon–3pm and 5:30pm–midnight (last order). Tube: Leicester Sq.

INEXPENSIVE

Cork & Bottle Wine Bar ☆ *Value* INTERNATIONAL   Don Hewitson, a connoisseur of fine wines for more than 30 years, presides over this fine wine find. The ever-changing wine list features an excellent selection of Beaujolais *crus* from Alsace, 30 selections from Australia, 30 champagnes, and a good selection of California labels. If you want something to wash down, the most successful dish is a yeast-raised cheese-and-ham pie, with a cream cheese–like filling and crisp well-buttered pastry—not your typical quiche. There's also chicken and apple salad, Lancashire hotpot, Mediterranean prawns with garlic and asparagus, lamb in ale, and tandoori chicken.

44–46 Cranbourn St., WC2. ☏ 020/7734-7807. Reservations not accepted after 6:30pm. Main courses £6.50–£11.95 ($9.75–$17.90); glass of wine from £3.50 ($5.25). AE, DC, MC, V. Mon–Sat 11am–11:30pm; Sun noon–10:30pm. Tube: Leicester Sq.

SOHO

The restaurants of Soho are conveniently located for those rushing to have both dinner and an evening at one of the West End theaters.

VERY EXPENSIVE

Spoon + ⍟ AMERICAN   In Ian Schrager's Sanderson Hotel, this is a branch of the Spoon that master chef Alain Ducasse lures *tout Paris* to. Like its namesake, this is Ducasse's take on American fusion cuisine. A waiter told us, "We prefer to cater mainly to bright young things, but try to be democratic as well." This is the only place you can go in London to eat a French version of that American classic—macaroni and cheese. Of course, there's lobster in banana leaves if you want to go native. Also who can beat Spoon + when it comes to dishing up the best bubble-gum ice cream in London? We don't mean to make a caricature of the food, although some items seemed designed to shock. Much of what is offered is really good, especially the crab ceviche or the iced tomato soup. Spoon + chefs allow you to compose your own meal or at least pair up ingredients—perhaps a beautiful sole with a crushed lemon confit, or do you prefer it with satay sauce? You choose from a trio of columns—main course, sauce, and accompanying side dish. On our last visit we found the restaurant ridiculously overpriced, but reconsidered when our fellow diners turned out to be Madonna and her young groom, Guy Ritchie.

50 Berners St., W1. ⍒ 020/7300-1400. Reservations required. Main courses £30–£50 ($45–$75). AE, DC, MC, V. Mon-Sat noon–3pm and 6–11:30pm (till 10:30pm Sun). Tube: Leicester Sq. or Covent Garden.

EXPENSIVE

Teatro Club & Restaurant ⍟ MODERN BRITISH   This is still London's restaurant of the moment even though it's been around since the last century (1998) when it was acclaimed for its contemporary British fare. Having Gordon Ramsay, one of London's top chefs, as its consultant helped. The chef is Stuart Gillies, an artist who cooks with flavor, precision, and skill.

The cuisine is richer than the minimalist interior, beginning with such starters as warm carpaccio of monkfish and squid with herb and chili dressing. The crab bisque is velvety smooth, as is the *foie gras* du jour. Salmon appears with a lemony couscous. You can venture into the roast fillet of cod with girolle mushrooms, peas, and spinach or perhaps the leg of Barbary duck with wild mushrooms, borlotti beans, and basil. Horseradish butter gives added zest to the grilled halibut. Desserts are a journey into nostalgia: fresh plum tartlet with custard, banana sticky toffee, and the like. The best deal is the £13.50 ($20.25) fixed-price dinner.

93–107 Shaftesbury Ave., W1. ℂ 020/7494-3040. Fax 020/7494-3050. Reservations required. Main courses £18–£35 ($27–$52.50); fixed-price menus (lunch or dinner) £13.50–£16.95 ($20.25–$25.45). AE, DC, MC, V. Mon–Fri noon–3pm and Mon–Sat 6–11:30pm. Tube: Piccadilly Circus.

MODERATE

Bam-Bou 🞕 VIETNAMESE/FRENCH London's best Vietnamese-inspired eatery is spread over a series of dining rooms, alcoves, and bars in this townhouse with French colonial decor. A favorite of young London, the restaurant is so popular you may have to wait for 30 minutes to an hour for a table. The smell of lime and lemongrass lures you to a table—the combination married perfectly in the chicken in lemongrass. Equally worthy is the caramelized ginger chicken. One of our party ordered tempura of softshell crab with pemlo and mizuna salad, and fellow diners nibbled so much he had to order another helping. Lemongrass and chicken are wed again, very effectively, in a brochette with peanuts. The stuffed cod with tamarind is aromatically appealing, as is the monkfish flavored with an exotic turmeric, onion, and fill. Our favorite starter is spicy raw beef with aromatic basil, lime, and chili, or fried marinated squid. A winner for dessert is the sweet banana rolls with chocolate sauce.

1 Percy St., W1. ℂ 020/7323-9130. Reservations required. Main courses £10.95–£12.95 ($16.40–$19.40); 2-course lunch and pre-theater menu £12.50 ($18.75). AE, DC, MC, V. Mon–Fri noon–11:15pm; Sat 6–11:15pm. Tube: Tottenham Court Rd.

Mezzo MODERN EUROPEAN/ASIAN This 750-seat Soho restaurant—the creation of Sir Terence Conran—is the biggest in London. The mammoth space, the former site of rock's Marquee club, contains several restaurants: **Mezzonine** upstairs, serving a Thai/Asian cuisine with European; swankier **Mezzo** downstairs, offering a modern European cuisine in an atmosphere of 1930s Hollywood; and **Mezzo Cafe,** where you can stop in for a sandwich.

The food is at its most ambitious downstairs, where 100 chefs work behind glass to feed up to 400 diners at a time. This is dinner-as-theater. Not surprisingly, the cuisine tends to be uneven. We suggest the rotisserie rib of beef with red wine and creamed horseradish, or the roast cod, crisp skinned and cooked to perfection. For dessert, you can't beat the butterscotch ice cream with a pitcher of hot fudge. A live jazz band entertains after 10pm from Wednesday to Saturday, and the world of Marlene Dietrich and Noel Coward comes alive again.

100 Wardour St., W1. ✆ 020/7314-4000. Reservations accepted. Mezzo 3-course fixed-price dinner £15.50 ($23.25); Mezzonine 3-course dinner £11.90 ($17.85). AE, DC, MC, V. Mezzo: Wed–Fri noon–3pm; Sun 12:30–3pm; Mon–Thurs 6pm–midnight; Fri–Sat 6pm–3am; Sun 6–11pm. Mezzonine: Mon–Fri noon–3pm; Sat noon–4pm; Mon–Thurs 5:30pm–1am; Fri–Sat 5:30pm–3am. Tube: Piccadilly Circus.

Quo Vadis ✪ MODERN BRITISH This trendy restaurant occupies the former apartment house of Karl Marx, who would never recognize it. It was an Italian restaurant from 1926 until the mid-1990s, when its interior was transformed into the stylish postmodern place you'll find today. The street-level dining room is a showcase for the paintings of controversial Damien Hirst and other contemporary artists. Many bypass the restaurant for the upstairs bar, where Hirst has put a severed cow's head and a bull's head on display in separate aquariums. Why? They're catalysts to conversation, satirical odes to the destructive effects of mad cow disease, and perhaps satirical commentaries on the flirtatious games that patrons conduct here.

Quo Vadis is associated with Marco Pierre White, but don't expect to see the culinary superstar; he functions as a consultant. Also, don't expect the overburdened staff to pamper you; they're preoccupied dealing with the glare of publicity. And the food? It's well presented and good, but not as artful or innovative as the setting might suggest. We suggest the tomato and red mullet broth perfumed with basil or the terrine of *foie gras* and duck confit. Try the escallop of tuna with tapenade and eggplant "caviar" (actually eggplant and black olives puréed and seasoned) or the roast chicken a la souvaroff, truffle oil, herb dumplings, and vegetable broth.

26–29 Dean St., W1. ✆ 020/7437-9585. Reservations required. Main courses £15–£27.50 ($22.50–$41.25); fixed-price lunches and pre- and post-theater £14.95–£17.95 ($22.40–$26.90). AE, MC, V. Mon–Fri noon–3pm; Mon–Sat 6–11pm; Sun 6–10:30pm. Tube: Leicester Sq. or Tottenham Court Rd.

Soho Spice SOUTH INDIAN One of central London's most stylish Indian restaurants combines a sense of media and fashion hip with the flavors and scents of southern India. You might opt for a drink at the cellar bar before heading to the street-level dining room decorated in saffron, cardamom, bay, and pepper hues. A staff member dressed in a similarly vivid uniform will propose a wide array of choices, including slow-cooked Indian tikkas that feature combinations of spices with lamb, chicken, fish, or vegetables. The a la carte menu offers a variety of courses, including Jhinga Hara

Pyaz, spicy queen prawns with fresh spring onions, and Paneer Pasanda, cottage cheese slices stuffed with spinach and served with almond sauce. The cuisine will satisfy traditionalists, but has a modern flair. The presentation takes it a step above typical Indian restaurants.

124–126 Wardour St., W1. ℂ 020/7434-0808. Reservations recommended. Main courses £8.50–£14.50 ($12.75–$21.75); set lunch £7.50 ($11.25); set dinner £16.95 ($25.45). AE, V. Sun–Thurs 11:30am–12:30am; Fri–Sat 11:30am–3am; Sun 12:30–10:30pm. Tube: Tottenham Court Rd.

YO! Sushi SUSHI *Kids*   This is sushi Disneyland, with high-tech gadgets, gimmicks, and good sushi. If you've got a kid, and you want to indoctrinate him or her into the ways of raw fish, this is the place to go. YO! Sushi has the longest sushi bar in the world, with a *kaiten* (conveyor belt) serving 130 guests. You're allowed to choose two pieces of sushi from five price categories. Plates have colors that match the prices. Lime is the cheapest, pink the most expensive. Service robots move around and take your drink orders. Some of the chefs are human beings, although they turn out sushi at automated speeds. They stand behind a counter where you can order everything from fresh clams to avocado and salmon hand rolls. You can have your fill of cuttlefish, eel, shrimp, salmon roe, octopus, or whatever. Vegetarian sushi includes pickled turnip and cucumber. Wash it all down with Sapporo beer, Japanese tea, or iced or hot sake. Live footage from Japan on Sony wide-screen TVs keeps you amused.

52 Poland St., W1. ℂ 020/7287-0443. Reservations recommended. Sushi £1.50–£3.50 ($2.25–$5.25). AE, DC, MC, V. Daily noon–12:30am. Tube: Oxford Circus.

INEXPENSIVE

Balans MODERN BRITISH   On one of the gayest streets in London, Old Compton Street, Balans is the best known gay restaurant, and has been since 1993. Some of its fans take all their meals here. Its hours of service are almost without equal in London. Although the food is British, it is an eclectic cuisine, borrowing from whatever kitchen it chooses, from the Far East to America. You can fill up on one of the succulent pastas, especially the black-ink tortellini sprinkled with scallops. Grills delight the mostly male patrons, especially the tuna teriyaki or the charred roast chicken. Balans has a party pub atmosphere and is a good place to meet people.

60 Old Compton St., W1. ℂ 020/7437-5212. Reservations recommended. Main courses £5–£12 ($7.50–$18). AE, MC, V. Mon–Sat 8am–5am; Sun 8am–2am. Tube: Piccadilly Circus or Leicester Sq.

Mildreds *⊛ Finds* VEGETARIAN   Mildreds may sound like a 1940s Joan Crawford movie, but it's one of London's most enduring vegetarian and vegan dining spots. It was vegetarian long before such restaurants became trendy. Jane Muir and Diane Thomas worked in restaurants together before opening their own place. Today they run a bustling diner with friendly service. Sometimes it's a bit crowded and tables are shared. They do a mean series of delectable stir-fries. The ingredients are naturally grown, and strongly emphasize the best seasonal produce. The menu changes daily, but features an array of soups, casseroles, and salads. Organic wines are served, and the portions are large. Save room for dessert, especially the nutmeg-and-mascarpone ice cream or the chocolate rum and amaretto pudding.

58 Greek St., W1. ℂ 020/7494-1634. Reservations not accepted. Main courses £5.30–£6.50 ($7.95–$9.75). Mon–Sat noon–11pm. No credit cards. Tube: Tottenham Court Rd.

TRAFALGAR SQUARE
MODERATE

Crivelli's Garden *⊛* ITALIAN/FRENCH   In the National Gallery at Trafalgar Square, this hot dining choice lies over the foyer of the Sainsbury Wing, providing a view of the fabled square. The view's a bonus—it's the cuisine that attracts visitors. The restaurant is named for a mural by Paulo Rego which takes up one side of a wall. The chefs are at home in both the French and Italian kitchens, offering wood-fired pizzas and bruschetta or something more imaginative, such as gnocchi with rocket and wild mushrooms. Try the grilled rib of pork, marinated and served with baby artichokes. The lightly batter fried sole is a worthy choice as well. The steamed salmon with leeks, cilantro, and ginger is an excellent dish, as is the red pepper ravioli in a chive sauce. A cafe is in the basement of the main building, and is a good choice for sandwiches, pastas, soups, and pastries.

In the National Gallery, Trafalgar Square WC2. ℂ 020/7747-2869. Reservations required. Fixed-price lunch and Wed dinner £14.50–£18.50 ($21.75–$27.75). AE, DC, MC, V. Daily noon–3pm and Wed 6–8pm. Tube: Charing Cross.

National Portrait Gallery Restaurant *⊛* MODERN BRITISH If anything, tables here open onto a better view than those at the National Gallery's restaurant (see above). Along with the view (Nelson's Column, Big Ben, and the like), you get superb meals. This rooftop restaurant is a sought after dining ticket on the fifth floor of the Gallery's Ondaatje Wing. Patrons usually go for lunch, not knowing that the chefs also cook on Thursday and Friday nights. Start with goat cheese fritters with tomato and fennel or grilled baby leeks. In spring there's nothing finer than English asparagus. The main courses are filled with flavor, but the natural goodness of the food comes out in such dishes as grilled baby chicken or peppered rump of lamb with a summer bean cassoulet. Chefs aren't afraid of simple preparations mainly because they are assured of the excellence of their products. The wine list features some organic bottles.

In the National Portrait Gallery, Trafalgar Square. © 020/7313-2490. Reservations recommended. Main courses £12–£16 ($18–$24). AE, DC, MC, V. Daily 11:45am–2:45pm and Thurs–Fri 5:30–8:30pm. Tube: Leicester Sq.

MAYFAIR
VERY EXPENSIVE

Le Gavroche 🌟🌟🌟 CLASSICAL FRENCH   Although challengers come and go, this *luxe* dining room remains the number one choice in London for classical French cuisine. There's always something special coming out of the kitchen of Michel Roux; the service is faultless and the ambience chic, not stuffy. The menu changes constantly, depending on the fresh produce available and the inspiration of the chef. But it remains classically French, although not of the "essentially old-fashioned bourgeois repertoire" that some critics suggest. Try the soufflé Suissesse, *papillote* of smoked salmon, or whole Bresse chicken with truffles and a Madeira cream sauce. Game is often served, depending on availability. New menu options include cassoulet of snails with frog thighs, seasoned with herbs; mousseline of lobster in champagne sauce; pavé of braised turbot with red Provençal wine and smoked bacon; and fillet of red snapper with caviar and oyster-stuffed tortellini.

Desserts, including the sablé of pears and chocolate, are sublime. The wine cellar is among the most interesting in London, with many Burgundies and Bordeaux. The *menu exceptionnel* is, in essence, a tasting menu for the entire table. It usually consists of four to five smaller courses, followed by one or two desserts and coffee.

43 Upper Brook St., W1. © 020/7408-0881. Fax 020/7491-4387. Reservations required as far in advance as possible. Main courses £29.10–£38 ($43.65–$57); fixed-price lunch £38.50 ($57.75); menu exceptionnel for entire table £78 ($117) per person. AE, MC, V. Mon–Fri noon–2pm and 7–11pm. Tube: Marble Arch.

Petrus 🌟🌟 MODERN FRENCH   Clubby and not at all stuffy, this is the domain of Marcus Wareing, a former boxer from Lancashire. The restaurant serves nouvelle French food in the grand tradition of Wareing's mentor, Gordon Ramsay, London's hottest chef. In a sleek, opulent setting, you get reasonably priced food prepared with a technical precision but also a touch of whimsy. It's best to order the chef's six-course tasting menu to appreciate his culinary ambitions. You'll be dazzled with everything from marinated *foie gras* to an apple and artichoke salad, from Bresse pigeon in a truffle confit to a Valhrona chocolate fondant. We've delighted in all the dishes sampled here, from the eggplant caviar to crisp roast sea bass paired with caramelized endive and plump oysters.

33 St. James's St., SW1. © 020/7930-4272. Reservations required. Fixed-price menu £26–£45 ($39–$67.50) for 3 courses, or £55 ($82.50) for 6-course tasting menu. Mon–Fri noon–2:30pm, daily 6:45–10:45pm. AE, DC, MC, V. Tube: Green Park.

The Square ✦✦✦ CONTINENTAL   This restaurant is on the rise, though it's been around for more than a decade. It doesn't scare Le Gavroche, but food critics think The Square will emerge as a great restaurant. Chef Philip Howard delivers the goods. This is the restaurant to visit on the London gastronomic circuit. You get immaculate food in a cosseting atmosphere with abstract modern art on the walls. Howard has a magic touch with pasta—it appears as a bulging roll of cannelloni stuffed with shredded trout and green leeks, or as a ravioli of partridge on a pool of creamy game-flavored sauce with finely shredded cabbage. A surprise awaits in every corner of the menu—for example, risotto of calf's tail with fillet of veal and butternut squash. His fish is stunningly fresh, and the Bresse pigeon is as good as it is in its hometown in France. If you're a vegetarian, stay clear. Many dishes are aimed at the true carnivore, who digs into such a gamy mixture as sautéed liver and other offally bits.

6–10 Bruton St., W1. © 020/7495-7100. Reservations required. Main courses £16.50–£20 ($24.75–$30). Fixed-price dinner £45–£65 ($67.50–$97.50). AE, DC, MC, V. Mon–Fri noon–2:45pm, Mon–Sat 7–11pm. Tube: Bond St.

MODERATE

Greenhouse MODERN BRITISH   Chef Paul Merrett is inspired by modern British food. The fare from the heart of England includes a roast breast of pheasant that Henry VIII would have loved, and grilled farmhouse pork—we're also fond of the wilted greens wrapped in bacon. The menu is backed up by a well-chosen wine list. Some of the delightfully sticky desserts, including a moist bread-and-butter pudding and a baked ginger loaf with orange marmalade, would have pleased a Midlands granny. Simply conceived dishes with a resolutely British slant draw a never-ending line of satisfied customers. The ingredients are first-class and beautifully prepared, without ever destroying the natural flavor of a dish.

27A Hays Mews, W1. © 020/7499-3331. Reservations required. Main courses £13.50–£22 ($22.95–$37.40). Fixed-price lunch £17.50–£21 ($29.75–$35.70). AE, DC, MC, V. Mon–Fri noon–2:30pm and 6:30–11pm; Sat 6:30–11pm; Sun 12:30–2:30pm and 6:30–11pm. Closed Christmas, bank holidays. Tube: Green Park.

Momo MOROCCAN/NORTH AFRICAN   You'll be greeted by a friendly and casual staff member in a black-and-white T-shirt and fatigue pants. The setting is like Marrakesh, with stucco walls, a wood-and-stone floor, patterned wood window shades, burning candles, and banquettes. You can fill up on the fresh baked bread along with appetizers such as garlicky marinated olives and pickled carrots spiced with pepper and cumin. These starters are a gift from the chef. Other appetizers are also tantalizing, especially the *briouat:* paper-thin and crisp packets of puff pastry filled with saffron-flavored chicken and other treats. One of the chef's specialties is *pastilla au pigeon,* a poultry pie with almonds. Many diners visit for the couscous maison, among the best in London. Served in a decorative pot, this aromatic dish of raisins, meats (including merguez sausage), chicken, lamb, and chickpeas is given added flavor with that powerful hot sauce of the Middle East, marissa. After all this, the refreshing cinnamon-flavored orange slices are a tempting treat for dessert.

25 Heddon St., W1. © 020/7434-4040. Reservations required 2 weeks in advance. Main courses £10.50–£16.50 ($15.75–$24.75); fixed-price 2-course lunch £15 ($22.50); fixed-price 3-course lunch £17 ($25.50). AE, DC, MC, V. Daily noon–2:30pm; Mon–Sat 7–11pm, Sun 6:30–10:30pm. Tube: Piccadilly Circus or Oxford Circus.

INEXPENSIVE

Bubbles PACIFIC RIM   This interesting wine bar lies between Upper Brook Street and Oxford Street. The owners attach equal importance to their food and their impressive wine list (some wines are sold by the glass). On the ground floor, you can enjoy fine wines along with a selection of bar food. The menu has been upgraded and made more sophisticated and appealing. A basket of homemade bread is placed before you with olives, goat cheese, salami, and roasted pepper. Begin perhaps with the zesty tandoori prawns, to follow with such delights as Japanese mirin omelet with pickled vegetables and a sweet ginger mayonnaise, or duck breast on parsnip mash with a tamarillo sauce.

41 N. Audley St., W1. © 020/7491-3237. Reservations recommended. Main courses £8.95–£12.95 ($13.40–$19.40); vegetarian main courses £7–£10 ($10.50–$15). AE, MC, V. Mon–Sat 11am–9:30pm. Tube: Bond St.

ST. JAMES'S
EXPENSIVE

L'Oranger *🍊* CONTINENTAL This bistro-cum-brasserie occupies a high-ceilinged space in an affluent neighborhood near the bottom of St. James's Street. Amid touches of paneling, burnt-orange paint, patterned carpeting, immaculate linens, flowers, and uniformed waiters, you'll appreciate the set menus of executive chef Kamel Benamar. His arrangement of flavors has been praised by a clientele pundits call "people who have made it." All menus are fixed-price: Depending on the chef's inspiration, they may include *foie gras* poached in a red Pessac wine sauce or pan-fried fillet of sea bass with zucchini, tomatoes, basil, and a black-olive vinaigrette. Other staples include crispy fillets of cod with bouillabaisse sauce and new potatoes, and braised leg of rabbit in Madeira sauce with whole cloves of yellow garlic *en confit* and braised cabbage. Starters include a terrine of ham and tongue served with gherkins and parsley, bound with a layer of spinach and served on a bed of choron sauce.

5 St. James's St., SW1A. *©* **020/7839-3774.** Reservations recommended. Fixed-price lunches £19.50–£23.50 ($29.25–$35.25); fixed-price dinner £35.50 ($53.25). AE, DC, MC, V. Mon–Fri noon–2:30pm; Mon–Sat 6–11:15pm. Tube: Green Park.

MODERATE

Circus MODERN BRITISH/INTERNATIONAL This place buzzes during pre- and post-theater hours with foodies anxious to sample the wares of chef Richard Lee. A minimalist haven for power design and eating in the heart of London, this restaurant took over the ground floor and basement of the Granada Television building. The place evokes a London version of a Left Bank Parisian brasserie. For some country cousins from the north of England who missed out on the food, Lee offers braised faggot with bubble-and-squeak (bubble-and-squeak is cabbage and potatoes, and faggots are highly seasoned squares of pig's liver, pork, onion, herbs, and nutmeg—bound with an egg and baked wrapped in a pig's caul). You might taste the skate wing with crushed new potatoes accompanied by a thick pesto-like medley of rocket blended with black olives. Or try the sautéed chili-flavored squid with bok choi, heavenly with a tamarind dressing. The sorbets are a nice finish to a meal, especially the mango and pink grapefruit version. Of course, if you're ravenous, there's the velvety smooth amaretto cheesecake with a coffee sauce. Service is a delight.

1 Upper James St., W1. ☎ **020/7534-4000.** Reservations required. Main courses £11.50–£18.50 ($19.55–$31.45); fixed-price menus 5:45–7:15pm and 10:30pm–midnight. Fixed-price dinner £10.50–£12.50 ($17.85–$21.25). AE, DC, MC, V. Daily noon–2:30pm; Mon–Sat 6pm–midnight. Bar menu daily noon–1:30am. Tube: Piccadilly Circus.

Quaglino's ⍟ CONTINENTAL   It's vast, it's convivial, it's fun. Giovanni Quaglino established a restaurant here in 1929. Personalities who paraded through in ermine and pearls could fill a between-the-wars roster of who's who in Europe. In 1993, restaurateur and designer Sir Terence Conran brought the place into the postmodern age with a new decor—eight artists were commissioned to decorate the massive columns supporting the soaring ceiling. A mezzanine with a bar features live jazz on Friday and Saturday nights and live piano music the rest of the week. An altar in the back is devoted to the most impressive display of crustaceans and shellfish in Britain.

Everything seems to be served in bowls. Menu items have been criticized for their quick preparation and standard format. But considering that on some nights up to 800 people might dine, the marvel is that the place functions as well as it does. That's not to say there isn't an occasional delay. Come for fun, not subtlety and finesse. The menu changes often, but your choices might include goat cheese and caramelized onion tart, seared salmon with potato pancakes, crab tartlet with saffron, and roasted cod and ox cheek with chargrilled vegetables. The prawns and oysters—delectable and fresh—are the most ordered items.

16 Bury St., SW1. ☎ **020/7930-6767.** Reservations recommended. Main courses £12–£18 ($18–$27); fixed-price menu (available only for lunch and pre-dinner theater between 5:30 and 6:30pm) 2-courses £12.50 ($18.75), 3 courses £15 ($22.50). AE, DC, MC, V. Daily noon–2:30pm; Mon–Thurs 5:30–11:30pm; Fri–Sat 5:30pm–12:30am; Sun 5:30–11pm. Tube: Green Park.

3 Westminster & Victoria

EXPENSIVE

Rhodes in the Square ⍟⍟⍟ MODERN BRITISH   In this discreet residential district, super-chef Gary Rhodes strikes again. Rhodes is known for taking traditional British cookery and giving it daring twists and adding new flavors. You can count on delightful surprises from this major talent. The glitterati can be seen in the apartment-block-cum-hotel, sampling his offerings in a high-ceilinged room done in midnight blue. You never know what's available—maybe his whole red mullet stuffed with a medley of eggplant, anchovies, fresh garlic, and peppers, appearing with a cream-laced sauce flavored with fennel. Start, perhaps, with chicken liver parfait with *foie gras,* and go on to an open omelet with chunky bits of lobster topping it along with a Thermidor sauce and cheese crust. His glazed duck served with bitter orange jus is how this dish is supposed to taste. For dessert, make your selection from the British pudding plate that ranges from lemon meringue tart to a simple seared carpaccio of pineapple oozing with good flavor.

Dolphin Sq., Chichester St., SW1. ℂ 020/7798-6767. Reservations required. Fixed-price meals £27.50 ($41.25) for 2 courses, £33.50 ($50.25) for 3 courses. AE, DC, MC, V. Tues–Fri noon–2:30pm; Tues–Sat 7–10pm. Tube: Pimlico.

Simply Nico ⭐ *Value* FRENCH   Simply Nico is the brainchild of master chef Nico Ladenis, run by his sous chef. We think it's the best value in town. In Nico's own words, it's "cheap and cheerful." The wood floors reverberate with the din of contented diners, who pack in at snug tables to enjoy the simply prepared food. The fixed-price menu changes frequently, but options might include starters such as pan-fried *foie gras* followed by shank of lamb with parsnips, or the ever-popular monkfish.

48A Rochester Row, SW1. ℂ 020/7630-8061. Reservations required. Fixed-price 2-course lunch £20.50 ($30.75); fixed-price 3-course lunch £23.50 ($35.25); fixed-price 3-course dinner £26.50 ($39.75). AE, DC, MC, V. Mon–Fri noon–2pm; Mon–Sat 6–10pm. Tube: Victoria or St. James's Park.

MODERATE

Tate Gallery Restaurant ⭐ *Value* MODERN BRITISH   This restaurant is particularly attractive to wine fanciers. It offers what may be the best bargains for superior wines in Britain. Bordeaux and Burgundies are in abundance, and management keeps the markup between 40% and 65%, rather than the 100% to 200% added in most restaurants. In fact, the prices here are lower than they are in most wine shops. Wine begins at £13.50 ($20.25) per bottle, or £4.95 ($7.45) per glass. Oenophiles frequently come just for lunch. The restaurant specializes in an English menu that changes about every month. Dishes might include pheasant casserole, Oxford sausage with mashed potatoes, pan-fried skate with black butter and capers, and a selection of vegetarian dishes. One critic found the staff and diners as traditional "as a Gainsborough landscape." Access to the restaurant is through the museum's main entrance on Millbank.

Millbank, SW1. ℂ 020/7887-8877. Reservations recommended. Main courses £9–£16 ($13.50–$24); fixed-price 2-course lunch £16.75 ($25.15); fixed-price 3-course lunch £19.50 ($29.25). Minimum charge £16.75 ($25.15). AE, DC, MC, V. Mon–Sat noon–3pm; Sun noon–4pm. Tube: Pimlico. Bus 77 or 88.

4 Knightsbridge to South Kensington

KNIGHTSBRIDGE
VERY EXPENSIVE

La Tante Claire ★★★ FRENCH   In swanky new digs, "Aunt Claire" is again one of the stellar restaurants of London. Pierre Koffmann remains the chef behind this place, more interested in turning out culinary fireworks than in creating a media frenzy. David Collins designed the restaurant with lilac walls and soothing green floors as a backdrop to the cuisine, which uses the freshest and best produce in London. The standards of Chef Koffmann are the benchmark others aspire to. To sample perfection, dishes bringing out mouthwatering flavors and precise textures try his legendary ravioli langoustine or pig's trotters. Who would have thought that the pig's foot could be transformed into such a sublime concoction? His soup made with truffles is to make gourmands cry for joy. His *nage de homard* (lobster) with sauternes and fresh ginger is a culinary work of skill, as is his steamed lamb with a vegetable couscous. For dessert, his hot pistachio soufflé served with its own ice cream will linger in your memory. The service proceeds like a perfectly trained orchestra.

Wilton Place, Knightsbridge, SW1. ✆ 020/7823-2003. Reservations required. Main courses £27–£40 ($45.90–$68). AE, DC, MC, V. Mon–Fri 12:30–2pm; Mon–Sat 7–11pm. Tube: Hyde Park Corner or Knightsbridge.

INEXPENSIVE

Le Metro INTERNATIONAL   Located around the corner from Harrods, Le Metro draws a fashionable crowd to its basement precincts. The place serves good, solid, and reliable food prepared with flair. The menu changes frequently, but try the mushroom risotto or confit of duck with lentils, garlic, and shallots if you can. You can order special wines by the glass.

28 Basil St., SW3. ✆ 020/7589-6286. Main courses £8.50–£10.50 ($12.75–$15.75). AE, DC, MC, V. Mon–Sat 7:30am–10:30pm. Tube: Knightsbridge.

CHELSEA
VERY EXPENSIVE

Gordon Ramsay ★★★ FRENCH   One of the city's most innovative and talented chefs is Gordon Ramsay. He has taken over the former location of La Tante Claire (see above), and serves a cuisine more innovative and exciting than the long-established La Tante herself. London is rushing to sample Mr. Ramsay's wares. Lord

Andrew Lloyd Webber has visited and acclaimed Ramsay as one of Europe's grandest chefs, saying "you can get better food here than anywhere else in London."

Every dish from this kitchen is gratifying, reflecting subtlety and delicacy without any sacrifice to the food's natural essence. Try, for example, Ramsay's celebrated cappuccino of white beans with grated truffles. His appetizers are likely to dazzle: salad of crispy pig's trotters with calf's sweetbreads, fried quail eggs, and a cream vinaigrette, or *foie gras* three ways—sautéed with quince, *mi-cuit* with an Earl Grey consommé, or pressed with truffle peelings. From here, you can grandly proceed to fillet of brill poached in red wine, grilled fillet of red mullet on a bed of caramelized endives, or caramelized Challandaise duck cooked with dates. Desserts are stunning, especially the pistachio soufflé with chocolate sorbet or the passion fruit and chocolate parfait.

68 Royal Hospital Rd., SW3. © 020/7352-4441. Reservations required (1 month in advance). Fixed-price lunch £30 ($45) for 3 courses; fixed-price dinner £60 ($90) for 3 courses, £75 ($112.50) for 7 courses. AE, DC, MC, V. Mon–Fri noon–2:30pm and 6:45–11pm. Tube: Sloane Sq.

EXPENSIVE

Blue Bird ☞ MODERN CONTINENTAL This enormous space resounds with clinking silverware and peals of laughter from a loyal clientele. Locals and staff alike refer to it as a *restaurant de gare*—a railway station restaurant. Although there's a cafe and an upscale delicatessen and housewares store on the street level, the heart and soul is in the restaurant. It holds up to 275 diners at a time, and you'll find a color scheme of red and blue canvas cutouts that replicate birds in flight. Tables are close together, but the scale of the place makes dining private and intimate. The menu emphasizes savory, cooked-to-the-minute cuisine, some emerging from a wood-burning stove used to roast everything from lobster to game. An immense shellfish bar stocks every crustacean you can think of, and a bar does a thriving business with the Sloane Square subculture. Perennial favorites include the marinated lamb with baked beans and aïoli, as well as versions of pasta and fresh fish. Before it was a restaurant, the site was as a garage that repaired the legendary Bluebird, an English sports car that is, alas, no longer produced.

350 King's Rd., SW3. © 020/7559-1000. Reservations recommended. Main courses £13.50–£21.50 ($22.95–$36.55). AE, DC, MC, V. Mon–Fri noon–3:30pm and 6–10:30pm; Sat 11am–3:30pm and 6–11pm; Sun 11am–3:30pm and 6–10:30pm. Tube: Sloane Sq.

The House ⓖ CONTINENTAL   In a quiet area of Chelsea, this restaurant is like dining in someone's townhouse. Two ground-floor alcoves make up the main dining room, with a trio of small private rooms upstairs. With its floral fabrics on the walls, antiques, and fireplaces, it couldn't get more English. The menu is eclectic, borrowing freely from whatever sounds and tastes good. Ingredients and flavors appear in surprising medleys for a harmonious whole. Expect such oddities (good tasting, too) as a soup of curried parsnips with crispy chicken wings, or salt cod fritters with a red pepper hummus. The potato terrine layered with capers and parsley in a caper dressing is another divine way to launch your meal. For a main dish, we chose roast scallops with a confit of belly pork, served with fresh fennel and a garlic purèe. For a classic English (or German) dish, you can select venison pie with pickled red cabbage. For something old English to finish, make it a banana and toffee crumble.

3 Milner St., SW3. ⓒ **020/7584-3002.** Reservations required. Fixed-price lunch £17.50 ($26.25); set dinner £25 ($37.50). Mon–Fri noon–2:30pm; Mon–Sat 6–11pm. Tube: South Kensington.

INEXPENSIVE
Chelsea Kitchen INTERNATIONAL   This simple restaurant feeds large numbers of Chelsea residents in a setting that's little changed since 1961. The food and the clientele move fast, almost guaranteeing that the entire inventory of ingredients is sold out at the end of each day. Menu items usually include leek-and-potato soup, chicken Kiev, chicken parmigiana, steaks, sandwiches, and burgers. The clientele includes a broad cross-section of patrons—all having a good and cost-conscious time.

98 King's Rd., SW3. ⓒ **020/7589-1330.** Reservations recommended. Main courses £3–£5.50 ($4.50–$8.25); fixed-price menu £7 ($10.50). No credit cards. Daily 8am–11:45pm. Tube: Sloane Sq.

KENSINGTON & SOUTH KENSINGTON
EXPENSIVE
Bibendum/The Oyster Bar ⓖ FRENCH/MEDITERRANEAN In trendy Brompton Cross, this still-fashionable restaurant occupies two floors of a garage that's an Art Deco masterpiece. Although it's still going strong, Bibendum's heyday was in the early 1990s. But the white-tiled room, with stained-glass windows, sunlight, and a chic clientele, is still pleasant. The eclectic cuisine, known for its freshness and simplicity, is based on what's available seasonally.

Dishes might include roast pigeon with celeriac purée and apple sauté; rabbit with anchovies, garlic, and rosemary; or grilled lamb cutlets with a delicate sauce. Some of the best dishes are for dining *à deux,* including Bresse chicken flavored with fresh tarragon or grilled veal chops with truffle butter.

Simpler meals and cocktails are available in the **Oyster Bar** on the building's street level. The bar-style menu stresses fresh shellfish presented in the traditional French style, on ice-covered platters occasionally adorned with seaweed. It's a crustacean-lover's lair.

81 Fulham Rd., SW3. ℂ 020/7581-5817. Reservations required in Bibendum; not accepted in Oyster Bar. Main courses £15–£25 ($22.50–$37.50); fixed-price 3-course lunch £28 ($42); cold seafood platter in Oyster Bar £45 ($67.50) for 2. AE, DC, MC, V. Bibendum Mon–Fri noon–2:30pm and 7–11:15pm; Sat 12:30–3pm and 7–11:15pm; Sun 12:30–3pm and 7–10:15pm. Oyster Bar Mon–Sat noon–10:30pm; Sun noon–3pm and 7–10pm. Tube: South Kensington.

Clarke's ⓖ MODERN BRITISH   Sally Clarke is one of the finest chefs in London, and this is one of the hottest restaurants around. *Still.* Clarke honed her skills at Michael's in Santa Monica and the West Beach Cafe in Venice (California) before heading back to her native land. In this excellent restaurant, everything is bright and modern, with wood floors, discreet lighting, and additional space in the basement where tables are more spacious and private. Some people are put off by the fixed-price menu, but the food is so well prepared that diners rarely object to what ends up in front of them. The menu, which changes daily, emphasizes chargrilled foods with herbs and seasonal veggies. You might begin with an appetizer salad of blood orange with red onion, watercress, and black olive-anchovy toast, then follow with grilled breast of chicken with black truffle, crisp polenta, and arugula. Desserts are likely to include a warm pear and raisin puff pastry with maple syrup ice cream. Just put yourself in Clarke's hands—you'll be glad you did.

124 Kensington Church St., W8. ℂ 020/7221-9225. Reservations recommended. Fixed-price lunches £8.50–£14 ($12.75–$21); fixed-price 4-course dinner £44 ($66). AE, DC, MC, V. Mon–Fri 12:30–2pm and 7–10pm. Tube: High St. Kensington.

MODERATE

Blue Elephant ⓖ THAI   This is the counterpart of the famous **L'Eléphant Bleu** in Brussels. Located in a converted factory building in West Brompton, it has been all the rage since 1986. It remains the leading Thai restaurant in London, where the competition seems to grow daily. In an almost magical setting of tropical foliage, diners are treated to an array of MSG-free Thai dishes. You can begin with a "Floating Market" (shellfish in clear broth flavored with chili paste and lemongrass), then go on to a splendid selection of main courses, for which many of the ingredients have been flown in from Thailand. We recommend the roasted duck curry served in a clay cooking pot.

4–6 Fulham Broadway, SW6. ℂ 020/7385-6595. Reservations required. Main courses £10–£25 ($15–$37.50); Royal Thai banquet £32–£36 ($48–$54); Sun buffet £19.50 ($29.25). AE, DC, MC, V. Mon–Fri noon–2:30pm; Mon–Sat 6:30pm–12:30am; Sun noon–3pm and 6:30–10:30pm. Tube: Fulham Broadway.

The Enterprise TRADITIONAL BRITISH/EUROPEAN   Its proximity to Harrods attracts regulars and out-of-town shoppers. Although the joint swarms with singles at night, during the day it attracts the ladies who lunch. With banquettes, white linen, and fresh flowers on the tables, you won't mistake it for a boozer. The kitchen serves traditional English fare as well as European favorites, all prepared with fresh ingredients. Featured dishes include fried salmon cakes with perfectly done fries and grilled steak with fries and salad. They're not so grand that they won't prepare an entrecôte with frites if that's what pleases you—the juicy, properly aged, and flavorful thin French-style slice of beef is about the best you can have in London.

35 Walton St., SW3. ℂ 020/7584-3148. Reservations accepted only for lunch. Main courses £9.65–£14.95 ($14.50–$22.40). AE, MC, V. Daily 12:30–2:30pm; Sat–Sun 12:30–3:30pm; Mon–Sat 7–11pm; Sun 7–10:30pm (the bar is open all day). Tube: South Kensington.

INEXPENSIVE

Admiral Codrington ⓡ Finds MODERN BRITISH/CONTI-NENTAL   Once a lowly pub, this stylish bar and restaurant is all the rage. The exterior has been maintained, but the old "Cod," as it is known, has emerged to offer plush dining with a revitalized decor by Nina Campbell and a glass roof that rolls back on sunny days. The bartenders still offer a traditional pint, but the menu features such delectable fare as linguine with zucchini, crab, and chile peppers, or rib-eye steak with slow-roasted tomatoes. Opt for the grilled breast of chicken salad with bean sprouts, apple, or cashews, or the grilled tuna with a couscous salad and eggplant "caviar."

17 Mossop St., SW3. ℂ 020/7581-0005. Reservations recommended. Main courses £3.95–£12.75 ($5.95–$19.15). MC, V. Mon–Sat noon–11:30pm; Sun noon–10:30pm. Tube: South Kensington.

5 Marylebone to Notting Hill Gate

MARYLEBONE
EXPENSIVE

Nico Central ☞ FRENCH/MODERN BRITISH   This brasserie is inspired by London's legendary chef, Nico Ladenis. Nico Central delivers earthy French cuisine that's "haute but not haughty" and praised for its "absurdly good value." Guests sit on bentwood chairs at linen-covered tables. Nearly a dozen starters will tempt you. The menu changes seasonally and according to the chef's inspiration, but might include grilled duck with mushroom-Parmesan risotto, pan-fried *foie gras* with brioche and a caramelized orange, braised knuckle of veal, and baked fillet of brill with assorted vegetables. Save room for a dessert—they are, in the words of one devotee, "divine."

35 Great Portland St., W1. ☎ 020/7436-8846. Reservations required. Set lunch £18.50 ($27.75); dinner main courses £17–£20 ($25.50–$30). AE, DC, MC, V. Mon–Fri noon–2:30pm; Mon–Sat 6–10pm. Tube: Oxford Circus.

Orrey ☞☞ INTERNATIONAL/CLASSICAL FRENCH   With ingredients imported from France, this is one of London's classic French restaurants. Sea bass from Montpellier, olive oil from Maussane-les-Alpilles, mushrooms from Calais, and poultry from Bresse, it all turns up on this refined menu, the creation of chef Chris Galvin who is enjoying his first Michelin star. On the second floor of The Conran Shop in Marylebone, the restaurant changes its menu seasonally to take advantage of the best produce. Galvin is a purist in terms of ingredients. Our favorites are Bresse pigeon with savoy cabbage and mushroom ravioli or duckling with an endive tatin and cepe (flap mushrooms) sauce. Where but here can you get a good caramelized calf's sweetbreads salad in a truffle vinaigrette any more? Everything has a brilliant, often whimsical, touch as evoked by the sautéed leeks in pumpkin oil. A wild mushroom consommé arrives with a medley of such fungi as *pieds de bleu, pieds de mouton,* chanterelles, and *trompettes de morte,* all from French forests. Skipping the blueberry soufflé, we ended with a cheese plate that featured a Banton goat cheese from Provence so fresh that it oozed onto the plate. Summer evenings are to be enjoyed on a fourth-floor terrace where you can drink and order light fare from the bar menu.

55 Marylebone High St., W1. ☎ 020/7616-8088. Reservations required. Main courses £15.50–£24.50 ($23.25–$36.75). Fixed-price 3-course menu £23.50 ($35.25), 5-course set menu £45 ($67.50). AE, DC, MC, V. Daily noon–3pm; Mon–Sat 7–11pm, Sun 7–10:30pm. Tube: Baker St.

MODERATE

Mash ☆ *(Finds)* MODERN CONTINENTAL   What is it, you ask? A bar? A deli? A microbrewery? All of the above, and a restaurant. Breakfast and weekend brunch are the highlights, but don't ignore dinner. The novelty decor includes the likes of curvy sci-fi lines and lizard-eye lighting fixtures, but ultimately the food is the attraction. The owners of the hot Atlantic Bar & Grill and the Coast restaurant have opened this place that invites diners to a "sunken chill-out zone" created by leading designer John Currin.

Suckling pig with spring cannellini stew made us forget all about the trendy mirrored bathrooms. So did the terrific pizzas emerging from the wood-fired oven. On another occasion, we returned for the fish freshly grilled over wood. It was sea bass and presented enticingly with grilled artichoke. Try also the chargrilled tuna, sautéed new potatoes, wilted spinach, and puttanesca dressing.

19–21 Great Portland St., W1. ℂ 020/7637-5555. Reservations required. Main courses £12–£18 ($18–$27); fixed-price lunch £25 ($37.50). AE, DC, MC, V. Mon–Sat 7:30am–11pm. Tube: Oxford Circus.

Union Cafe CONTINENTAL   After shopping along Oxford Street, restore your spirits with the quality ingredients and exceptional food at this sleek spot. The mainly female chefs use the finest ingredients in any season. Everything from English cheeses to free-range meat will tempt you. Rarely is any item oversauced. The natural, fresh flavors come to the fore. In most cases, the fresh fish and meat are chargrilled to perfection. The pepper tuna steaks, served rare, are a taste sensation, as are the oak-smoked salmon with fresh horseradish sauce and the wild boar and apple sausage. A daily vegetarian pizza is offered, including one filled with mozzarella, spinach, tomatoes, and eggplant. If you don't want wine, you can choose homemade drinks that might have delighted Dickens, like an elderflower cordial. Desserts, such as caramelized pear cake or blood orange sorbet, are worth the trek across town.

96 Marylebone Lane, W1. ℂ 020/7486-4860. Reservations recommended. Main courses £10–£15 ($15–$22.50). AE, MC, V. Mon–Sat 10:30am–10:30pm. Tube: Bond St.

PADDINGTON & BAYSWATER
MODERATE

Veronica's ☆ *(Finds)* TRADITIONAL BRITISH   Called the "market leader in cafe salons," Veronica's offers traditional—and historical—fare at prices you won't mind paying. It's a celebration of

British cuisine over a 2,000-year period, with some dishes based on medieval, Tudor, and even Roman recipes, given an imaginative twist by owner Veronica Shaw. One month she'll focus on Scotland, another month on Victorian foods, yet another on Wales, and the next on Ireland. Your appetizer might be a salad called *salmagundy*, made with crunchy pickled vegetables, that Elizabeth I enjoyed in her day. Another concoction might be "Tweed Kettle," a 19th-century recipe to improve the monotonous taste of salmon. Many dishes are vegetarian, and everything tastes better when followed with a British farmhouse cheese or a pudding. The restaurant offers a moderated menu to help keep cholesterol down. It is brightly and attractively decorated, and the service warm and ingratiating.

3 Hereford Rd., W2. (©) **020/7229-5079.** Reservations required. Main courses £11.50–£18.50 ($17.25–$27.75); fixed-price meals £14.50–£18.50 ($21.75–$27.75). AE, DC, MC, V. Tues–Fri and Sun 12:30–3pm; Mon–Sat 6:30–11pm. Tube: Bayswater.

NOTTING HILL GATE
EXPENSIVE

Pharmacy Restaurant and Bar 🍷 MODERN EUROPEAN The theme of this medical-chic restaurant evokes a small-town pharmacy or a drug lord's secret stash of mind-altering pills. That ambiguity is appreciated by the arts-conscious crowd that flocks here, partly because they're interested in what Damien Hirst (*enfant terrible* of London's art world) has created, and partly because the place can be a lot of fun. You'll enter the street-level bar, where a drink menu lists lots of highly palatable martinis as well as a concoction known as a Cough Syrup (cherry liqueur, honey, and vodka that's shaken, not stirred, over ice). Bottles of pills, bar stools with aspirin-shaped seats, and painted representations of fire, water, air, and earth decorate the scene. Upstairs in the restaurant, the theme is less pronounced but subtly present. Menu items include trendy but comforting food items such as carpaccio of whitefish, lamb cooked with Provençal vegetables, pan-fried cod in red wine with Jerusalem artichokes and shallots, and roast saddle of hare in pear sauce.

150 Notting Hill Gate, W11. (©) **020/7221-2442.** Reservations required Fri–Sat; strongly recommended other nights. Main courses £11.50–£25 ($17.25–$37.50). AE, DC, DISC, MC, V. Daily noon–2:45pm and 6:45–10:45pm. Tube: Notting Hill Gate.

MODERATE

The Cow 🍷 *Finds* MODERN BRITISH   You don't have to be a young fashion victim to enjoy the superb cuisine here. Tom Conran (son of entrepreneur Sir Terence Conran) holds forth in this hip Notting Hill watering hole. It looks like an Irish pub, but the accents you'll hear are trustafarian rather than Dublin. With a pint of Fuller's or London Pride, you can linger over the modern European menu, which changes daily but is likely to include ox tongue poached in milk; mussels in curry and cream; or a mixed grill of lamb chops, calf's liver, and sweetbreads. The seafood selections are delectable. "The Cow Special"—a half-dozen Irish rock oysters with a pint of Guinness or a glass of wine for £8.50 ($12.75)—is the star of the show. A raw bar downstairs serves other fresh seafood choices. To finish, skip the filtered coffee served upstairs (it's wretched), and opt for an espresso downstairs.

89 Westbourne Park Rd., W2. ⓒ 020/7221-0021. Reservations required. Main courses £10–£24 ($17–$40.80). MC, V. Mon–Sat 7–11pm; Sun 12:30–3:30pm (brunch) and 7:30–10:30pm; bar daily noon–11pm. Tube: Westbourne Grove.

6 Teatime

Everyone should indulge in a formal afternoon tea at least once in London. It's a relaxing, civilized affair that usually consists of three courses, elegantly served on delicate china: first, finger sandwiches (with the crusts cut off, of course), then fresh-baked scones served with jam and deliciously decadent clotted cream (Devonshire cream), and third, an array of bite-sized sweets. All the while, an indulgent server keeps the pot of tea of your choice fresh at hand. Sometimes ports and aperitifs are on offer to accompany your final course. It's a quintessential British experience; we've listed our favorites below. Note that for the most popular hotels (especially the Ritz), make reservations as far in advance as possible. If you go to a place that doesn't take reservations, show up at least a half hour early, especially between April and October. Jacket and tie are often required for gentlemen, and jeans and sneakers are usually frowned upon.

HIGH TEA
COVENT GARDEN & THE STRAND
Palm Court at the Waldorf Meridien   The Waldorf's Palm Court combines afternoon tea with afternoon dancing (the foxtrot, quickstep, and the waltz). The Palm Court is compared to a 1920s movie set (which it has been several times in its long life). You can order tea on a terrace or in a pavilion the size of a ballroom lit by skylights. On tea-dancing days, the orchestra leader will conduct

such favorites as "Ain't She Sweet" and "Yes, Sir, That's My Baby," as a butler in a cutaway asks if you want a cucumber sandwich.

In the Waldorf Hotel, Aldwych, WC2. © 020/7836-2400. Reservations required for tea dance. Jacket and tie required for men at tea dance. Afternoon £21 ($31.50); tea dance £25–£28 ($37.50–$42). AE, DC, MC, V. Afternoon tea Mon–Fri 3–5:30pm; tea dance Sat 3–5:30pm, Sun 4–6:30pm. Tube: Covent Garden or Temple.

MAYFAIR

Brown's Hotel ⓡ   Along with the Ritz, Brown's ranks as one of the most chic venues for tea in London. Tea is served in the drawing room · done in English antiques, oil paintings, and floral chintz—much like the drawing room of a country estate. Give your name to the concierge upon arrival; he'll seat you at one of the sofas and settees or at low tables. There's a choice of 10 teas, plus sandwiches, scones, and pastries (all made in the hotel kitchens) rolled around on a trolley for your selection.

29–34 Albemarle St., W1. © 020/7518-4108. Reservations not accepted. Afternoon tea £18.95 ($28.40). AE, DC, MC, V. Daily 3pm and 4:45pm. Tube: Green Park.

The Palm Court   This is one of the great London favorites for tea. Restored to its former charm, the lounge has an atmosphere straight from 1927, with a domed yellow-and-white glass ceiling, *torchères*, and palms in Compton stoneware *jardinières*. A delightful afternoon repast that includes a long list of different teas is served daily. A pianist plays every weekday afternoon.

In the Sheraton Park Lane Hotel, Piccadilly, W1. © 020/7290-7328. Reservations recommended. Afternoon tea £18 ($27); with a glass of Park Lane champagne £23 ($34.50). AE, DC, MC, V. Daily 3–6pm. Tube: Hyde Park Corner or Green Park.

ST. JAMES'S

Ritz Palm Court ⓡⓡⓡ   This is the most fashionable place in London to order afternoon tea—and the hardest to get into without reserving way in advance. Its spectacular setting is straight out of *The Great Gatsby,* complete with marble steps and columns and a baroque fountain. You have your choice of a long list of teas served with delectable sandwiches and luscious pastries.

In The Ritz Hotel, Piccadilly, W1. © 020/7493-8181. Reservations required at least 8 weeks in advance. Jeans and sneakers not acceptable. Jacket and tie required for men. Afternoon tea £27 ($40.50). AE, DC, MC, V. Three seatings daily at 2, 3:30, and 5pm. Tube: Green Park.

St. James Restaurant & The Fountain Restaurant   This pair of tea salons functions as a culinary showplace for London's most prestigious grocery store, Fortnum & Mason. The more formal of the two, the St. James, on the fourth floor, is a pale green and beige homage to Edwardian taste. More rapid and less formal is The Fountain Restaurant, on the street level, where a sense of tradition and manners is a part of the teatime experience, but in a less opulent setting. The quantities of food served in both are usually ample enough to be defined as early suppers for most theatergoers.

In Fortnum & Mason, 181 Piccadilly, W1. (C) 020/7734-8040. In the St. James, full tea £18.95 ($28.40); in The Fountain, full tea £11.95 ($17.90). AE, DC, MC, V. St. James, Mon–Sat 3–5pm; The Fountain, Mon–Sat 3–6pm. Tube: Piccadilly Circus.

KNIGHTSBRIDGE

The Georgian Restaurant   As long as anyone can remember, teatime at Harrods has been a distinctive feature of Europe's most famous department store. A flood of visitors is gracefully herded into a high-volume but elegant room. Many come here for the tea ritual, where staff members haul silver pots and trolleys laden with pastries and sandwiches through the cavernous dining hall. Most exotic is Betigala tea, a rare blend from China, similar to Lapsang Souchong.

On the 4th floor of Harrods, 87–135 Brompton Rd., SW1. (C) 020/7225-6800. High tea £18 ($27) or £25 ($37.50) with Harrods champagne, per person. AE, DC, MC, V. Mon–Sat 3–5:15pm (last order). Tube: Knightsbridge.

KENSINGTON

The Orangery (R) (Finds)   In its own way, the Orangery is the most amazing place for afternoon tea in the world. Set 50 yards north of Kensington Palace, it occupies a long narrow garden pavilion built in 1704 by Queen Anne. In homage to her original intentions, rows of potted orange trees bask in sunlight from soaring windows, and tea is served amid Corinthian columns, ruddy-colored bricks, and a pair of Grinling Gibbons woodcarvings. There are even some urns and statuary the royal family imported from Windsor Castle. The menu includes soups and sandwiches, with a salad and a portion of upscale potato chips known as kettle chips. There's an array of different teas, served with high style, accompanied by fresh scones with clotted cream and jam and Belgian chocolate cake.

In the gardens of Kensington Palace, W8. (C) 020/7376-0239. Reservations not accepted. Pot of tea £1.70 ($2.55); summer cakes and puddings £1.95–£4.25 ($2.95–$6.40); sandwiches £4.70 ($7.05). MC, V. Daily 10am–5pm; closing time 1/2 hour before gates close (usually between 4 and 5pm) in winter. Mar–Oct 10am–6pm; Nov–Mar 10am–4pm. Tube: High St. Kensington or Queensway.

CASUAL TEAROOMS
COVENT GARDEN & THE STRAND

MJ Bradley's   Although it defines itself as a coffeehouse, many of MJ Bradley's fans resolutely drop in for a cup of as many as 20 different kinds of tea, everything from Earl Grey and Assam to such herbal brews as peppermint. Outfitted like a brasserie, it manages to mingle nostalgia with modern wall sculptures. If you're hungry, consider one of the imaginative sandwiches with fillings of herb-flavored cream cheese with sun-dried tomatoes.

9 King St., WC2. ✆ 020/7240-5178. Cup of tea 95p ($1.40); sandwiches £1.85–£4.50 ($2.80–$6.75) each. AE, DC, DISC, MC, V. Daily 8am–11pm. Tube· Covent Garden or Charing Cross.

SOHO

The Blue Room   Nothing about this place has been patterned on the grand tearooms above, where tea-drinking is an intricate and elaborate social ritual. What you'll find here is a cozy, eccentric enclave lined with the artworks of some of the regular patrons, battered sofas that might have come out of a college dormitory, and a gathering of likable urban hipsters to whom very little is sacred. You can enjoy dozens of varieties of tea, including herbals, served in steaming mugs. Lots of arty types gather here during the late afternoon, emulating some of the rituals of the old-fashioned tea service but with absolutely none of the hauteur.

3 Bateman St., W1. ✆ 020/7437-4827. Reservations not accepted. Cup of tea £1.20 ($1.80); cakes and pastries 60p–£2.50 (90¢–$3.75); sandwiches £3–£4.50 ($4.50–$6.75). No credit cards. Mon–Sat 9am–10:30pm; Sun 11am–10pm. Tube: Leicester Sq.

CHELSEA

The Tearoom at the Chelsea Physic Garden   It encompasses only 3½ acres, crisscrossed with gravel paths and ringed with a high brick wall that shuts out the roaring traffic of Royal Hospital Road. These few spectacular acres, however, revere the memory of industries that were spawned from seeds developed and tested within its walls. Founded in 1673 as a botanical education center, the Chelsea Physic Garden's list of successes includes the exportation of rubber from South America to Malaysia and tea from China to India.

On the 2 days a week it's open, the tearoom is likely to be filled with botanical enthusiasts sipping cups of tea as fortification for their garden treks. The setting is a banal-looking Edwardian building. Because the tearoom is only an adjunct to the garden itself, don't expect the lavish rituals of teatime venues. But you can carry your cakes and cups of tea out into a garden that, despite meticulous care, always looks a bit unkempt. (Herbaceous plants within its hallowed precincts are left untrimmed to encourage bird life and seed production.) Botanists and flower lovers in general find the place fascinating.

66 Royal Hospital Rd., SW3. ℂ 020/7352-5646. Tea with cake £4 ($6). MC, V (in shop only). Wed noon–5pm; Sun 2–6pm. Closed Nov–Mar. Tube: Sloane Sq.

NOTTING HILL

The Garden Cafe This is the most unusual of the places we recommend, and one of the most worthwhile. The Garden Cafe is in The Lighthouse, the largest center in Europe for people with HIV and AIDS. The cafeteria is open to the public and is less institutional looking than you might expect; French doors open onto a garden with fountains and summertime tables. Tea is available throughout the day, although midafternoon, between 3:30 and 5:30pm, seems to be the most convivial time. Its Notting Hill location is a short walk from Portobello Road.

London Lighthouse, 111–117 Lancaster Rd., W11. ℂ 020/7792-1200. Cup of tea 60p (90¢); platter of food £2–£4.50 ($3–$6.75). No credit cards. Mon–Fri 9am–5pm; Sat 10am–5pm. Tube: Ladbroke Grove.

5

Exploring London

Dr. Samuel Johnson said, "When a man is tired of London, he is tired of life, for there is in London all that life can afford." It would take a lifetime to explore every alley, court, street, and square in this city, and volumes to discuss them. Since you don't have a lifetime to spend, we've chosen the best of what London has to offer.

1 The Top Attractions

British Museum ✪✪✪   Set in scholarly Bloomsbury, this immense museum grew out of a private collection of manuscripts purchased in 1753 with the proceeds of a lottery. It grew and grew, fed by legacies, discoveries, and purchases, until it became one of the most comprehensive collections of art and artifacts in the world. It's impossible to take in this museum in a day.

The overall storehouse splits basically into the national collections of antiquities; prints and drawings; coins, medals, and bank notes; and ethnography. Special treasures you may want to seek out on your first visit include the **Rosetta Stone,** whose discovery led to the deciphering of hieroglyphs, in the Egyptian Room; the **Elgin Marbles,** a series of pediments, metopes, and friezes from the Parthenon in Athens, in the Duveen Gallery; and the legendary **Black Obelisk,** dating from around 860 B.C., in the Nimrud Gallery. The exhibits change throughout the year, so if your heart is set on seeing a specific treasure, call to make sure it's on display.

Insider's Tip: If you're a first-time visitor, you will, of course, want to concentrate on some of these fabled treasures. But we duck into the British Museum several times on our visits to London, even if we have only an hour or two to see the less heralded exhibits. These include wandering rooms 33 and 34 and 91 to 94 to take in the glory of the Orient, covering Taoism, Confucianism, and Buddhism. A new gallery nearby for the North American collection has just opened. Finally, the museum has opened a new money Gallery in room 68, tracing the story of money. The center of the

The Top Attractions

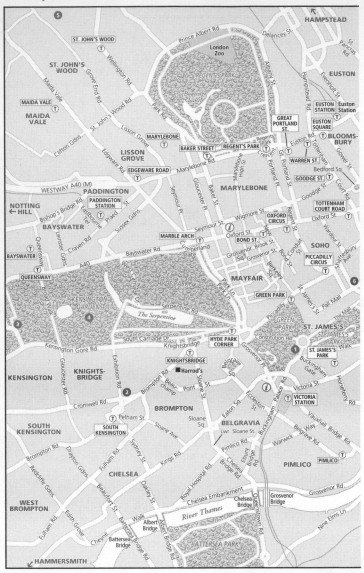

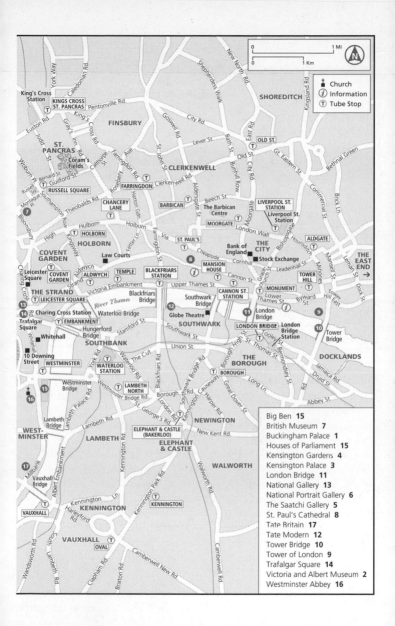

Big Ben **15**
British Museum **7**
Buckingham Palace **1**
Houses of Parliament **15**
Kensington Gardens **4**
Kensington Palace **3**
London Bridge **11**
National Gallery **13**
National Portrait Gallery **6**
The Saatchi Gallery **5**
St. Paul's Cathedral **8**
Tate Britain **17**
Tate Modern **12**
Tower Bridge **10**
Tower of London **9**
Trafalgar Square **14**
Victoria and Albert Museum **2**
Westminster Abbey **16**

Great Court features the Round Reading Room restored to its original decorative scheme.

Great Russell St., WC1. © **020/7323-8299** or 020/7636-1555 for recorded information. www.thebritishmuseum.ac.uk. Free admission. Sat–Wed 10am–5:30pm, Thurs–Fri 10am–8:30pm. Tube: Holborn, Tottenham Court Rd., or Goodge St.

Buckingham Palace 𝕱𝕱 This massive, graceful building is the official residence of the queen. The redbrick palace was built as a country house for the notoriously rakish duke of Buckingham. In 1762, King George III, who needed room for his 15 children, bought it. It didn't become the official royal residence, though, until Queen Victoria took the throne; she preferred it to St. James's Palace. From George III's time, the building was continuously expanded and remodeled, faced with Portland stone, and twice bombed (during the Blitz). Located in a 40-acre garden, it's 360 feet long and contains 600 rooms. You can tell whether the Queen is at home by whether the Royal Standard is flying.

For most of the year, you can't visit the palace without an official invitation. Since 1993, though, much of it has been open for tours during an 8-week period in August and September, when the royal family is usually vacationing outside London. The admission charges help pay for repairs to Windsor Castle, damaged by fire in 1992. You have to buy a timed-entrance ticket the same day you tour the palace. Tickets go on sale at 9am, but rather than lining up at sunrise with all the other tourists—this is one of London's most popular attractions—book by phone with a credit card and save yourself a dreary morning.

Buckingham Palace's most famous spectacle is the overrated **Changing of the Guard** (daily April through July and every other day the rest of the year). The ceremony begins at 11:30am, although it's frequently canceled for bad weather, state events, and other harder-to-fathom reasons. We like the changing of the guards at Horse Guards better (see page 126), where you can actually see the men marching and don't have to battle such tourist hordes. However, few first-time visitors can resist the Buckingham Palace changing of the guard. If that's you, arrive as early as 10:30am and claim territorial rights to a space in front of the palace. *Insider's Tip:* You can avoid the long queues at Buckingham Palace by purchasing tickets before you go through **Global Tickets,** 234 W. 44th St., Suite 1000, New York, NY 10034 (© **800/223-6108** or 212/332-2435). You'll have to pick the exact date on which you'd like to go. Visitors with disabilities can reserve tickets directly through the palace by calling ✆ **020/7930-5526.**

At end of The Mall (on the road running from Trafalgar Sq.). ✆ **020/7389-1377.** www.royal.gov.uk. Palace tours £11 ($16.50) adults, £9 ($13.50) seniors, £5.50 ($8.25) children under 17. Changing of the Guard free. Palace open for tours April 8–Sept 30 daily 9:30am–4:30pm. Tube: St. James's Park, Green Park, or Victoria.

Houses of Parliament 🛈🛈

The Houses of Parliament, along with their trademark clock tower, are the ultimate symbol of London. Both the House of Commons and the House of Lords are in the former royal Palace of Westminster, the king's residence until Henry VIII moved to Whitehall. The current Gothic Revival buildings date from 1840 and were designed by Charles Barry. Assisting Barry was Augustus Welby Pugin, who designed the paneled ceilings, tiled floors, stained glass, clocks, fireplaces, umbrella stands, and even the inkwells. There are more than 1,000 rooms and 2 miles of corridors.

The clock tower at the eastern end houses the world's most famous timepiece. **"Big Ben"** refers not to the clock tower itself, but to the largest bell in the chime, which weighs close to 14 tons and is named for the first commissioner of works.

You may observe debates from the **Stranger's Galleries** in both houses. Sessions usually begin in mid-October and run to the end of July, with recesses at Christmas and Easter. The debates in the House of Commons are often lively (seats are at a premium during crises). The chances of getting into the House of Lords when it's in session are generally better than for the more popular House of Commons.

Those who'd like to book a tour can do so, but it takes a bit of work. Both houses are open to the general public for guided tours only for a limited season in August and September. The palace is open Monday to Saturday from 9:30am with the last entry at 4:15pm during those times. All tour tickets cost £3.50 ($5.25) per person. You need to send a written request for tours to Public Information Office, 1 Derby Gate, Westminster, London SW1A 2TT. The staff is prompt in replying but only if you include a self-addressed stamped envelope (international postage only). Tickets for postal delivery must be booked up to 3 days in advance of a visit when collected from the British Visitor Centre at 1 Regent St., SW1; Tube: Piccadilly Circus. Tickets can also be booked through London's TicketMaster (✆ **020/7344-9966;** www.ticketmaster.co.uk).

If you arrive just to attend a session, these are free. You line up at Stephen's Gate, heading to your left for the entrance into the Commons or to the right for the Lords. The London daily newspapers announce sessions of Parliament.

Insider's Tip: The hottest ticket is during "Prime Minister's Question Time" on Wednesdays, which is from 3 to 3:30pm but which must seem like hours to Tony Blair on the hot seat. It's not quite as thrilling as it was when Margaret Thatcher exchanged barbs with the MPs, but Blair holds his own against any and all who are trying to embarrass him and his government.

Westminster Palace, Old Palace Yard, SW1. House of Commons ℂ **020/ 7219-4272.** House of Lords ℂ **020/7219-3107.** www.parliament.uk. Free admission. House of Lords open Mon–Wed from 2:30pm, Thurs from 11:30am, and sometimes Fri (check by phone). House of Commons open Mon–Tues 2:30–10:30pm, Wed 9:30am–10:30pm, Thurs 11:30am–4:30pm, Fri call ahead—not always open. Join line at St. Stephen's entrance. Tube: Westminster.

Kensington Palace 𝔾 Once the residence of British monarchs, Kensington Palace hasn't been the official home of reigning kings since George II. It was acquired in 1689 by William III and Mary II as an escape from the damp royal rooms along the Thames. Since the end of the 18th century, the palace has housed various members of the royal family, and the State Apartments are open for tours.

You can view a collection of Victoriana, including some of her memorabilia. In the apartments of Queen Mary II is a striking 17th-century writing cabinet inlaid with tortoiseshell. Paintings from the Royal Collection line the walls. A rare 1750 lady's court dress and splendid examples of male court dress from the 18th century are on display in rooms adjacent to the State Apartments as part of the Royal Ceremonial Dress Collection, featuring royal costumes dating as far back as 200 years.

Kensington Palace is the London home of Princess Margaret as well as the Duke and Duchess of Kent. *Warning:* You don't get to see the apartments where Princess Di lived or where both Di and Charles lived until they separated.

Kensington Gardens are open to the public for leisurely strolls through the manicured grounds and around the Round Pond. One of the most famous sights is the controversial Albert Memorial, a lasting tribute not only to Victoria's consort but also to the questionable artistic taste of the Victorian era. There's a wonderful afternoon tea offered in The Orangery; see "Teatime" in chapter 4, "Dining."

The Broad Walk, Kensington Gardens, W8. © 020/7937-9561. www.hrp.org.uk. Admission £8.50 ($12.75) adults, £6.70 ($10.05) seniors/students, £6.10 ($9.15) children, £26.10 ($39.15) family. June–Sept daily 10am–5pm; off-season daily 10am–4pm. Tube: Queensway or Notting Hill Gate; High St. Kensington on south side.

National Gallery ✸✸✸ This stately neoclassical building contains an unrivaled collection of Western art spanning 7 centuries—from the late 13th to the early 20th—and covers every great European school.

The largest part of the collection is devoted to the Italians, including the Sienese, Venetian, and Florentine masters. They're now housed in the Sainsbury Wing. On display are such works as Leonardo's *Virgin of the Rocks;* Titian's *Bacchus and Ariadne;* Giorgione's *Adoration of the Magi;* and unforgettable canvases by Bellini, Veronese, Botticelli, and Tintoretto. Botticelli's *Venus and Mars* is eternally enchanting.

Of the early Gothic works, the Wilton Diptych (French or English school, late 14th century) is the rarest treasure; it depicts Richard II being introduced to the Madonna and Child by John the Baptist and the Saxon kings, Edmund and Edward the Confessor.

Then there are the Spanish giants: El Greco's *Agony in the Garden* and portraits by Goya and Velázquez. The Flemish-Dutch school is represented by Brueghel, Jan van Eyck, Vermeer, Rubens, and de Hooch; the Rembrandts include two of his immortal self-portraits. There's also a French impressionist and postimpressionist collection that includes works by Manet, Monet, Degas, Renoir, and Cézanne. Particularly charming is the peep-show cabinet by Hoogstraten in one of the Dutch rooms: It's like spying through a keyhole.

British and modern art are the specialties of the Tate Gallery (see below), but the National Gallery does have some fine 18th-century British masterpieces, including works by Hogarth, Gainsborough, Reynolds, Constable, and Turner.

Guided tours of the National Gallery are offered daily at 11:30am and 2:30pm. The Gallery Guide Soundtrack is also available. A portable CD player provides audio information on paintings of your choice with the mere push of a button. Although this service is free, voluntary contributions are appreciated.

Insider's Tip: The National Gallery has a computer information center where you can design your own personal tour map. The program includes four indexes that are cross-referenced for your convenience. Using a touch-screen computer, you design your own personalized tour by selecting a maximum of 10 paintings you would like to view. Once you have made your choices, you print a personal tour map with your selections; this mapping service is free.

Northwest side of Trafalgar Sq., WC2. ✆ 020/7747-2885. www.nationalgallery. org.uk. Free admission. Thurs–Tues 10am–6pm; Wed 10am–9pm. Tube: Charing Cross, Embankment, Leicester Sq., or Piccadilly Circus.

National Portrait Gallery 🌟🌟 In a gallery of remarkable and unremarkable pictures (they're collected for their subjects rather than their artistic quality), a few paintings tower over the rest, including Sir Joshua Reynolds's portrait of Samuel Johnson ("a man of most dreadful appearance"). Among the best are Nicholas Hilliard's miniature of Sir Walter Raleigh and a full-length Elizabeth I, along with the Holbein cartoon of Henry VIII. There's also a portrait of William Shakespeare (with a gold earring) by an unknown artist that bears the claim of being the "most authentic contemporary likeness" of its subject. One of the most famous pictures in the gallery is the group portrait of the Brontë sisters (Charlotte, Emily, and Anne) by their brother, Bramwell. An idealized portrait of Lord Byron by Thomas Phillips is also on display.

The galleries of Victorian and early-20th-century portraits display portraits from 1837 (when Victoria took the throne) to present day; later 20th-century portraiture includes major works by such artists as Warhol and Hambling. Some of the more flamboyant personalities of the past 2 centuries are on show: T. S. Eliot; Disraeli; Macmillan; Sir Richard Burton (the explorer, not the actor); Elizabeth Taylor; and our two favorites, G. F. Watts's famous portrait of his great actress wife, Ellen Terry, and Vanessa Bell's portrait of her sister, Virginia Woolf. The late Princess Diana is on the Royal Landing; this portrait seems to attract the most viewers. The Gallery has recently opened a new cafe and art bookshop.

In 2000, Queen Elizabeth opened the Ondaatje Wing of the gallery, granting the gallery over 50 percent more exhibition space. The most intriguing new space is the splendid Tudor Gallery, opening with portraits of Richard III and Henry II, his conqueror in the Battle of Bosworth in 1485. There's also a portrait of Shakespeare that the gallery acquired in 1856. Rooms lead through centuries of English monarchs, with literary and artistic figures thrown in. A Balcony Gallery displays more recent figures.

St. Martin's Place, WC2. ✆ 020/7306-0055. www.npg.org.uk. Free admission; fee for some temporary exhibitions. Mon–Wed 10am–6pm; Thurs–Fri 10am–9pm; Sat 10am–6pm; Sun noon–6pm. Tube: Charing Cross or Leicester Sq.

The Saatchi Gallery ✮✮✮   In the world of contemporary art, this collection is unparalleled. Charles Saatchi is one of Britain's greatest private collectors, and this museum features rotating displays from his vast holdings. Enter through the unmarked metal gateway of a former paint warehouse. Saatchi's aim is to introduce new and unfamiliar art to a wider audience. The collection comprises more than 1,000 paintings and sculptures.

The main focus is works by young British artists, including such controversial ones as Damien Hirst's 14-foot tiger shark preserved in a formaldehyde-filled tank. Also on occasional exhibit is Marc Quinn's frozen "head," cast from nine pints of plasma taken from the artist. Art critics were shocked at Richard Wilson's art when it was introduced: 2,500 gallons of used sump oil that flooded an entire gallery. The work of young American and European artists, often controversial, is also represented..

98A Boundary Rd., NW8. ✆ **020/7624-8299.** Admission £5 ($8.50) adults, £3 ($5.10) students and seniors, children under 12 free. Thurs–Sun noon–6pm. Tube: St. John's Wood or Swiss Cottage.

St. Paul's Cathedral ✮✮✮   That St. Paul's survived World War II at all is a miracle, it was badly hit during the early years of the bombardment of London. But St. Paul's is accustomed to calamity, having been burned down three times and destroyed once by invading Norsemen. It was during the Great Fire of 1666 that the old St. Paul's was razed, making way for a structure designed by Sir Christopher Wren built between 1675 and 1710. It's the architectural genius's ultimate masterpiece.

The classical dome of St. Paul's dominates the City's square mile. The golden cross surmounting it is 365 feet above the ground; the golden ball on which the cross rests measures 6 feet in diameter yet looks like a marble from below. Surrounding the interior of the dome is the Whispering Gallery, an acoustic marvel in which the faintest whisper can be heard clearly on the opposite side. You can climb to the top of the dome for a 360-degree view of London.

The interior houses a vast number of monuments. The duke of Wellington is entombed here, as are Lord Nelson and Sir Christopher Wren himself. At the east end of the cathedral is the American Memorial Chapel, honoring the 28,000 U.S. service personnel who lost their lives while stationed in Britain in World War II.

Guided tours last 1½ hours and include parts of the cathedral not open to the public. They take place Monday to Saturday at 11am,

11:30am, 1:30pm, and 2pm. Recorded tours lasting 45 minutes are available throughout the day.

St. Paul's is an Anglican cathedral with services at the following times: matins at 7:30am Monday to Friday, 8:30am on Saturday; Holy Communion Monday to Saturday at 8am and 12:30pm; and evensong Monday to Saturday at 5pm. On Sunday, there's Holy Communion at 8am and at 11:30am, matins at 10:15am, and evensong at 3:15pm. Admission charges don't apply if you're attending a service.

St. Paul's Churchyard, EC4. ℭ **020/7236-4128**. www.stpauls.co.uk. Cathedral and galleries £5 ($7.50) adults, £2.50 ($3.75) children 6–16. Guided tours £2.50 ($3.75) adults, £2 ($3) students and seniors, £1 ($1.50) children; recorded tours £3.50 ($5.25). Free for children 5 and under. Sightseeing Mon–Sat 8:30am–4pm; galleries Mon–Sat 9:30am–4pm. No sightseeing Sun (services only). Tube: St. Paul's.

Tate Britain 𝓡𝓡𝓡 Fronting the Thames near Vauxhall Bridge in Pimlico, the Tate looks like a smaller, more graceful relation of the British Museum. It houses the national collections, covering British art from the 16th century to the present, as well as an array of international artists. In spring of 2000, the Tate moved its collection of 20th- and 21st-century art to the **Tate Modern** (see below).

The older works include some of the best of Gainsborough, Reynolds, Stubbs, Blake, and Constable. William Hogarth is well represented, particularly by his satirical *O the Roast Beef of Old England* (known as *The Gate of Calais*). The illustrations of William Blake for such works as *The Book of Job, The Divine Comedy,* and *Paradise Lost* are here. The collection of works by J. M. W. Turner is its largest collection of works by a single artist; Turner himself willed most of the paintings and watercolors to the nation.

Also on display are the works of many major 19th- and 20th-century painters, including Paul Nash. In the modern collections are works by Matisse, Dalí, Modigliani, Munch, Bonnard, and Picasso. Truly remarkable are the several enormous abstract canvases by Mark Rothko, the group of paintings and sculptures by Giacometti, and the paintings of one of England's best-known modern artists, the late Francis Bacon. Sculptures by Henry Moore and Barbara Hepworth are also occasionally displayed.

Insider's Tip: Drop in to the Tate Gallery Shop for some of the best art books and postcards in town. The gallery sells T-shirts with art masterpieces on them. Invite your friends for tea at the Coffee Shop with its excellent cakes and pastries. At lunch in the Tate

Gallery Restaurant, enjoy good food, Rex Whistler art, and the best and most reasonably priced wine list in London.

Millbank, SW1. © 020/7887-8000. www.tate.org.uk. Free admission; special exhibitions sometimes incur a charge varying from £3–£6 ($4.50–$9). Daily 10:30am–5:50pm. Tube: Vauxhall.

Tate Modern 𝄢𝄢𝄢   In a transformed Bankside Power Station in Southwark, this museum draws some 2 million visitors a year to see the greatest collection of international 20th-century art in Britain. As such, it is one of the three or four most important modern art galleries in the world. Tate Modern is also viewer friendly with eye-level hangings. All the big painting stars are here, ranging from Dalí to Duchamp, from Giacometti to Matisse and Mondrian, from Picasso and Pollock to Rothko and Warhol. The Modern is also a gallery of 21st-century art, displaying exciting art recently created.

You can cross the Millennium Bridge, a pedestrian-only walk from the steps of St. Paul's, over the Thames to the gallery. The Tate Modern makes extensive use of glass for its exterior and interior, offering panoramic views. Galleries are arranged over three levels and provide different kinds of space. Instead of exhibiting art chronologically and by school, the Tate Modern takes a thematic approach. This allows displays to cut across movements.

Bankside., SE1. © 020/7887-8008. www.tate.org.uk. Free admission. Sun–Thurs 10am–6pm, Fri–Sat 10am–10pm. Tube: Southwark.

Tower Bridge 𝄢𝄢   This is one of the world's most celebrated landmarks, and possibly the most photographed and painted bridge on earth. In spite of its medieval look, Tower Bridge was built in 1894.

In 1993, an exhibition opened inside the bridge to commemorate its history; it takes you up the north tower to high-level walkways between the two towers with spectacular views of St. Paul's, the Tower of London, and the Houses of Parliament. You're then led down the south tower and on to the bridge's original engine room, with its Victorian boilers and steam engines that used to raise and lower the bridge for ships to pass. Exhibits in the bridge's towers use advanced technology, including animatronic characters, video, and computers to illustrate the history of the bridge.

At Tower Bridge, SE1. © 020/7403-3761. Tube: Tower Hill. Admission to the **Tower Bridge Experience** (© 020/7403-3761) £6.25 ($9.43) for adults, £4.25 ($6.43) for children 5 to 15, students, and seniors; family tickets start at £18.25 ($27.43); it's free for children 4 and under. Open April to October daily 10am to 6:30pm, November to March daily 9:30am to 6pm; last entry is 1½ hours before closing. Closed Good Friday and January 1 to 28 as well as a few days around Christmas.

Tower of London 𝕽𝕽𝕽 This ancient fortress continues to pack in the crowds, with its macabre associations with the legendary figures imprisoned and/or executed here. There are more spooks here per square foot than in any other building in Britain. Headless bodies, bodiless heads, phantom soldiers, icy blasts, clanking chains—you name them, the Tower has them.

The Tower is actually a compound of structures built mostly as expressions of royal power. The oldest is the **White Tower,** begun by William the Conqueror in 1078 to keep London's native Saxon population in check. Later rulers added other towers, more walls, and fortified gates, until the building became like a small town within a city. Until the reign of James I, the Tower was also one of the royal residences. But above all, it was a prison for distinguished captives.

Every stone tells a story—usually a gory one. In the **Bloody Tower,** according to Shakespeare, the two little princes (the sons of Edward IV) were murdered by henchmen of Richard III. Richard knew his position as king could not be secure as long as his nephews were alive. There seems no doubt that the little princes were murdered in the Tower on orders of their uncle.

Sir Walter Raleigh spent 13 years before his date with the executioner in the Bloody Tower. On the walls of the **Beauchamp Tower,** you can still read the last messages scratched by prisoners. Through **Traitors' Gate** passed such ill-fated figures as Robert Devereux, the second Earl of Essex, a favorite of Elizabeth I. A plaque marks the eerie place at **Tower Green** where two wives of Henry VIII, Anne Boleyn and Catherine Howard, Sir Thomas More, and the 4-day queen, Lady Jane Grey, all lost their lives.

The Tower, besides being a royal palace, a fortress, and a prison, was also an armory, a treasury, a menagerie, and, in 1675, an astronomical observatory. Reopened in 1999, the White Tower holds the **Armouries,** which date from the reign of Henry VIII, as well as a display of instruments of torture and execution. In the Jewel House, you'll find the tower's greatest attraction, the **Crown Jewels.** Here, some of the world's most precious stones are set into robes, swords, scepters, and crowns. The Imperial State Crown is the most famous crown on earth; made for Victoria in 1837, it's worn today by Queen Elizabeth when she opens Parliament. Studded with some 3,000 jewels (principally diamonds), it includes the Black Prince's Ruby, worn by Henry V at Agincourt. The 530-carat Star of Africa, a cut diamond on the Royal Sceptre with Cross, would make Harry

---

Tips **Tower Tips**

You can spend as little time as possible in the Tower's long lines if you buy your ticket in a kiosk at any Tube station. Even so, choose a day other than Sunday—crowds are at their worst then, and arrive as early as you can in the morning.

Winston turn over in his grave. You'll have to stand in long lines to catch just a glimpse of the jewels.

In the latest development here, the presumed prison cell of Sir Thomas More opened to the public. More left this cell in 1535 to face his executioner after he'd fallen out with King Henry VIII over the monarch's desire to divorce Catherine of Aragon. More is believed to have lived in the lower part of the Bell Tower, here in this whitewashed cell, during the last 14 months of his life.

A **palace** once inhabited by Edward I in the late 1200s stands above Traitors' Gate. It's the only surviving medieval palace in Britain. Guides are dressed in period costumes. Reproductions of furniture and fittings, including Edward's throne, evoke the era.

Don't forget to look for the ravens. Six of them (plus two spares) are registered as official Tower residents. According to a legend, the Tower of London will stand as long as those ominous birds remain, so to be on the safe side, one of the wings of each raven is clipped.

A 21st-century addition to the Tower complex is the New Armories restaurant, offering a range of snacks and meals, including the traditional cuppa for people about to lose their heads from too many attractions and not enough to eat.

One-hour guided tours of the entire compound are given by the Yeoman Warders (also known as "Beefeaters") every half-hour, starting at 9:25am from the Middle Tower near the main entrance. The last guided walk starts about 3:25pm in summer, 2:25pm in winter, weather permitting, of course.

You can attend the nightly **Ceremony of the Keys,** the ceremonial locking-up of the Tower by the Yeoman Warders. For free tickets, write to the Ceremony of the Keys, Waterloo Block, Tower of London, London EC3N 4AB, and request a specific date, but also list alternate dates. At least 6 weeks' notice is required. All requests must be accompanied by a stamped, self-addressed envelope (British stamps only) or two International Reply Coupons. With ticket in hand, you'll be admitted by a Yeoman Warder at 9:35pm. Frankly, we think it's not worth the trouble you go through to see this rather cheesy ceremony, but we know some who disagree with us.

Tower Hill, EC3. © 020/7709-0765. www.hrp.org.uk. Admission £11.30 ($19.20) adults, £8.50 ($14.45) students and seniors, £7.50 ($12.75) children, free for children under 5, £33 ($49.50) family ticket for 5 (but no more than 2 adults). Mar–Oct Mon–Sat 9am–5pm, Sun 10am–5pm; off-season Tues–Sat 9am–4pm, Sun–Mon 10am–4pm. Tube: Tower Hill.

Victoria and Albert Museum 𝓡𝓡𝓡   The Victoria and Albert is the greatest museum in the world devoted to the decorative arts. It's also one of the liveliest and most imaginative museums in London—where else would you find the quintessential "little black dress" in the permanent collection?

The medieval holdings include such treasures as the early-English Gloucester Candlestick; the Byzantine Veroli Casket, with its ivory panels based on Greek plays; and the Syon Cope, a unique embroidery made in England in the early 14th century. An area devoted to Islamic art houses the Ardabil Carpet from 16th-century Persia.

The V&A houses the largest collection of Renaissance sculpture outside Italy. A highlight of the 16th-century collection is the marble group *Neptune with Triton* by Bernini. The cartoons by Raphael, which were conceived as designs for tapestries for the Sistine Chapel, are owned by the queen and are on display here. The museum has the greatest collection of Indian art outside India, plus Chinese and Japanese galleries as well. In complete contrast are suites of English furniture, metalwork, and ceramics, and a superb collection of portrait miniatures, including the one Hans Holbein the Younger made of Anne of Cleves for the benefit of Henry VIII, who was again casting around for a suitable wife.

V&A has recently opened 15 new galleries—the British Galleries—unfolding the story of British design from 1500 to 1900. From Chippendale to Morris, all of the top British designers are featured in some 3,000 exhibits, ranging from the 17-foot-high Melville Bed (1697) with its luxurious wild silk damask and red silk velvet hangings, to 19th-century classics such as furniture by Charles Rennie Mackintosh. Don't miss the V&A's most bizarre gallery, Fakes and Forgeries. The impostors here are amazing—in fact, we'd judge some of them as better than the old masters themselves.

Cromwell Rd., SW7. © 020/7942-2000. www.vam.ac.uk. Admission £5 ($7.50) adults; £3 ($4.50) seniors; free for children under 18, seniors, and persons with disabilities. Daily 10am–5:45pm (Wed until 10pm). Tube: South Kensington.

Westminster Abbey ✮✮✮ With its square twin towers and superb archways, this early-English Gothic abbey is one of the greatest examples of ecclesiastical architecture on earth. It's also the shrine of a nation, the place in which most of its rulers were crowned and where many lie buried.

Nearly every figure in English history has left his or her mark on the Abbey. Edward the Confessor founded the Benedictine abbey in 1065 on this spot. The first English king crowned in the abbey was Harold in January 1066. The man who defeated him at the Battle of Hastings later that year, William the Conqueror, was also crowned here. The coronation tradition has continued to the present day, broken only twice (Edward V and Edward VIII). The essentially early-English Gothic structure existing today owes more to Henry III's plans than to those of any other sovereign, although many architects, including Wren, have contributed to the abbey.

Built on the site of the ancient Lady Chapel in the early 16th century, the **Henry VII Chapel** is one of the loveliest in Europe, with its fan vaulting, Knights of Bath banners, and Torrigiani-designed tomb of the king himself, over which hangs a 15th-century Vivarini painting, *Madonna and Child.* Also here, ironically buried in the same tomb, are Catholic Mary I and Protestant Elizabeth I (whose archrival, Mary Queen of Scots, is entombed on the other side of the Henry VII Chapel).

You can also visit the most hallowed spot in the abbey, the **shrine of Edward the Confessor** (canonized in the 12th century). In the chapel is the Coronation Chair, made at the command of Edward I in 1300 to display the Stone of Scone. Scottish kings were once crowned on it (it has since been returned to Scotland).

When you enter the transept on the south side of the nave and see a statue of the Bard with one arm resting on a stack of books, you've arrived at **Poets' Corner.** Shakespeare himself is buried at Stratford-upon-Avon, but resting here are Chaucer, Ben Jonson, Milton, Shelley, and monuments to just about everybody: Chaucer, Shakespeare, "O Rare Ben Johnson" (his name misspelled), Samuel Johnson, George Eliot, Charles Dickens, and others. The most stylized monument is Sir Jacob Epstein's sculptured bust of William Blake. More recent tablets commemorate poet Dylan Thomas and Lord Laurence Olivier.

Statesmen and men of science—Disraeli, Newton, Charles Darwin—are also interred in the abbey or honored by monuments. Near the west door is the 1965 memorial to Sir Winston Churchill.

In the vicinity of this memorial is the tomb of the **Unknown Warrior,** commemorating the British dead of World War I.

Although most of the Abbey's statuary commemorates notable figures of the past, ten new statues were unveiled in July 1998. Placed in the Gothic niches above the West Front door, these statues honor ten modern-day martyrs. Designed by Tim Crawley, the sculptures include Elizabeth of Russia, Janani Luwum, and Martin Luther King, representatives of those who have sacrificed their lives for their beliefs.

Off the Cloisters, the **College Garden** is the oldest garden in England, under cultivation for more than 900 years. Established in the 11th century as the abbey's first infirmary garden, this was once a source of fruits, vegetables, and medicinal herbs. Surrounded by high walls, flowering trees dot the lawns, and park benches provide comfort. It's open only on Tuesday and Thursday, April to September, 10am to 6pm and October to March, 10am to 4pm.

Insider's Tip: Far removed from the pomp and glory is the **Abbey Treasure Museum,** with a bag of oddities. They're displayed in the undercroft or crypt. Here are royal effigies that were used instead of the real corpses for lying-in-state because they smelled better. You'll see the almost lifelike effigy of Admiral Nelson and even that of Edward III, his lip warped by the stroke that felled him. Other oddities include the much-used sword of Henry VI, and the Essex Ring Elizabeth I gave to her favorite when she was feeling good about him.

On Sunday, the Royal Chapels are closed, but the rest of the church is open unless a service is being conducted. For times of services, phone the **Chapter Office** (© **020/7222-5152**). Up to six tours of the abbey are conducted by the vergers Monday to Saturday, beginning at 10am and costing £3 ($4.50) per person.

Broad Sanctuary, SW1. © **020/7222-7110.** www.westminster-abbey.org. Admission £6 ($10.20) adults; £3 ($4.50) for students, seniors, and children 11–18; free for children under 11; family ticket £12 ($18). Mon–Fri 9:30am–3:45pm; Sat 9:30am–1:45pm. Tube: Westminster or St. James's Park.

2 More Central London Attractions

CHURCHES & CATHEDRALS

Many of London's churches offer free lunchtime concerts; a list is available from the London Tourist Board. It's customary to leave a small donation.

All Hallows Barking-by-the-Tower   The brass-rubbing center at this fascinating church next door to the Tower has a crypt museum, Roman remains, and traces of early London, including a Saxon arch predating the Tower. Samuel Pepys, the famed diarist, climbed to the spire to watch the raging fire of London in 1666. In 1644, William Penn was baptized here, and in 1797, John Quincy Adams was married here. Bombs destroyed the church in 1940, leaving only the tower and walls standing. The church was rebuilt from 1949 to 1958.

Byward St., EC3. ℂ 020/7481-2928. Free admission; crypt museum tour £2.50 ($3.75). Museum Mon–Fri 11am–4pm, Sat 10am–5pm, Sun 1–4:30pm; church Mon–Fri 9am–6pm, Sat–Sun 10am–5pm. Tube: Tower Hill.

St. Bride's ⌖

Known as "the church of the press" thanks to its location at the end of Fleet Street, St. Bride's is a remarkable landmark. The current church is the eighth that has stood here. After it was bombed in 1940, an archeologist excavated the crypts and was able to confirm much of the site's history: A Roman house was discovered, and it was established that St. Brigit of Ireland had founded the first Christian church here. A crypt with evidence of six earlier churches was discovered. Among the famous parishioners have been writers John Dryden, John Milton, Richard Lovelace, and John Evelyn; the diarist Samuel Pepys was baptized here; novelist Samuel Richardson is buried here. After the Great Fire destroyed it, Christopher Wren rebuilt the church with a spire that has been described as a "madrigal in stone." The crypt was a burial chamber and charnel house for centuries; today, it's a museum. Concerts are given on Tuesday and Friday, and there's an organ recital on Wednesday. Concerts are often suspended during Lent and Christmas.

Fleet St., EC4. ℂ 020/7427-0133. Free admission. Mon–Fri 8am–4:45pm, Sat 10am–4pm, Sun 10am–12:30pm and 6–7:30pm. Concerts at 1:15pm Tues and Fri. Tube: Blackfriars.

St. Giles Cripplegate ⌖

Named for the patron saint of cripples, St. Giles was founded in the 11th century. The church survived the Great Fire, but the Blitz left only the tower and walls standing. Oliver Cromwell was betrothed to Elizabeth Bourchier here in 1620, and John Milton, author of *Paradise Lost,* was buried here in 1674. More than a century later, someone opened his grave, knocked out his teeth, stole a rib bone, and tore hair from his skull. Guided tours are available on most Tuesday afternoons. Call to confirm.

At Fore and Wood sts., London Wall, EC2. ℂ 020/7638-1997. www. stgilescripplegate.com. Free admission. Mon–Fri 11am–4pm; Sat–Sun 9am–noon for services. Tube: Moorgate or St. Paul's.

St. James's Church ⓡ   When the aristocratic area known as St. James's was developed in the late 17th century, Sir Christopher Wren was commissioned to build its parish church. Diarist John Evelyn wrote of the interior, "There is no altar anywhere in England, nor has there been any abroad, more handsomely adorned." The reredos (a screen with religious icons placed behind the altar), organ case, and font were all carved by Wren's master carver Grinling Gibbons. The poet William Blake and William Pitt, the first Earl of Chatham, who became England's youngest prime minister at age 24, were both baptized here; caricaturist James Gillray, auctioneer James Christie, and coffeehouse founder Francis White are all buried here. One of the more colorful marriages celebrated here was that of explorer Sir Samuel Baker and the woman he had bought at a slave auction in a Turkish bazaar. St. James's Church is a radical, inclusive Anglican church. It's also the Centre for Health and Healing and holds seminars on New Age and Creation Spirituality. There's a Bible Garden and a craft market in the courtyard. The Wren Cafe is open daily, and lunchtime and evening concerts are held.

197 Piccadilly, W1. ⓒ 020/7734-4511. Free admission. Recitals on Mon, Wed, and Fri 1:10pm. Tube: Piccadilly Circus or Green Park.

St. Martin-in-the-Fields ⓡ   Designed by James Gibbs, a disciple of Christopher Wren, and completed in 1726, this classical temple stands at the northeast corner of Trafalgar Square, opposite the National Gallery. Its spire, added in 1824, towers 185 feet. The steeple became the model for many churches in colonial America. Since the first year of World War I (1914), the homeless have sought "soup and shelter" at St. Martin, a tradition that continues.

At one time, the crypt held the remains of Charles II (he's in Westminster Abbey now), who was christened here, giving St. Martin a claim as a royal parish church. His mistress, Nell Gwynne, and the highwayman Jack Sheppard are both interred here. The floors of the crypt are gravestones, and the walls date from the 1500s. The little restaurant, **Café in the Crypt,** is still called "Field's" by its devotees. Also in the crypt is **The London Brass Rubbing Centre** (ⓒ **020/7930-9306**) with 88 copies of bronze portraits ready for use. Paper, rubbing materials, and instructions are furnished, and there's classical music for you to enjoy as you proceed. The charges range from £2.90 to £15 ($4.35–$22.50), the latter price for the largest, a life-size Crusader knight. There's also a gift shop with brass-rubbing kits for children, budget-priced ready-made rubbings, Celtic jewelry, miniature brasses, and model knights. The center is open Monday to Saturday, 10am to 6pm and Sunday, noon to 6pm.

Insider's Tip: In back of the church is a craft market. Lunchtime and evening concerts are staged Monday, Tuesday, and Friday at 1:05pm, and Thursday to Saturday at 7:30pm. Tickets cost £6 to £15 ($9–$22.50).

Trafalgar Sq., WC2. © **020/7766-1100.** Mon–Fri 7:45am–6pm, Sat–Sun 8:45am–8pm as long as no service is taking place. Tube: Charing Cross.

St. Mary-le-Bow *★★*   A true Cockney is said to be born within the sound of this church's bells. The church has been buffeted by the series of disasters that mark its sometimes gruesome history. In 1091, its roof was ripped off in a storm; the church tower collapsed in 1271 and 20 people were killed; in 1331, Queen Philippa and her ladies-in-waiting fell to the ground when a balcony collapsed during a joust celebrating the birth of the Black Prince. It was rebuilt by Wren after being engulfed by the Great Fire; and the original "Cockney" Bow bells were destroyed in the Blitz, but have been replaced. The church was rededicated in 1964 after extensive restoration work.

Cheapside, EC2. © **020/7248-5139.** Free admission. Mon–Thurs 6:30am–5:30pm, Fri 6:30am–4pm. Tube: St. Paul's or Bank.

Westminster Cathedral *★*   This spectacular brick-and-stone church (1903) is the headquarters of the Roman Catholic Church in Britain. Adorned in early-Byzantine style, it's massive: 360 feet long and 156 feet wide. One hundred different marbles compose the interior, and eight columns support the nave. The huge baldachino over the high altar is lifted by eight yellow marble columns. Mosaics emblazon the chapels and the vaulting of the sanctuary. If you take the elevator to the top of the 273-foot-tall campanile, you're rewarded with views that take in Buckingham Palace, Westminster Abbey, and St. Paul's Cathedral. There is a cafe serving light snacks and soft drinks from 9am to 5pm and a gift shop open from 9:30am to 5:15pm.

Ashley Place, SW1. © **020/7798-9055.** www.westminstercathedral.org.uk. Cathedral free. Audio tours £2.50 ($3.75). Tower £2 ($3). Cathedral, daily 7am–7pm. Tower, May–Nov daily 9am–1pm and 2–5pm; otherwise, Thurs–Sun only. Tube: Victoria.

HISTORIC BUILDINGS

Banqueting House ⭑⭑ The feasting chamber in Whitehall Palace is probably the most sumptuous dining hall on earth. (Unfortunately, you can't dine here unless you're a visiting head of state.) Designed by Inigo Jones and decorated with, among other things, original ceiling paintings by Rubens, the hall is dazzling enough to make you forget food altogether. Among the historic events that took place here were the beheading of King Charles I, who stepped through a window onto the scaffold outside, and the restoration ceremony of Charles II, marking the return of monarchy after Cromwell's brief Puritan Commonwealth.

Whitehall Palace, Horse Guards Ave., SW1. ℂ 020/7930-4179. www. hrp.org.uk/bh. Admission £3.90 ($6.65) adults, £3.10 ($5.25) seniors and students, £2.30 ($3.45) children. Mon–Sat 10am–5pm (last admission 4:30pm). Tube: Westminster, Charing Cross, or Embankment.

Cabinet War Rooms This is the bombproof bunker from which Sir Winston Churchill and his government ran the nation during World War II. Many of the rooms are exactly as they were in September 1945: Imperial War Museum curators studied photographs to put notepads, files, typewriters, even pencils, pins, and clips, in their correct places.

Along the tour, you'll have a personal sound guide that provides a detailed account of the function and history of each room of this nerve center. They include the Map Room, with its huge wall maps. Next door is Churchill's bedroom/office; it has a basic bed and a desk with two BBC microphones for those famous broadcasts that stirred the nation. The Transatlantic Telephone Room is little more than a closet, but it held the extension linked to the special scrambler phone on which Churchill conferred with Roosevelt.

Clive Steps, at end of King Charles St. (off Whitehall near Big Ben), SW1. ℂ 020/ 7930-6961. www.iwm.org.uk. Admission £5.40 ($9.20) adults, £3.90 ($6.65) seniors and students, free for children 16 and under. Apr–Sept daily 9:30am–6pm (last admission at 5:15pm); Oct–Mar daily 10am–6pm. Tube: Westminster or St. James's.

Horse Guards ⭑ North of Downing Street, on the west side of Whitehall, is the building of the Horse Guards, designed by William Kent, chief architect to George II, as the headquarters of the British Army. The draw here is the Horse Guards themselves: the Household Cavalry Mounted Regiment, a union of the oldest and most senior regiments in the British Army—the Life Guards and the Blues and Royals. In theory, their duty is to protect the sovereign. Life Guards wear red tunics and white plumes and Blues and Royals are attired in blue tunics with red plumes. Two mounted members of the Household Cavalry keep watch daily from 10am to 5pm. The sentries change duty every hour as a benefit to the horses. Foot sentries change every 2 hours. The chief guard rather grandly inspects the troops here daily at 4pm. The guard, with flair and fanfare, dismounts at 5pm.

We prefer the **changing of the guards** here to the ceremony at Buckingham Palace. Beginning around 11am Monday to Saturday and 10:30am on Sunday, a new guard leaves the Hyde Park Barracks, rides down Pall Mall, and arrives at the Horse Guards building, all in about 30 minutes. The old guard then returns to the barracks.

If you pass through the arch at Horse Guards, you'll find yourself at the **Horse Guards Parade,** which opens onto St. James's Park. This court provides the best view of the various architectural styles that make up Whitehall. Regrettably, the parade ground itself is now a parking lot.

The military pageant known as **Trooping the Colour,** which celebrates the queen's birthday, takes place in June at the Horse Guards Parade (see the "London Calendar of Events" in chapter 1). The "Colour" refers to the flag of the regiment. "Beating the Retreat" is staged here 3 or 4 evenings a week during the first 2 weeks of June. It's only a dress rehearsal, though, for Trooping the Colour.

Whitehall, SW1. ℂ 020/7414-2396. www.plus44.co.uk. Tube: Charing Cross, Westminster, or Embankment.

⌢Fun Fact Legal London

The smallest borough in London, **Holborn** ✿ (ho-burn) is often referred to as "Legal London." It's home to the majority of the city's barristers, solicitors, and law clerks as well as the ancient **Inns of Court** (Tube: Holborn or Chancery Lane). All barristers (litigators) must belong to one of these institutions, and many work from their dignified ancient buildings: **Gray's Inn, Lincoln's Inn** (the best preserved of the three), and the **Middle and Inner Temple** (just over the line inside the City). They were severely damaged during World War II, and the razed buildings were replaced with modern offices, but the borough still retains pockets of its former days.

Gray's Inn 🐾 Gray's Inn is the fourth of the ancient Inns of Court still in operation. As you enter, you'll see a late-Georgian terrace lined with buildings that serve as both residences and offices. Gray's was restored after suffering heavy damage in World War II. It contains a rebuilt Tudor Hall, but its greatest attraction is the tree-shaded lawn and handsome gardens. The 17th-century atmosphere exists today only in the square. Scientist-philosopher Francis Bacon (1561 to 1626) was the inn's most eminent tenant.

Gray's Inn Rd. (north of High Holborn; entrance on Theobald's Rd.), 8 South Sq., WC1. ℂ 020/7458-7800. www.online-law.co.uk. Free admission to squares and gardens. To enter the hall, guests must make a written application. Gardens Mon–Fri 9am–2:30pm; squares Mon–Fri 9am–5pm. Tube: Chancery Lane.

Lincoln's Inn 🐾🐾 Lincoln's Inn is the oldest of the four Inns of Court. Between the City and the West End, Lincoln's Inn comprises 11 acres, including lawns, squares, gardens, a 17th-century chapel (open Mon–Fri noon–2pm), a library, and two halls. The Old Hall dates from 1490 and has remained almost unaltered with its linen-fold paneling, stained glass, and wooden screen by Inigo Jones. It was once the home of Sir Thomas More, and where barristers met, ate, and debated 150 years before the *Mayflower* sailed on its epic voyage. Old Hall set the scene for the opening chapter of Charles Dickens's *Bleak House*. The other hall, Great Hall, remains one of the finest Tudor Revival buildings in London and was opened by Queen Victoria in 1843. It's now the center of the inn and is used for the formal ceremony of calling students to the bar.

Lincoln's Inn Fields, WC2. ℂ 020/7405-1393. www.lincolnsinn.org.uk. Free admission to grounds. Mon–Fri 7am–7pm. Tube: Holborn or Chancery Lane.

Old Bailey This courthouse replaced the infamous Newgate Prison, once the scene of hangings and other forms of "public entertainment." It's known as the "Old Bailey" after a street that runs nearby. It's fascinating to watch the bewigged barristers presenting their cases to the high-court judges. Entry is strictly on a first-arrival basis, and guests line up outside; security will then direct you to one of the rooms where cases are being tried. It's impossible to predict how long a line you might face. If there's a London equivalent of the O.J. Simpson trial, forget about it. You'll never get in. On a day with trials attracting little attention, you can often enter after only 15 minutes or so. You never know until you show up. The best time to line up is 10am. You enter courts 1 to 4, 17, and 18 from Newgate Street, and the balance from Old Bailey (the street).

Newgate St., EC4. ℭ **020/7248-3277.** Free admission. Court in session Mon–Fri 10:30am–1pm and 2–4:30pm. Children under 14 not admitted; those 14–16 must be accompanied by an adult. No cameras, tape recorders, or cell phones (and there are no coat-checking facilities). Tube: St. Paul's. To get here from the Temple, travel east on Fleet St., which becomes Ludgate Hill; cross Ludgate Circus and turn left at the Old Bailey, a domed structure with the figure of *Justice* atop it.

LITERARY LANDMARKS

You can visit other homes of the celebrated in London, notably Apsley House, the former mansion of the duke of Wellington (see below). The most fascinating private home of a famous person that's open to the public is Sir John Soane's Museum (see page 137), where this legendary architect used to live.

Dickens House   Here in Bloomsbury stands the simple abode in which Charles Dickens wrote *Oliver Twist* and finished *The Pickwick Papers* (his American readers waited at the dock for the ship that brought in each new chapter). The place is almost a shrine: It contains his study, manuscripts, and personal relics, as well as reconstructed interiors. During Christmas week (including Christmas day), the museum is decorated in the style of Dickens's first Christmas there. The admission price of £10 ($15) for adults and £5 ($7.50) for children includes hot mince pies and a few glasses of "smoking Bishop," Dickens's favorite hot punch, as well as a copy of the museum's guidebooks.

48 Doughty St., WC1. ℭ **020/7405-2127.** www.dickensmuseum.com. Admission £4 ($6) adults, £3 ($4.50) students, £2 ($3) children, £9 ($13.50) families. Mon–Sat 10am–5pm. Tube: Russell Sq.

Samuel Johnson's House ⟨⟩   Dr. Johnson and his copyists compiled his famous dictionary in this Queen Anne house, where the lexicographer, poet, essayist, and fiction writer lived from 1748 to 1759. Although Johnson also lived at Staple Inn in Holborn and at a number of other places, the Gough Square house is the only one of his residences remaining in London. The 17th-century building has been painstakingly restored, and it's well worth a visit.

17 Gough Sq., EC4. ℭ **020/7353-3745.** www.drjh.dircon.co.uk. Admission £4 ($6) adults, £3 ($4.50) students and seniors, £1 ($1.50) children, free for children 10 and under. Apr–Oct Mon–Sat 11am–4:45pm; Nov–Mar Mon–Sat 11am–5:15pm. Tube: Blackfriars or Chancery Lane. Walk up New Bridge St. and turn left onto Fleet; Gough Sq. is tiny and hidden, north of Fleet St.

MUSEUMS & GALLERIES

Apsley House, The Wellington Museum ⟨⟩   This was the mansion of the duke of Wellington, one of Britain's greatest generals.

The "Iron Duke" defeated Napoleon at Waterloo, but later, for a short period while prime minister, he had to have iron shutters fitted to his windows to protect him from the mob outraged by his autocratic opposition to reform.

The house is crammed with art treasures, including three Velázquez paintings, and military mementos including the duke's medals and battlefield orders. Apsley House also holds some of the finest silver and porcelain pieces in Europe in the Plate and China Room. Grateful to Wellington for saving their thrones, European monarchs rewarded him with these. The collection includes a Sèvres Egyptian service intended as a divorce present from Napoléon to Josephine (but she refused it); Louis XVIII later gave it to Wellington.

149 Piccadilly, Hyde Park Corner, SW1. ℂ 020/7499-5676. www.vam.ac.uk/collections/apsley. Admission £4.50 ($6.75) adults, £3 ($4.50) seniors, free for children under 18. Tues–Sun 11am–5pm. Tube: Hyde Park Corner.

British Library ﴾﴿ In December 1996, one of the world's great libraries began moving its collection of some 12 million books, manuscripts, and other items from the British Museum to its own home in St. Pancras. In the new building, you get modernistic beauty rather than the fading glamour and the ghosts of Karl Marx, Thackeray, and Virginia Woolf of the old library at the British Museum. Academics, students, writers, and bookworms from the world over come here.

The bright, roomy interior is more inviting than the dull redbrick exterior suggests. The writer Alain de Botton likened the exterior to a supermarket, and Prince Charles made it the subject of one of his screeds against modern architecture. Still, the architect, Colin St. John Wilson, says he has been delighted by the positive response. The most spectacular room is the Humanities Reading Room, constructed on three levels and with daylight filtered through the ceiling.

The fascinating collection includes such items of historic and literary interest as two of the four surviving copies of the Magna Carta (1215), a Gutenberg Bible, Nelson's last letter to Lady Hamilton, and the journals of Captain Cook. Almost every major author—Dickens, Jane Austen, Charlotte Brontë, Keats, and hundreds of others—is represented in the section devoted to English literature. Beneath Roubiliac's 1758 statue of Shakespeare stands a case of documents relating to the Bard, including a mortgage bearing his signature and a copy of the First Folio of 1623.

Value **Money-Saving Passes**

If you're coming to London to pubcrawl, forget doing it cheaply, but if you plan to visit a lot of museums, you can save money with the **London GoSee Card.** It's valid at some of London's major attractions, including the Museum of Moving Images, the Victoria and Albert Museum, the Science Museum, the Design Museum, and more. Validity ranges from 3 to 7 days. An adult 3-day card costs £16 ($24), and a 7-day card goes for £26 ($39). Families of two adults and up to four children can purchase a 3-day card for £32 ($48) or a 7-day card for £50 ($75). Cards are sold at British tourist information centers, London Transport centers, airports, and various attractions. For more details, call ✆ **800/223-6108** in the U.S. or ✆ **020/7923-0807** in the U.K. Or try them on the Web: www.london-gosee.com.

The **London Pass** provides admission to 60 attractions in and around London, £5 worth of phone calls, "timed" admission at some attractions, bypassing the queues, plus free travel on public transport (buses, tubes, and trains), and a pocket guidebook. It costs £22 ($33) for 1 day, £49 ($73.50) for 3 days, or £79 ($118.50) for 6 days (children pay £14/$21, £30/$45, or £42/$63) and includes admission to St. Paul's Cathedral, *HMS Belfast,* the Jewish Museum, and the Thames Barrier Visitor Centre—and many more. Visit the website at www.londonpass.com or call ✆ **870/242-9988.** *Tip:* Purchase the pass before you go because passes purchased in London do not include free transportation.

Visitors can also view the Diamond Sutra, dating from 868, said to be the oldest surviving printed book. Using headphones set around the room, you can also hear thrilling audio snippets such as James Joyce reading a passage from *Finnegans Wake.* Curiosities include the earliest known tape of a birdcall, dating from 1889. Particularly intriguing is an exhibition called "Turning the Pages." You can, for example, electronically read a complete Leonardo da Vinci notebook, putting your hands on a special computer screen that flips from one page to another. There is a copy of *The Canterbury Tales* from 1410, and even manuscripts from *Beowulf* (ca. 1000). Illuminated texts from some of the oldest known Biblical displays include the Codex Sinaitticus and Codex Alexandrius, 3rd-century Greek gospels. In the music displays, you can seek out works by Beethoven, Handel, Stravinsky, and Lennon and McCartney.

Walking tours of the library cost £4.50 ($6.75) for adults or £3 ($4.50) for seniors, students, and children. They are conducted Wednesday to Monday at 3pm, Tuesday at 6:30pm, with an extra tour on Sunday at 3pm. Reservations are advised 3 weeks in advance.

96 Euston Rd., NW1. ℂ 020/7412-7000. www.bl.uk. Free admission. Mon 10am–8pm, Tues–Thurs 9:30am–8pm, Fri–Sat 9:30am–5pm. Tube: King's Cross/ St. Pancras, or Euston.

Courtauld Gallery 🅰🅰 Although surprisingly little-known, the Courtauld contains a wealth of paintings. It has one of the world's great collections of impressionist works outside Paris. There are French impressionists and postimpressionists, with masterpieces by Monet, Manet, Degas, Renoir, Cézanne, van Gogh, and Gauguin. The gallery also has a superb collection of old-master paintings and drawings, with works by Rubens, Michelangelo, and Tiepolo; early-Italian paintings, ivories, and majolica; the Lee collection of old masters; and early-20th-century English and French paintings, as well as 20th-century British paintings.

Like the Frick Collection in New York, it's a superb display, a visual feast in a jewel-like setting. We come here at least once every season to revisit one painting in particular: Manet's exquisite *A Bar at the Folies-Bérgere*. Many paintings are displayed without glass, giving the gallery a more intimate feel than most.

The Hermitage of St. Petersburg is opening a series of eight rooms here for rotating exhibits from its vast collections, opening with the treasures of Catherine the Great.

Somerset House, The Strand, WC2. ℂ 020/7848-2526. www.courtauld.ac.uk. Admission £4 ($6) adults, £3 ($4.50) students, free for children under 18. Mon–Sat 10am–6pm, Sun noon–6pm; last admission 5:15pm. Tube: Temple or Covent Garden.

Guildhall Art Gallery 🅰 In 1999, Queen Elizabeth opened a new £70 million gallery in the City, a continuation of the original gallery launched in 1886 that was burned down in a severe air raid in May 1941. Many famous and much-loved pictures that for years were known only through temporary exhibitions and reproductions are again available for the public to see in a permanent setting. The new gallery can display only 250 of the 4,000 treasures it owns. A curiosity is the huge double-height wall built to accommodate Britain's largest independent oil painting, John Singleton Copley's *The Defeat of the Floating Batteries at Gibraltar, September 1782.* The Corporation of London in the City owns these works and has been collecting them since the 17th century. The most popular art is in the Victorian collection, including such well-known favorites as Millais's *My First Sermon* and *My Second Sermon,* and Landseer's *The First Leap.* There is also a landscape of Salisbury Cathedral by John Constable. Since World War II, all paintings acquired by the gallery concentrate on London subjects.

Guildhall Yard, EC ✆ **020/7332-3700.** www.corpoflondon.gov.uk/gag_july/index.htm. Admission £2.50 ($3.75) adults, £1 ($1.50) children. Mon–Sat 10am–5pm, Sun noon–4pm. Tube: Bank, St. Paul's, Mansion House, or Moorgate.

Hermitage Rooms at Somerset House ⭐⭐⭐ This is a virtual outstation of St. Petersburg's State Hermitage Museum, which owns a great deal of the treasure trove left over from the czars, including possessions of art-collecting Catherine the Great. Now you don't have to journey all the way to Russia to see some of Europe's great treasures. There will be a series of rotating exhibitions from the Hermitage acquired over a period of 3 centuries by Russian czars. The actual exhibitions will change, but you'll get to see such treasures as medals, jewelry, portraits, porcelain, clocks, and furniture. There will be a rotating "visiting masterpiece" overshadowing all the other collections. Some items that amused us on our first visit (and you are likely to see similar novelties) were a wig made entirely out of silver thread for Catherine the Great, a Wedgwood "Green Frog" table service, and two Chinese silver filigree toilet sets. The rooms themselves have been designed in the style of the Winter Palace at St. Petersburg. Because this exhibit attracts so much interest, tickets should be purchased in advance. Tickets are available from TicketMaster at ✆ **020/7413-3398** (24 hours). You can book online at www.ticketmaster.co.uk. Somerset House also contains the priceless Gilbert Collection (see page 132).

The Strand, WC2. ✆ **020/7845-4600.** Admission £6 ($9) adults, £4 ($6) students and seniors. Mon–Sat 10am–6pm, Sun noon–6pm. Tube: Temple, Covent Garden, or Charing Cross.

Imperial War Museum ⭐ This museum occupies 1 city block the size of an army barracks, greeting you with 15-inch guns from the battleships *Resolution* and *Ramillies.* The large domed building, constructed in 1815, was the former Bethlehem Royal Hospital for the insane, known as "Bedlam."

A wide range of weapons and equipment is on display, along with models, decorations, uniforms, posters, photographs, and paintings. You can see a Mark V tank, a Battle of Britain Spitfire, and a German one-man submarine, as well as a rifle carried by Lawrence of Arabia. In the Documents Room, you can view the self-styled "political testament" that Hitler dictated in the chancellery bunker in the closing days of World War II, witnessed by henchmen Joseph Goebbels and Martin Bormann, as well as the famous "peace in our time" agreement that Neville Chamberlain brought back from Munich in 1938. (Of his signing the agreement, Hitler later said, "[Chamberlain] was a nice old man, so I decided to give him my autograph.") It's a world of espionage and clandestine warfare in the major new permanent exhibit known as the "Secret War Exhibition," where you can discover the truth behind the image of James Bond—and find out why the real secret war is even stranger and more fascinating than fiction. Displays include many items never before seen in public: coded messages, forged documents, secret wirelesses, and equipment used by spies from World War I to the present day.

Public film shows take place on weekends at 3pm and on certain weekdays during school holidays and on public holidays.

One of the latest additions opened in June 2000. The permanent Holocaust exhibition occupies two floors. Through original arti-facts, documents, film, and photographs, some lent to the museum by former concentration camps in Germany and Poland, the display relates the story of Nazi Germany and the persecution of the Jews. In addition, the exhibition brings attention to the persecution of other groups under Hitler's regime, including Poles, Soviet prison-ers of war, people with disabilities, and homosexuals. Among the items on display are a funeral cart used in the Warsaw Ghetto, a sec-tion of railcar from Belgium, a sign from the extermination camp at Belzec, and the letters of an 8-year old French Jewish boy who hid in an orphanage before being sent to Auschwitz.

Lambeth Rd., SE1. ☎ **020/7416-5000**. www.iwm.org.uk. Admission £5.50 ($8.25) adults, £4.50 ($6.75) seniors and students, £2.60 ($3.90) children; free daily 4:30–6pm. Daily 10am–6pm. Tube: Baker Line to Lambeth North or Elephant and Castle.

Madame Tussaud's ⛵ ⏰(Kids)   Madame Tussaud's is not so much a wax museum as an enclosed amusement park. A weird, moving, sometimes terrifying (to children) collage of exhibitions, panora-mas, and stage settings, it manages to be most things to most peo-ple, most of the time.

Madame Tussaud attended the court of Versailles and learned her craft in France. She personally took the death masks from the guillotined heads of Louis XVI and Marie Antoinette (still among the exhibits). She moved her museum from Paris to England in 1802. Madame herself molded the features of Benjamin Franklin, whom she met in Paris. All the rest—from George Washington to John F. Kennedy, Mary Queen of Scots to Sylvester Stallone—have been subjects for the same painstaking (and breathtaking) replication.

In the well-known Chamber of Horrors are all kinds of instruments of death, along with figures of their victims. The shadowy presence of Jack the Ripper lurks in the gloom as you walk through a Victorian London street. Present-day criminals are portrayed within the confines of prison. The latest attraction to open here is "The Spirit of London," a musical ride that depicts 400 years of London's history, using special effects that include audio-animatronic figures. Visitors take "time-taxis" that allow them to see and hear "Shakespeare" as he writes and speaks lines, be received by Queen Elizabeth I, and feel and smell the Great Fire of 1666 that destroyed London.

We've seen these exhibitions so many times that we're well over them, but we still remember how fascinated we were the first time we were taken here as kids.

Insider's Tip: To avoid the long lines, sometimes more than an hour in summer, call in advance and reserve a ticket for fast pickup at the entrance. If you don't want to bother with that, be aggressive and form a group of 9 people waiting in the queue. With 9, you constitute a group and can go in almost at once through the "group door." Otherwise, go when the gallery first opens or late in the afternoon when crowds have thinned.

Marylebone Rd., NW1. © 020/7935-6861. www.madame-tussauds.com. Admission £11.50 ($17.25) adults, £9 ($13.50) seniors, £8 ($12) children under 16, free for children under 5. Combination tickets including the new planetarium £13.95 ($20.95) adults, £10.80 ($16.20) seniors, £8 ($12) children under 16. Mon–Fri 10am–5:30pm, Sat–Sun 9:30am–5:30pm. Tube: Baker St.

Museum of London 🕸🕸   In London's Barbican district near St. Paul's Cathedral, overlooking the city's Roman and medieval walls, the museum traces the history of London from prehistoric times to the 20th century through archeological finds; paintings and prints; social, industrial, and historic artifacts; and costumes, maps, and models. Exhibits are arranged so that you can begin and end your chronological stroll through 250,000 years at the main entrance to the museum. The museum's pièce de résistance is the Lord Mayor's

Coach, a gilt-and-scarlet fairy-tale coach built in 1757 and weighing in at 3 tons, but you can also see the Great Fire of London in living color and sound; the death mask of Oliver Cromwell; cell doors from Newgate Prison, made famous by Charles Dickens; and most amazing of all, a shop counter showing pre–World War II prices.

150 London Wall, EC2. ℂ 020/7600-3699. www.museumoflondon.org.uk. Admission £5 ($7.50) adults, £3 ($4.50) students and seniors, children free. Mon–Sat 10am–5:50pm, Sun noon–5:50pm. Tube: St. Paul's or Barbican.

Natural History Museum 𝒦𝒦 *Kids*   This is the home of the national collections of living and fossil plants, animals, and minerals, with many magnificent specimens on display. Exciting exhibits designed to encourage people of all ages to learn about natural history include *"Human Biology—An Exhibition of Ourselves," "Our Place in Evolution," "Origin of the Species," "Creepy Crawlies,"* and *"Discovering Mammals."* The Mineral Gallery displays marvelous examples of crystals and gemstones. Visit the Meteorite Pavilion, which exhibits fragments of rock that have crashed into the earth. What attracts the most attention is the dinosaur exhibit, displaying 14 complete skeletons. The center of the show depicts a trio of robotic Deinonychus enjoying a freshly killed Tenontosaurus. The latest addition is *"Earth Galleries,"* an exhibition outlining humankind's relationship with planet Earth. Here in the exhibition *"Earth Today and Tomorrow,"* visitors are invited to explore the planet's history from the big bang to its inevitable death.

Cromwell Rd., SW7. ℂ 020/7942-5000. www.nhm.ac.uk. Admission £9 ($13.50) adults, £4.50 ($6.75) seniors and students, free for children 17 and under, £18 ($27) family ticket; free to everyone Mon–Fri after 4:30pm and Sat–Sun after 5pm. Mon–Sat 10am–5:50pm, Sun 11am–5:50pm. Tube: South Kensington.

Science Museum 𝒦𝒦𝒦   This museum traces the development of science and industry and their influence on everyday life. These collections are among the most comprehensive, and most significant anywhere. On display is Stephenson's original rocket, the prototype railroad engine; you can also see Whittle's original jet engine and the Apollo 10 space module. The King George III collection of scientific instruments is the highlight of a gallery on science in the 18th century. Health Matters is a permanent gallery on modern medicine. The museum has two hands-on galleries, as well as working models and video displays.

Insider's Tip: A large addition to this museum explores such topics as genetics, digital technology, and artificial intelligence. Four floors of a Welcome Wing shelter half a dozen exhibition areas and a 450-seat Imax theater. One exhibition explores everything from the use of drugs in sports to how engineers observe sea life with robotic submarines. On an upper floor, visitors can learn how DNA was used to identify living relatives of the Bleadon Man, a 2,000-year-old Iron Age man. On the third floor is the computer that Tim Berners-Lee used to design the first browser for the World Wide Web.

Exhibition Rd., SW7. ℭ **020/7938-8000**. www.sciencemuseum.org.uk. Admission £7.95 ($11.95) adults, £4.95 ($8.40) students, free for children under 17 and for people over 60; free to all after 4:30pm. Daily 10am–6pm. Tube: South Kensington.

Shakespeare's Globe Theatre & Exhibition ✸ This is a recent recreation of what was probably the most important public theater ever built—on the exact site where many of Shakespeare's plays opened. The late American filmmaker Sam Wanamaker worked for some 20 years to raise funds to re-create the theater as it existed in Elizabethan times, thatched roof and all. A fascinating exhibit tells the story of the Globe's construction, using the material (including goat hair in the plaster), techniques, and craftsmanship of 400 years ago. The new Globe isn't an exact replica: It seats 1,500 patrons, not the 3,000 who regularly squeezed in during the early 1600s, and this thatched roof has been specially treated with a fire retardant. Guided tours of the facility are offered throughout the day.

See "The Play's the Thing: London's Theater Scene" in chapter 7, "London After Dark," for details on attending a play here.

New Globe Walk, Southwark, SE1. ℭ **020/7902-1500**. www.shakespeares-globe.org. Exhibition and tour admission £7.50 ($11.25) adults, £5 ($7.50) children 15 and under, £6 ($9) seniors and students. Guided tours £5 ($7.50) adults, £4 ($6) students and seniors, £3 ($4.50) children 15 and under. Daily 10am–6pm (guided tours every 30 minutes or so). Tube: Mansion House or London Bridge.

Sir John Soane's Museum ✸ This is the former home of Sir John Soane (1753 to 1837), an architect who rebuilt the Bank of England (not the present structure). With his multiple levels, fool-the-eye mirrors, flying arches, and domes, Soane was a master of perspective and a genius of interior space (his picture gallery, for example, is filled with three times the number of paintings that a room of similar dimensions would be likely to hold). One prize of the collection is William Hogarth's satirical series *The Rake's Progress,* which includes his much-reproduced *Orgy and The Election,* a satire on mid-18th-century politics. Soane also filled his house with classical sculpture: The sarcophagus of Pharaoh Seti I, found in a burial chamber in the Valley of the Kings, is here. Also on display are architectural drawings from Soane's collection of 30,000.

13 Lincoln's Inn Fields, WC2. ℭ 020/7405-2107. Free admission (donations invited). Tues–Sat 10am–5pm; first Tues of each month 6–9pm. Tours given Sat at 2:30pm; £3 ($4.50) tickets distributed at 2pm on a first-come, first-served basis (group tours by appointment only). Tube: Holborn.

Wallace Collection ⟨R⟩⟨R⟩ Located in a palatial setting (the modestly described "town house" of the late Lady Wallace), this collection is a contrasting array of art and armaments. The art collection (mostly French) includes works by Watteau, Boucher, Fragonard, and Greuze, as well as such classics as Frans Hals's *Laughing Cavalier* and Rembrandt's portrait of his son Titus. The paintings of the Dutch, English, Spanish, and Italian schools are outstanding. The collection also contains 18th-century French decorative art, including furniture from a number of royal palaces, Sévres porcelain, and gold boxes. The European and Asian armaments, on the ground floor, are works of art in their own right: superb inlaid suits of armor, some obviously for parade rather than battle, with more businesslike swords, halberds, and magnificent Persian scimitars.

Manchester Sq., W1. ℭ 020/7935-0687. www.the-wallace-collection.org.uk. Free admission. Mon–Sat 10am–5pm, Sun 2–5pm. Tube: Bond St. or Baker St.

PARKS & GARDENS

London's parks are the most advanced system of "green lungs" of any large city on the globe. Although not as rigidly maintained as those of Paris (Britons traditionally prefer a more natural look), they're cared for with a loving hand that puts their American equivalents to shame.

The largest of the central London parks is **Hyde Park** ⟨R⟩⟨R⟩ (Tube: Marble Arch, Hyde Park Corner, or Lancaster Gate), once a favorite deer-hunting ground of Henry VIII. With the adjoining Kensington Gardens (see below), it covers 615 acres of central London with velvety lawns interspersed with ponds, flowerbeds, and trees. Running through its width is a 41-acre lake known as the **Serpentine,** where you can row, sail model boats, or swim (provided you don't mind sub-Florida water temperatures). **Rotten Row,** a 1½-mile sand riding track, attracts some skilled equestrians on Sunday. You can rent a paddleboat or a rowboat from the boathouse (open March to October) on the north side of **Hyde Park's Serpentine** (ℭ 020/7262-1330).

At the northeastern tip, near Marble Arch, is **Speakers' Corner.** Since 1855 (before the legal right to assembly was guaranteed), people have been getting on their soapboxes about any subject under the sky. Hecklers, often aggressive, are part of the fun. Anyone can speak; just don't blaspheme, use obscene language, or start a riot.

Blending with Hyde Park and bordering on the grounds of Kensington Palace, **Kensington Gardens** (Tube: High Street Kensington or Queensway) contains the famous statue of Peter Pan, with the bronze rabbits that toddlers are always trying to kidnap. It's also home to that Victorian extravaganza, the Albert Memorial. The Orangery is an ideal place to take afternoon tea (see "Teatime" in chapter 4, "Dining").

East of Hyde Park, across Piccadilly, stretch **Green Park** ⍟ (Tube: Green Park) and **St. James's Park** ⍟ (Tube: St. James's Park), forming an almost unbroken chain of landscaped beauty. They are ideal for picnics; you'll find it hard to believe that this was once a festering swamp near a leper hospital. There's a romantic lake stocked with ducks and some surprising pelicans, descendants of the pair that the Russian ambassador presented to Charles II in 1662.

Regent's Park ⍟⍟⍟ (Tube: Regent's Park or Baker Street) covers most of the district of that name, north of Baker Street and Marylebone Road. Designed by the 18th-century genius John Nash to surround a palace for the prince regent that never materialized, this is the most classically beautiful of London's parks. Its core is a rose garden planted around a small lake alive with waterfowl and spanned by Japanese bridges; in early summer, the rose perfume in the air is as heady as wine. The park is home to the **Open-Air Theatre** and the **London Zoo.** As at all the local parks, hundreds of deck chairs are scattered around the lawns, waiting for sunbathers. The deck-chair attendants, who collect a small fee, are mostly college students on break. Rowboats and sailing dinghies are available in **Regent's Park** (© **020/7486-4759**). Sailing and canoeing cost £5 ($7.50) for 1½ hours.

3 Sightseeing & Boat Tours Along the Thames

RIVER CRUISES

A trip up or down the river will give you an entirely different view of London from the one you get from land. You'll see how the city grew along and around the Thames and how many of its landmarks turn their faces toward the water. Several companies operate motor launches from the Westminster piers (Tube: Westminster), offering panoramic views of one of Europe's most historic waterways en route.

Westminster-Greenwich Thames Passenger Boat Service, Westminster Pier, Victoria Embankment, SW1 (✆ **020/7839-3572**), concerns itself with downriver traffic from Westminster Pier to such destinations as Greenwich. The most popular excursion departs for Greenwich (a 50-minute ride) at half-hour intervals between 10am and 4pm April to October, between 10:30am and 5pm from June to August; from November to March, boats depart at 40-minute intervals daily from 10:40am to 3:20pm. One-way fares are £6.30 ($9.45) for adults, £3.30 ($4.95) for children under 16, and £5 ($7.50) for seniors. Round-trip fares are £7.60 ($11.40) for adults, £3.80 ($5.70) for children, and £6.30 ($9.45) for seniors. A family ticket for two adults and up to three children under 15 costs £16.80 ($25.20) one-way, £20 ($30) round-trip.

Westminster Passenger Association (Upriver) Ltd., Westminster Pier, Victoria Embankment, SW1 (✆ **020/7930-2062** or 020/7930-4721), offers the only riverboat service upstream from Westminster Bridge to Kew, Richmond, and Hampton Court. There are daily sailings from the Monday before Easter until the end of October on traditional riverboats, all with licensed bars. Trip time can be as little as 1½ hours to Kew and between 2½ to 4 hours to Hampton Court, depending on the tide. Cruises from Westminster Pier to Hampton Court via Kew Gardens leave daily at 10:30am, 11:15am, and noon. Round-trip tickets are £10 to £14.50 ($15–$21.75) adults, £7.50 to £12 ($11.25–$18) seniors, and £5 to £9 ($7.50–$13.50) children 4 to 14; one child under 4 accompanied by an adult goes free. Evening cruises from May to September are also available, departing Westminster Pier at 7:30 and 8:30pm (9:30pm on demand) for £6.50 ($9.75) adults and £5 ($7.50) children.

THAMES-SIDE SIGHTS

THE BRIDGES

Some of the Thames bridges are household names. **London Bridge,** contrary to the nursery rhyme, never fell down, but it has been replaced a number of times and is vastly different from the original London Bridge, which was lined with houses and shops. The one that you see now is the ugliest of them; the previous incarnation was dismantled and shipped to Lake Havasu, Arizona, in the 1960s.

Also on the Thames, you can visit London's newest park, Thames Barrier Park, SE1, the city's first riverside park in years. It lies on the north bank of the Thames alongside the Thames Barrier, that steel and concrete movable flood barrier inaugurated in 1982. Spread across 22 acres, the park has water fountains that flow into a 1,300-foot sunken landscaped garden. There's also a riverside promenade and a playground. The park is open daily from sunrise to sunset (reached via bus no. 69 from the Canning Town tube station).

4 Especially for Kids

London has fun places for kids of all ages. In addition to what's listed below, kids love **Madame Tussaud's,** the **Science Museum,** the **Natural History Museum,** and the **Tower of London,** discussed above.

The London Dungeon   This ghoulish place was designed to chill the blood while reproducing the conditions of the Middle Ages. Under the arches of London Bridge Station, it presents a series of tableaux more grisly than the ones in Madame Tussaud's. The rumble of trains overhead adds to the atmosphere, and tolling bells bring a note of melancholy; dripping water and caged rats make for even more atmosphere. Naturally, there's a burning at the stake and a torture chamber with racking, branding, and fingernail extraction, and a "Jack the Ripper Experience." The special effects were conceived for major film and TV productions. They've recently added a new show called "Judgment Day." You are sentenced to death (by actors) and taken on a boat ride to meet your fate. If you survive, there's a Pizza Hut on the premises and a souvenir shop selling certificates that testify you made it through Judgment Day.

28–34 Tooley St., SE1. (C) **020/7403-7221.** www.thedungeons.com. Admission £10.95 ($16.45) adults, £9.50 ($14.25) students and seniors, £6.95 ($10.45) children under 15. Admission includes Judgment Day boat ride. Daily 10:30am–5pm during winter, high season 10am 8pm daily. Tube: London Bridge.

London Zoo   One of the greatest zoos in the world, the London Zoo is more than 1½ centuries old. This 36-acre garden houses about 8,000 animals, including some of the rarest species on earth. There's an insect house (incredible bird-eating spiders), a reptile house (dragonlike monitor lizards), and others, such as the Sobell Pavilion for Apes and Monkeys and the Lion Terraces. In the Moonlight World, lighting simulates night for the nocturnal beasties while rendering them visible to onlookers.

In 1999, the Millennium Conservation Centre opened, combining animals, visuals, and displays demonstrating the nature of life on this planet. Many families budget almost an entire day here, watching the penguins being fed, enjoying an animal ride in summer, and meeting elephants on their walks around the zoo.

Regent's Park, NW1. ℂ **020/7722-3333**. www.londonzoo.co.uk. Admission £10 ($15) adults, £7 ($10.50) children and students, free for children aged 3–15. Mar–Sept daily 10am–5:30pm; Oct–Feb daily 10am–4pm. Tube: Regent's Park or Camden Town, then Bus C2 or 274.

Rock Circus   This outpost of Madame Tussaud's presents the history of rock and pop music from Bill Haley and the Beatles to Sting and Madonna through wax and animatronic figures, which move and perform golden oldies and more recent chart-toppers in an eerily lifelike way. Authentic memorabilia, videos, and personal stereo sound surround you.

London Pavilion, Piccadilly Circus, W1. ℂ **020/7734-7203**. www.rock–circus.com. Admission £8.25 ($12.43) adults, £7.25 ($10.93) seniors and students, £6.25 ($9.43) children under 16. Sun–Mon and Wed–Sat 10am–5:30pm; Tues 11am–5:30pm. Tube: Piccadilly Circus.

5 Organized Tours

BUS TOURS

For the first-timer, the quickest and most economical way to bring the city into focus is to take a bus tour. One of the most popular is the **Original London Sightseeing Tour,** which passes all the major sights in about 1½ hours. The tour, which uses a double-decker bus with live commentary, costs £12.50 ($18.75) for adults, £7.50 ($11.25) for children under 16, free for children under 5. The tour is hop on/hop off at any point. The tour plus admission to Madame Tussaud's is £22 ($33) for adults, £13.75 ($20.65) for children.

Departures are from convenient points within the city; you can choose your departure point when you buy your ticket. Tickets can be purchased on the bus or at a discount from any London Transport or London Tourist Board Information Centre. Most hotel concierges also sell tickets. For information or phone purchases, call ℂ **020/8877-1722.** It's also possible to write for tickets: **London Coaches,** Jews Row, London SW18 1TB.

A double-decker air-conditioned coach in the distinctive green-and-gold livery of **Harrods,** 87–135 Brompton Rd. (ℂ **020/ 7581-3603;** Tube: Knightsbridge), offers sightseeing tours around London. The first departure from Door 8 of Harrods is at 10:30am; afternoon tours begin at 1:30 and 4pm. Tea, coffee, and orange juice are served on board. It's £20 ($30) for adults, £10 ($15) for children under 14, free for those under 5. All-day excursions to Blenheim

Palace, Windsor, Stratford-upon-Avon, and outlying areas of London are available. You can purchase tickets at Harrods, Sightseeing Department, lower-ground floor.

Big Bus Company Ltd., Waterside Way, London SW17 (© **020/8944-7810**), operates a 2-hour tour in summer, departing frequently between 8:30am and 5pm daily from Marble Arch by Speakers Corner, Green Park by the Ritz Hotel, and Victoria Station (Buckingham Palace Road by the Royal Westminster Hotel). Tours cover the highlights—18 in all—ranging from the Houses of Parliament and Westminster Abbey to the Tower of London and Buckingham Palace (exterior looks only), accompanied by live commentary. The cost is £15 ($22.50) for adults, £6 ($9) for children. There's also a 1-hour tour that follows the same route, but covers only 13 sights. Tickets are valid all day; you can hop on and off the bus as you wish.

WALKING TOURS

The Original London Walks ℛ, 87 Messina Ave., P.O. Box 1708, London NW6 4LW (© **020/7624-3978**), the oldest established walking-tour company in London, is run by an Anglo-American journalist/actor couple, David and Mary Tucker. Their hallmarks are variety, reliability, reasonably sized groups, and—above all—superb guides. The renowned crime historian Donald Rumbelow, the leading authority on Jack the Ripper and the author of the classic guidebook *London Walks,* is a regular guide, as are several prominent actors (including classical actor Edward Petherbridge). Walks are regularly scheduled daily and cost £5 ($7.50) for adults, £3.50 ($5.25) for students and seniors; children under 15 go free. Call for schedule; no reservations needed.

Discovery Walks, 67 Chancery Lane, London WC2 (© **020/8530-8443;** www.Jack-the-Ripper-Walk.co.uk), are themed walks, led by Richard Jones, author of *Frommer's Memorable Walks in London.* **Stepping Out** (© **020/8881-2933;** www.walklon.ndirect.co.uk) offers a series of offbeat walks led by qualified historians, as does **Guided Walks in London,** 3 Chatham Close, London NW11 (© **020/7243-1097;** www.guided-walks-in-london.net). Tours generally cost £4 to £5 ($6–$7.50).

6

Shopping

Although London is one of the world's best shopping cities, it often seems made for wealthy visitors. Locals are more careful with their pounds. To find real values, do what most Londoners do: Wait for sales or search out specialty finds.

Your best bet is to concentrate on British goods. You can also do well with French products; values are almost as good as in Paris. Serious shoppers can find detailed advice and recommendations in *Frommer's Born to Shop London.*

1 Central London Shopping

THE WEST END   As a neighborhood, the West End includes Mayfair and is home to the core of London's big-name shopping. Most of the department stores, designer shops, and multiples (chain stores) have their flagships in this area.

The key streets are **Oxford Street** for affordable shopping (start at Marble Arch Tube station if you're ambitious, or Bond Street station if you only care to see some of it), and **Regent Street,** which intersects Oxford Street at Oxford Circus (Tube: Oxford Circus). The Oxford Street flagship (at Marble Arch) of the private-label department store Marks & Spencer is worth visiting for quality goods. Regent Street, which leads all the way to Piccadilly, has more upscale department stores (including Liberty of London), chains, and specialty dealers.

Parallel to Regent Street, **Bond Street** (Tube: Bond Street) connects Piccadilly with Oxford Street and is synonymous with the luxury trade. Divided into New and Old, it has experienced a recent revival and is the hot address for international designers; Donna Karan has two shops here. A slew of international hotshots from Chanel to Ferragamo to Versace have digs nearby.

Burlington Arcade (Tube: Piccadilly Circus), the glass-roofed, Regency-style passage leading off Piccadilly, looks like a period exhibition and is lined with shops and boutiques. Lit by wrought-iron lamps and decorated with ferns and flowers, its small, smart stores

Tips How to Get Your VAT Refund

Several readers have reported that merchants have told them they can get refund forms at the airport as they leave the country. *This is not true.* Don't leave the store without a form—it must be completed by the retailer on the spot. After you have asked if the store does VAT refunds and determined their minimum, request the paperwork.

Fill out your form and then present it—with the goods—at the Customs office in the airport. Allow a half-hour to stand in line. Remember: You're required to show the goods, so put them in your carry-on.

Once the paperwork has been stamped, you have two choices: You can mail the papers (remember to bring a stamp) and receive your refund as a British check (no!) or a credit-card refund (yes!), or go to the Cash VAT Refund desk at the airport and get your refund in cash. The bad news: If you accept cash other than sterling, you will lose money on the conversion.

Many stores charge a flat fee for processing your refund, so £3 to £5 may be automatically deducted from the total you receive. But because the VAT in Britain is 17.5%, it's worth the trouble to get the money back.

Note: If you're heading to other countries in the European Union, you go through this at your final destination in the EU, filing all your VAT refunds at once.

specialize in fashion, jewelry, Irish linen, cashmere, and more. If you linger there until 5:30pm, you can watch the beadles in their black-and-yellow livery and top hats place the iron grills that block off the arcade until 9am, at which time they just as ceremoniously remove them to start a new business day. Also at 5:30pm, a hand bell called the Burlington Bell is sounded, signaling the end of trading.

For a total contrast, check out **Jermyn Street** (Tube: Piccadilly Circus), on the far side of Piccadilly, a tiny 2-block-long street devoted to high-end men's haberdashers and toiletries shops; many have been doing business for centuries. Several hold royal warrants, including Turnbull & Asser, where HRH Prince Charles has his pj's made. A bit to the northwest, Savile Row (between Regent Street

---

⌒Tips **Tax-Free Shopping**

Global Refund (www.taxfree.so) is your best bet for getting VAT refunds at the airport. In London, you can shop where you see the Global Refund Tax-free Shopping sign. When leaving Britain, show your purchases, receipts, and passport to customs, and have your Global Refund checks stamped. You have several choices—immediate cash at one of Global Refund's offices, crediting to a credit card or bank account, or a bank check sent to a chosen address. Refund offices are situated at all major exit points such as Gatwick and Heathrow airports.

---

and New Bond Street) is synonymous with the finest in men's tailoring.

The West End theater district borders two more shopping areas: the still-not-ready-for-prime-time **Soho** (Tube: Tottenham Court Road), where the sex shops are slowly converting into cutting-edge designer shops, and **Covent Garden** (Tube: Covent Garden), a masterpiece unto itself. The original marketplace has overflowed its boundaries and eaten up the surrounding neighborhood; it's fun to wander the narrow streets and shop. Covent Garden is mobbed on Sundays.

Just a stone's throw from Covent Garden, **Monmouth Street** is somewhat of a shopping secret to Londoners who know they can find an array of stores in a space of only 2 blocks. Many shops here are outlets for British designers such as Alexander Campbell, who specializes in outfits made of wispy materials. Some shops along this street specialize in both used and new clothing. Other than clothing, stores specialize in everything from musical instruments from the Far East to palm and crystal ball readings.

KNIGHTSBRIDGE & CHELSEA The home of Harrods, Knightsbridge (Tube: Knightsbridge) is the second-most famous London retail district. (Oxford Street edges it out.) Nearby Sloane Street is chock-a-block with designer shops.

Walk southwest on **Brompton Road** (toward the Victoria and Albert Museum) and you'll find **Cheval Place,** lined with designer resale shops, and Beauchamp (*Bee*-cham) Place. It's only a block long, but it's very "Sloane Ranger," featuring the kinds of shops where young British aristocrats buy their clothing for the Season.

If you walk farther along Brompton Road, you connect to **Brompton Cross,** another hip area for designer shops. Also seek out

Walton Street, a tiny snake of a street running from Brompton Cross back toward the museums. Most of the street is devoted to fairytale shops for m'lady, where you can buy aromatherapy from Jo Malone, needlepoint, or costume jewelry.

King's Road (Tube: Sloane Square), the main street of Chelsea, will forever remain a symbol of the Swinging '60s. It's still popular with the young crowd, but there are fewer Mohawk haircuts, Bovver boots, and Edwardian ball gowns than before. More and more, King's Road is a lineup of markets and "multi-stores," conglomerations of indoor stands, stalls, and booths within one building. About a third of King's Road is devoted to these kinds of antiques markets; another third houses design-trade showrooms and stores of household wares; and the remaining third is faithful to the area's teeny-bopper roots.

Finally, don't forget all those museums in nearby **South Kensington**—they all have great gift shops.

KENSINGTON, NOTTING HILL & BAYSWATER

Kensington High Street (Tube: High Street Kensington) is the hangout of the classier breed of teen, one who has graduated from Carnaby Street and is ready for street chic. While there are a few staples of basic British fashion here, most of the stores feature items that stretch, are very short, very tight, and very black.

From Kensington High Street, you can walk up **Kensington Church Street,** which, like Portobello Road, is one of the city's main shopping avenues for antiques, selling everything from antique furniture to impressionist paintings.

Kensington Church Street dead-ends at the Notting Hill Gate Tube station, the jumping-off point for Portobello Road; the antiques dealers and weekend market are 2 blocks beyond.

Not far from Notting Hill Gate is **Whiteleys of Bayswater,** Queensway, W2 (© **020/7229-8844;** Tube: Bayswater or Queensway), an Edwardian mall whose chief tenant is Marks & Spencer. There are also 75 to 85 shops, mostly specialty outlets and restaurants, cafes, and bars, as well as an eight-screen movie theater.

2 The Department Stores

The British invented the department store, and they have lots of them, mostly in Mayfair, and each has its own customer profile.

Fortnum & Mason   The world's most elegant grocery store is a British tradition dating to 1707. It draws the carriage trade from Mayfair to Belgravia who seek such tinned treasures as *pâté de foie* *gras* or a boar's head. This store exemplifies the elegance and style you would expect from an establishment with three royal warrants. Enter and be transported to another world of deep-red carpets, crystal chandeliers, spiraling wooden staircases, and tail-coated assistants.

The grocery department is renowned for its selection of the finest foods from around the world—champagne, scrumptious Belgian chocolates, and Scottish smoked salmon. Wander through the four floors and inspect the bone china and crystal cut glass, find the perfect gift in the leather or stationery departments, or reflect on the changing history of furniture and ornaments in the antiques department. Dining choices include the Patio, the refurbished St. James Restaurant, the Fountain Restaurant, and the brand-new Salmon and Champagne Bar (for details on afternoon tea here, see "Teatime" in chapter 4, "Dining"). Fortnum & Mason now offers exclusive and specialty ranges for the home, as well as beauty products and women's and men's fashions. 181 Piccadilly, W1. ℂ 020/7734-8040. Tube: Piccadilly Circus.

Harrods Harrods remains an institution, but in the last decade or so it has grown increasingly dowdy and is not as cutting edge as it used to be. We always stop here anyway during our visits to London. As entrenched in English life as Buckingham Palace and the Ascot Races, it's still an elaborate emporium. Goods are spread across 300 departments. The range, variety, and quality can still dazzle.

The whole fifth floor is devoted to sports and leisure, with a wide range of equipment and attire. Toy Kingdom is on the fourth floor, along with children's wear. The Egyptian Hall, on the ground floor, sells crystal from Lalique and Baccarat, plus porcelain.

There's also a men's grooming room, a jewelry department, and a fashion department for younger customers. You also have a choice of 18 restaurants and bars. Best of all are the **Food Halls,** with a huge variety of foods and several cafes. Harrods began as a grocer in 1849, and that's still the heart of the business. The motto remains, "If you can eat or drink it, you'll find it at Harrods." 87–135 Brompton Rd., Knightsbridge, SW1. ℂ 020/7730-1234. Tube: Knightsbridge.

Liberty This department store is celebrated for its Liberty Prints, top-echelon, carriage-trade fabrics, often in floral patterns, prized by decorators for the way they add a sense of English tradition to a room. The front part of the Regent Street store isn't distinctive, but don't be fooled: Some parts of the place have been restored to Tudor-style splendor that includes half-timbering and interior paneling. There are six floors of fashion, china, and home furnishings, the famous Liberty Print fashion fabrics, upholstery fabrics, scarves, ties, luggage, and gifts. 214–220 Regent St., W1. © 020/ 7734-1234. Tube: Oxford Circus.

3 Goods A to Z

ANTIQUES

Alfie's Antique Market   This is one of the best-stocked conglomerates of dealers in London, crammed into the premises of a 19th-century store. It has more than 370 stalls, showrooms, and workshops in over 35,000 square feet of floor space. You'll find the biggest Susie Cooper (a designer of tableware and ceramics for Wedgwood) collection in Europe here. A whole antiques district has grown up around Alfie's along Church Street. 13–25 Church St., NW8. © 020/7723-6066. Fax 020/7724-0999. Tube: Marylebone or Edgware Rd.

Grays & Grays in the Mews   These markets have been converted into walk-in stands with independent dealers. The term "antique" covers items from oil paintings to, say, the 1894 edition of the *Encyclopedia Britannica*. Also sold are antique jewelry; silver; gold; maps and prints; bronzes and ivories; arms and armor; Victorian and Edwardian toys; furniture; Art Nouveau and Art Deco items; antique lace; scientific instruments; craft tools; and Asian, Persian, and Islamic pottery, porcelain, miniatures, and antiquities. There's a cafe in each building. Check out the 1950s-style **Victory Cafe** on Davies Street for the homemade cakes. 58 Davies St. and 1–7 Davies Mews, W1. © 020/7629-7034. Tube: Bond St.

ART & CRAFTS

ACAVA *Finds*   This is a London-based visual arts facility that provides studios and other services for professional artists, and represents about 250 artists working in spaces round the city. Call for individual open-studio schedules, as well as dates for the annual Open Studios weekend. © 020/8960-5015.

Contemporary Applied Arts   This association encourages traditional and progressive contemporary artwork. Many of Britain's best-established craftspeople, as well as promising talents, are represented in galleries that house a diverse display of glass, ceramics, textiles, wood, furniture, jewelry, and metalwork—all by contemporary artisans. Special exhibitions, including solo and group shows, focus on innovations in craftwork. There are new exhibitions every 6 weeks. 2 Percy St., W1. © 020/7436-2344. Tube: Goodge St.

Whitechapel Art Gallery   Since this East End gallery opened its Art Nouveau doors in 1901, collectors have been heading here to find out what's hot. It maintains its cutting edge; to some, it's the incubation chamber for some of the most talented of east London's artists. The collections are fun, hip, often sexy, and in your face. 80–82 Whitechapel High St., E1. ✆ 020/7522-7888 or 020/7522-7878 (recorded). Fax 020/7377-1685. Tube: District or Hammersmith & City Lines to Aldgate East.

BATH & BODY

The Body Shop   There's a branch of The Body Shop in every trading area and tourist zone in London. Some are bigger than others, but all are filled with politically—and environmentally—aware beauty, bath, and aromatherapy products. Prices are much lower in the U.K. than they are in the U.S. There's an entire children's line, a men's line, and lots of travel sizes and travel products. 374 Oxford St., W1. ✆ 020/7409-7868. Tube: Bond St. Other locations throughout London.

Boots the Chemist   This store has a million branches; we like the one across the street from Harrods for convenience and size. The house brands of beauty products are usually the best, be they Boots products (try the cucumber facial scrub), Boot's versions of The Body Shop (two lines, Global and Naturalistic), or Boot's versions of Chanel makeup (called No. 7). They also sell film, pantyhose (called tights), sandwiches, and all of life's little necessities. 72 Brompton Rd., SW3. ✆ 020/7589-6557. Tube: Knightsbridge. Other locations throughout London.

Floris   A variety of toilet articles and fragrances fill Floris's floor-to-ceiling mahogany cabinets, architectural curiosities in their own right. They were installed relatively late in the establishment's history—that is, 1851—long after the shop had received its royal warrants as suppliers of toilet articles to the king and queen. 89 Jermyn St., SW1. ✆ 020/7930-2885. Fax 020/7930-1402. Tube: Piccadilly Circus.

Penhaligon's   This Victorian perfumery, established in 1870, holds royal warrants to HRH Duke of Edinburgh and HRH Prince of Wales. All items sold are exclusive to Penhaligon's. It offers a large selection of perfume, aftershave, soap, and bath oils for women and men. Gifts include antique-silver scent bottles, grooming accessories, and leather traveling requisites. Penhaligon's is now in Saks Fifth Avenue stores across the United States. 41 Wellington St., WC2. ✆ 020/7836-2150, or 877/736-4254 in the U.S. for mail order. Tube: Covent Garden.

BOOKS, MAPS & ENGRAVINGS

In addition to the bookstores below, you'll also find well-stocked branches of the **Dillon's** chain around town, including one at 82 Gower St. (Tube: Euston Square).

Children's Book Centre   With thousands of titles, this is the best place to go for children's books. Fiction is arranged according to age, up to 16. There are also videos and toys for kids. 237 Kensington High St., W8. ✆ 020/7937-7497. Tube: Kensington.

Foyle's Bookshop   Claiming to be the world's largest bookstore, Foyle's has an impressive array of hardcovers and paperbacks, as well as travel maps, records, videotapes, and sheet music. They have opened a "hypermarket" where you can buy original artwork off the shelf. Works by some three-dozen Spanish and French artists are for sale at prices beginning at £60 ($90). 113–119 Charing Cross Rd., WC2. ✆ 020/7437-5660. Tube: Tottenham Court Rd.

Gay's the Word   Britain's leading gay and lesbian bookstore offers a large collection of books, as well as magazines, cards, and guides. There's also a used-books section. 66 Marchmont St., WC1. ✆ 020/7278-7654. Tube: Russell Sq.

The Map House of London   An ideal place to find an offbeat souvenir. Map House sells antique maps and engravings and a selection of old prints of London and England, both original and reproduction. A century-old engraving can cost as little as £6 ($10.20). 54 Beauchamp Place, SW3. ✆ 020/7589-4325. Tube: Knightsbridge.

Silver Moon Women's Bookshop   This place stocks thousands of titles by and about women, plus videos, jewelry, and a large selection of lesbian books. 64–68 Charing Cross Rd., WC2. ✆ 020/7836-7906. Tube: Leicester Sq.

Stanfords   Established in 1852, Stanfords is the world's largest map shop. Many maps, which include worldwide touring and survey maps, are unavailable elsewhere. It's also London's best travel bookstore (with a complete selection of Frommer's guides!). 12–14 Long Acre, WC2. ✆ 020/7836-1321. Tube: Covent Garden.

CASHMERE & WOOLENS

Scotch House   For top-quality woolen fabrics and garments, go to Scotch House, renowned for its wide selection of cashmere and wool knitwear for men, women, and children. Also available is a wide range of tartan garments and accessories, as well as Scottish tweed classics. 157–165 Regent St., W1. ✆ 020/7734-0203. Tube: Piccadilly Circus.

Westaway & Westaway   Stopping here is a substitute for a trip to Scotland. You'll find a range of kilts, scarves, waistcoats, capes, dressing gowns, and rugs in authentic tartans. The staff is knowledgeable about the clan symbols. They sell cashmere, camelhair, and Shetland knitwear, Harris tweed jackets, Burberry raincoats, and men's cashmere overcoats. 64–65 Great Russell St. (opposite the British Museum), WC1. ℂ 020/7405-4479. Tube: Tottenham Court Rd. or Holborn.

CHINA, GLASS & SILVER

Royal Doulton   Founded in the 1930s, this store has one of the largest inventories of china in Britain. A wide range of English bone china, as well as crystal and giftware, is sold. The firm specializes, of course, in Royal Doulton, plus Minton, Royal Crown Derby, and Aynsley china; Lladro figures; David Winter Cottages; Border Fine Arts; and other famous names. Royal Doulton also sells cutlery. The January and July sales are excellent. 154 Regent St., W1. ℂ 020/7734-3184. Tube: Piccadilly Circus or Oxford Circus.

London Silver Vaults *(Finds*   Don't let the out-of-the-way location or the façade's lack of charm slow you down. Downstairs, you go into vaults—40 in all—that are filled with tons of silver and silverplate, plus a collection of jewelry. It's a staggering selection of old to new, with excellent prices and friendly dealers. Chancery House, 53–64 Chancery Lane, WC2. ℂ 020/7242-3844. Tube: Chancery Lane.

Thomas Goode   This is one of the most famous emporiums in Britain; it's worth visiting for its architectural interest and nostalgic allure. Originally built in 1876, Goode's has 14 rooms loaded with porcelain, gifts, candles, silver, tableware, and even a private museum. There's also a tearoom-cum-restaurant tucked into the corner. 19 S. Audley St., W1. ℂ 020/7499-2823. Tube: Bond St., Green Park, or Marble Arch.

FASHION

Austin Reed   Austin Reed has long stood for superior-quality clothing and excellent tailoring. Chester Barrie's off-the-rack suits, for example, are said to fit like tailor-made. The polite employees are honest about telling you what looks good. The store has a wide variety of top-notch jackets and suits, and men can outfit themselves from dressing gowns to overcoats. For women, there are carefully selected suits, separates, coats, shirts, knitwear, and accessories. 103–113 Regent St., W1. ℂ 020/7734-6789. Tube: Piccadilly Circus.

Berk   This store boasts one of the largest collections of cashmere sweaters in London—at least the top brands. The outlet also carries capes, stoles, scarves, and camelhair sweaters. 46 Burlington Arcade, Piccadilly, W1. ☎ 020/7493-0028. Tube: Piccadilly Circus or Green Park.

Burberry   The name has been synonymous with raincoats ever since Edward VII ordered his valet to "bring my Burberry" when the skies threatened. An impeccably trained staff sells the famous raincoats, plus excellent men's shirts, sportswear, knitwear, and accessories. Raincoats are available in women's sizes and styles as well. Prices are high, but you get quality and prestige. 18–22 Haymarket, SW1. ☎ 020/7930-3343. Tube: Piccadilly Circus.

Dr. Marten's Department Store   Teens come to worship at Doc Marten's because the prices here are better than in the United States or Europe. The shoes have become so popular internationally that they have spawned an entire store selling dozens of styles of footwear, as well as accessories, gifts, and an ever-expanding range of clothes. 1–4 King St., WC2. ☎ 020/7497-1460. Tube: Covent Garden.

Hilditch & Key   The finest name in men's shirts, Hilditch & Key has been in business since 1899. The two shops on this street offer men's clothing (including a custom-made shirt service) and women's ready-made shirts. There's also an outstanding tie collection. Shirts go for half price during the twice-yearly sales; men fly in from all over the world for them. 37 and 73 Jermyn St., SW1. ☎ 020/7734-4707. Tube: Piccadilly Circus or Green Park.

Jigsaw   Branches of this fashion chain are numerous, but the Long Acre branch features trendy, middle-market womenswear and children's clothing. Around the corner, the Floral Street shop carries menswear, including a wide range of colored moleskin items. 21 Long Acre, WC2. ☎ 020/7240-3855. Tube: Covent Garden. Also at 9–10 Floral St., WC2 (☎ 020/7240-5651) and other locations throughout London.

Jigsaw Menswear   This store is for the male who wants to be a bit daring in his dress. You've heard of the gray flannel suit, but what about the gray flannel kilt with not a single tartan on it? The workers at Heathrow must have inspired the wool jumpsuits. There is also a selection of moleskin suits, black leather pants, and all the latest styles. 126 King's Rd., SW3. ☎ 020/7823-7304. Tube: Sloane Sq.

Next   This chain of "affordable fashion" stores saw its heyday in the 1980s, when it was celebrated for its main-street fashion revolution. No longer at its peak, it still merits a stopover. The look is still very contemporary, with a continental flair worn not only by men and women, but kids, too. 19–20 Long Acre, WC2. ☎ 020/7836-1516. Tube: Covent Garden. Other locations throughout London.

Reiss In a city where men's clothing often sells at celestial prices, Reiss is a relief for reasonable sporty and casual wear. Take your pick from everything from pullovers to rugged cargo pants. 114 King's Rd., SW3. ℂ 020/7225-4910. Tube: Sloane Sq.

SU214 If you find $5,000 a bit much for a Savile Row suit, you can buzz over here for a made-to-measure suit that evokes the look, with suits beginning at $500. In-house consultants are on hand for fittings, and you'll emerge looking quite English in a three-button pin-striped jacket and narrow pants. Of course, a mauve shirt and a mauve tie will help you achieve the look as well. 214 Oxford St., W1. ℂ 020/7927-0104. Tube: Bond St.

Thomas Pink This Jermyn Street shirtmaker, named after an 18th-century Mayfair tailor, gave the world the phrase "in the pink." It has a prestigious reputation for well-made cotton shirts, for men and women. The shirts are created from the finest two-fold Egyptian and Sea Island pure-cotton poplin. Some patterns are classic, others new and unusual. All are generously cut with long tails and finished with a choice of double cuffs or single-button cuffs. A small pink square in the tail tells all. 85 Jermyn St., SW1. ℂ 020/7930-6364. Tube: Green Park.

Turnbull & Asser Over the years, everyone from David Bowie to Ronald Reagan has been seen in a custom-made shirt from Turnbull & Asser. Excellent craftsmanship and simple lines—even bold colors—distinguish these shirts. The outlet also sells shirts and blouses to women, a clientele that has ranged from Jacqueline Bisset to Candice Bergen. Note that T&A shirts come in only one sleeve length and are then altered to fit. The sales department will inform you that its made-to-measure service takes 10 to 12 weeks, and you must order at least a half dozen. Of course, the monograms are included. 71–72 Jermyn St., SW1. ℂ 020/7808-3000. Tube: Piccadilly Circus or Green Park.

THE CUTTING EDGE

Currently the most cutting-edge shopping street in London is **Conduit Street,** W1 in Mayfair (Tube: Oxford Circus). Once known for its dowdy airline offices, it is now London's smartest fashion street. Trendy shops are opening between Regent Street and the "blue chip" boutiques of New Bond Street. Current stars include **Vivienne Westwood,** 44 Conduit St., W1 (ℂ 020/7439-1109), who has overcome her punk origins. She's now the grande dame of

English fashion. See below for her flagship store. **Krizia,** 24 Conduit St., W1 (*©* **020/7491-4989**), the fashion rage of Rome since the 1950s, operates this London flagship store, which displays not only Krizia's clothing lines but her luxury home goods as well.

For muted fashion elegance, **Yohji Yamamoto,** 14–15 Conduit St., W1 (*©* **020/7491-4129**), is hard to beat, and **Issey Miyake,** 52 Conduit St., W1 (*©* **020/7851-4600**), is the Japanese master of minimalist. **YMC,** 6 Conduit St., W1 (*©* **020/7499-0825**) stands for "You Must Create," and this shop's fresh, clean, simple fashions win new admirers every year.

Finally, one of the most avant garde British designers in history, **Alexander McQueen,** 47 Conduit St., W1 (*©* **020/7734-2340**), has moved in to give the neighborhood his blessing. No one pays more attention to detail and craftsmanship than the celebrated McQueen.

Anya Hindmarch   Although her bags are sold at Harvey Nichols, Liberty, Harrods, and throughout the U.S. and Europe, this is the only place to see the complete range of Anya Hindmarch's hand-bags, wallets, purses, and key holders. Smaller items start at about £45 ($67.50), whereas handbag prices start at £198 ($297), with alligator being the most expensive. There's a limited custom-made service; bring in your fabric if you want a bag to match. 15–17 Pont St., SW3. *©* 020/7838-9177. Tube: Sloane Sq. or Knightsbridge.

Browns   This is the only place in London to find the designs of Alexander McQueen, head of the House of Givenchy in Paris. Producing his own cottons, silks, and plastics, McQueen creates revealing, feminine women's couture and ready-to-wear, and has started a menswear line. McQueen made his reputation creating shock-value apparel more photographed than worn. But recently fashion critics have called his outfits more "consumer friendly." Browns has introduced "Browns Living," an array of lifestyle products. 23–27 S. Molton St., W1. *©* 020/7491-7833. Tube: Bond St.

Egg   This shop is hot, hot, hot with fashionistas. It features imag-inatively designed, contemporary clothing by Indian textile designer Asha Sarabhai and knitwear by Eskandar. Designs created from handmade textiles from a workshop in India range from everyday dresses and coats to hand-embroidered silk coats. Crafts and ceram-ics are also available. Closed Sunday and Monday. 36 Kinnerton St., SW1 *©* 020/7235-9315. Tube: Hyde Park Corner or Knightsbridge.

Hennes Here are copies of hot-off-the-catwalk fashions at afford-able prices. While the quality isn't to brag about, the prices are. For disposable cutting-edge fashion, you can't beat it. 261–271 Regent St., W1. ✆ 020/7493-4004. Tube: Oxford Circus.

Vivienne Westwood No one in British fashion is hotter than Vivienne Westwood. While it's possible to purchase some Westwood pieces around the world, her U.K. shops are the best places to find her full range of designs. The flagship location concentrates on her couture line, known as the Gold Label. Using a wide range of British resources, Westwood creates jackets, skirts, trousers, blouses, dresses, and evening dresses. She even came out with her own fragrance in 1997. The World's End branch carries casual designs, including T-shirts, jeans, and sportswear. 6 Davies St., W1. ✆ 020/7629-3757. Tube: Bond St; World's End branch: 430 King's Rd., SW3 ✆ 020/7352-6551; Tube: Sloane Sq.

VINTAGE & SECONDHAND

Note that there's no VAT refund on used clothing.

Annie's Vintage Costume and Textiles *Finds* The shop con-centrates on carefully preserved dresses from the 1920s and 1930s, but has a range of clothing and textiles from the 1880s through the 1960s. A 1920s fully-beaded dress will run you about £400 ($600), but there are scarves for £5 ($7.50), camisoles for £20 ($30), and a range of exceptional pieces priced between £50 and £60 ($75 and $90). Clothing is located on the main floor; textiles, including old lace, bed linens, and tapestries, are upstairs. 10 Camden Passage, N1. ✆ 020/7359-0796. Tube: Northern Line to Angel.

Pandora A London institution since the 1940s, Pandora stands in Knightsbridge, a stone's throw from Harrods. Several times a week, chauffeurs drive up with bundles packed by England's gentry. One woman voted best-dressed at Ascot several years ago was wear-ing a secondhand dress acquired here. Prices are generally one-third to one-half the retail value. Chanel and Anne Klein are among the designers represented. Outfits are usually no more than two seasons old. 16–22 Cheval Place, SW7. ✆ 020/7589-5289. Tube: Knightsbridge.

FOOD

English food has come a long way; it's worth enjoying and bringing home. Don't pass up the Food Halls in Harrods. Also, Fortnum & Mason is internationally famous as a food emporium. See "The Department Stores," above.

Charbonnel et Walker   Charbonnel et Walker is famous for its hot chocolate in winter (buy it by the tin) and its strawberries-and-cream chocolates during the Season. The firm will send messages of thanks or love spelled out on the chocolates themselves. Ready-made presentation boxes are also available. 1 The Royal Arcade, 28 Old Bond St., W1. ✆ 020/7491-0939. Tube: Green Park.

HOME DESIGN & HOUSEWARES

The Conran Shop   You'll find high style at reasonable prices from the man who invented it all for Britain: Sir Terence Conran. It's great for gifts, home furnishings, and tabletop. Michelin House, 81 Fulham Rd., SW3. ✆ 020/7589-7401. Tube: South Kensington.

Designers Guild   Often copied but never outdone—after more than 26 years in business, creative director Tricia Guild and her young designers still lead the pack in all that's bright and whimsical. There's an exclusive line of handmade furniture and accessories at the no. 267–271 location, and wallpaper and more than 2,000 fabrics at no. 275–277. The colors remain vivid, and the designs irreverent. Also available are children's accessories, toys, crockery, and cutlery. 267–271 and 275–277 King's Rd., SW3. ✆ 020/7351-5775. Tube: Sloane Sq.

JEWELRY

Asprey & Garrard   Previously known as Garrard & Co., this recently merged jeweler specializes in both antique and modern jewelry and silverware. The in-house designers also produce pieces to order and do repairs. You can have a pair of pearl earrings or silver cufflinks for a mere £60 ($102)—but the prices go nowhere but up from there. 167 New Bond St., W1. ✆ 020/7493-6767. Tube: Green Park.

Lesley Craze Gallery/Craze 2/C2 Plus   This complex has developed a reputation as a showcase of the best contemporary British jewelry and textile design. The gallery shop focuses on precious metals and includes pieces by such renowned designers as Wendy Ramshaw. Prices start at £60 ($90). Craze 2 features costume jewelry in materials ranging from bronze to paper, with prices starting at £12 ($18). C2 Plus features contemporary textile designs, including wall hangings, scarves, and ties by artists such as Jo Barker, Dawn DuPree, and Victoria Richards. C2 Plus has recently added a hanging gallery to display its textiles and wall hangings. 34 Clerkenwell Green, EC1. ✆ 020/7608-0393 (Gallery), 020/7251-0381 (Craze 2), 020/7251-9200 (C2 Plus). Tube: Farringdon.

LINENS

Irish Linen Company This royal-warrant boutique carries items crafted of Irish linen, including hand-embroidered handkerchiefs and bed and table linens. 35–36 Burlington Arcade, W1. ✆ **020/7493-8949.** Tube: Green Park or Piccadilly Circus.

MUSEUM SHOPS

Victoria and Albert Museum Gift Shop Run by the Craft Council, this is the best museum shop in London—indeed, one of the best in the world. It sells cards, a fabulous selection of art books, and the usual items, along with reproductions from the museum archives. Cromwell Rd., SW7. ✆ **020/7938-8500.** Tube: South Kensington.

MUSIC

Collectors should browse **Notting Hill;** there's a handful of good shops near the Notting Hill Gate Tube stop. Also browse **Soho** in the Wardour Street area, near the Tottenham Court Road Tube stop. Sometimes dealers show up at Covent Garden on the weekends.

In addition to the two below, also worth checking out is the ubiquitous **Our Price** chain, which offers only current chart-toppers, but usually at great prices.

Tower Records Attracting the throngs from a neighborhood whose pedestrian traffic is almost overwhelming, this is one of the largest record and CD stores in Europe. Sprawling over four floors, it's practically a tourist attraction in its own right. In addition to a huge selection, there's everything on the cutting edge of technology, hardware and software, CD-ROMs, and laser discs. 1 Piccadilly Circus, W1. ✆ **020/7439-2500.** Tube: Piccadilly Circus. Other locations throughout London.

Virgin Megastore If a record has just been released—and if it's worth hearing in the first place—chances are this store carries it. It's like a musical grocery store, and you get to hear the release on headphones at listening stations before purchase. Even rock stars come here to pick up new releases. A large selection of classical and jazz recordings is sold, as are computer software and video games. In between selecting your favorites, you can enjoy a coffee at the cafe or purchase an airline ticket from the Virgin Atlantic office. 14–16 Oxford St., W1. ✆ **020/7631-1234.** Tube: Tottenham Court Rd. Also at Kings Walk Shopping Centre, Kings Rd., Chelsea SW3. ✆ **020/7591-0957.** Tube: Sloane Sq.

SHOES

Also see **Dr. Marten's Department Store** in "Fashion," above.

Natural Shoe Store Shoes for men and women are stocked in this shop, which also does repairs. The selection includes all comfort and quality footwear, from Birkenstock to the British classics. 21 Neal St., WC2. ✆ 020/7836-5254. Tube: Covent Garden.

Shelly's This is the flagship of the mother of all London shoe shops, where they sell everything from tiny-tot hip shoes to grown-up hip shoes and boots at affordable prices. They're famous for their Dr. Marten's, but there's much more. 266–270 Regent St., W1. ✆ 020/7287-0939. Tube: Oxford Circus. Other locations throughout London.

STATIONERY & PAPER GOODS

Paperchase This flagship store has three floors of paper products, including handmade paper, wrapping paper, ribbons, picture frames, and a huge selection of greeting cards. It's the best of its kind in London. 213 Tottenham Court Rd., W1. ✆ 020/7467-6200. Tube: Goodge St. or Tottenham Court Rd. Other locations throughout London.

TEA

The Tea House This shop sells everything associated with tea, tea drinking, and teatime. It boasts more than 70 quality teas and tisanes, including whole-fruit blends, the best tea of China (Gunpowder, jasmine with flowers), India (Assam leaf, choice Darjeeling), Japan (Genmaicha green), and Sri Lanka (pure Ceylon), plus such longtime favorite English blended teas as Earl Grey. The shop also offers novelty teapots and mugs. 15 Neal St., WC2 ✆ 020/7420-7539. Tube: Covent Garden.

Of course, don't forget to visit **Fortnum & Mason** as well, (see "The Department Stores," above).

TOYS

Hamleys This flagship is the finest toyshop in the world—more than 35,000 toys and games on seven floors of fun and magic. The huge selection includes soft, cuddly stuffed animals as well as dolls, radio-controlled cars, train sets, model kits, board games, outdoor toys, and computer games. 188–196 Regent St., W1. ✆ 020/7494-2000. Tube: Oxford Circus. Also at Covent Garden and Heathrow Airport.

4 Street & Flea Markets

If Mayfair stores are not your cup of tea, you'll have more fun, and find a better bargain, at any of the city's street and flea markets.

THE WEST END Covent Garden Market (© 020/7836-9136; Tube: Covent Garden), the most famous market in England, offers several markets daily from 9am to 6:30pm (we think it's most fun to come on Sunday). It can be a little confusing until you dive in and explore. **Apple Market** is the bustling market in the courtyard, where traders sell, well, everything. Many of the items are what the English call collectible nostalgia; a wide array of glassware and ceramics, leather goods, toys, clothes, hats, and jewelry. Some of the merchandise is truly unusual. Many items are handmade, with some of the craftspeople selling their own wares—except on Mondays, when antiques dealers take over. Out back is **Jubilee Market** (© 020/7836-2139), also an antiques market on Mondays. Every other day, it's sort of a fancy hippie market with cheap clothes and books. Out front there are a few tents of cheap stuff, except on Monday.

The market itself (in a superbly restored hall) is one of the best shopping venues in London. Specialty shops sell fashions and herbs, gifts and toys, books and dollhouses, cigars, and much more. There are bookshops and branches of famous stores (Hamleys, The Body Shop), and prices are kept moderate.

St. Martin-in-the-Fields Market (Tube: Charing Cross) is good for teens and hipsters who can make do with imports from India and South America, crafts, and local football souvenirs. It's located near Trafalgar Square and Covent Garden; hours are Monday to Saturday from 11am to 5pm, and Sunday from noon to 5pm.

Berwick Street Market (Tube: Oxford Circus or Tottenham Court Road) may be the only street market in the world that's flanked by two rows of strip clubs, porno stores, and adult-movie dens. Don't let that put you off. Humming 6 days a week in the scarlet heart of Soho, this array of stalls and booths sells probably the best and cheapest fruit and vegetables in town. It also hawks ancient records, tapes, books, and old magazines, any of which may turn out to be collectors' items one day. It's open Monday to Saturday from 8am to 5pm.

On Sunday mornings along **Bayswater Road,** artists hang their work on the railings along the edge of Hyde Park and Kensington Gardens for more than a mile. If the weather's right, start at Marble Arch and walk. You'll see the same thing on the railings of Green Park along Piccadilly on Saturday afternoon.

NOTTING HILL Portobello Market (Tube: Notting Hill Gate) is a magnet for collectors of anything. It's mainly a Saturday event, from 6am to 5pm. You needn't be here at the crack of dawn; 9am is fine. Once known mainly for fruit and vegetables (still sold throughout the week), in the past decades Portobello has become synonymous with antiques.

The market is divided into three major sections. The most crowded is the antiques section, running between Colville Road and Chepstow Villas to the south. (*Warning:* Be careful of pickpockets in this area.) The second section (and the oldest part) is the fruit and vegetable market, lying between Westway and Colville Road. In the third and final section, there's a flea market where Londoners sell bric-a-brac and lots of secondhand goods they didn't really want in the first place. But looking around still makes for interesting fun.

The serious collector can pick up a helpful official guide, *Saturday Antique Market: Portobello Road & Westbourne Grove,* published by the Portobello Antique Dealers Association. It lists where to find what, be it music boxes, lace, or 19th-century photographs.

Note: Some 90 antiques and art shops along Portobello Road are open during the week when the street market is closed. This is a better time for the serious collector to shop because you'll get more attention from dealers and you won't be distracted by the organ grinder.

7

London After Dark

London's pulsating scene is the most vibrant in Europe. Although pubs still close at 11pm, the city is staying up later. More and more clubs extend partying into the wee hours. London is on a real high right now, especially in terms of music and dance; much of the current techno and electronica originated in London clubs.

London nightlife is always in a state of flux. What's hot today probably just opened and many clubs have the lifespan of fruit flies. London nightlife is not just music and dance clubs. The city abounds with the world's best theater, pubs oozing historic charm, and many more options for a night out.

1 The Play's the Thing: London's Theater Scene

Even more than New York, London is the theater capital of the world. The number and variety of productions and standards of acting and directing are unrivaled. The new Globe Theatre is an exciting addition to the theater scene. Because the Globe is also a sightseeing attraction, it's previewed in chapter 5, "Exploring London." Few things in London are as entertaining and rewarding as the theater.

TICKET AGENCIES If your heart is set on seeing a specific show, particularly a big hit, reserve in advance. For tickets and information before you go, try **Global Tickets,** 234 W. 44th St., Suite 1000, New York, NY 10036 (© **800/223-6108** or 212/332-2435; www. globaltickets.com). Their London office is at the British Visitors Center, 1 Regents St., W1 V1PJ (© 020/7734-4555), or at the Harrods ticket desk, 87–135 Brompton Rd. (© 020/7589-9109) opposite the British Airways desk. They'll mail your tickets, fax a confirmation, or leave them at the box office. Instant confirmations are available with "overseas" rates for most shows. A booking and handling fee of up to 20% is added to the price. You might also call **Keith Prowse/First Call** (© **800/669-8681** or 212/398-1430). They have offices in the U.S. where you can reserve months in advance: Suite 1000, 234 W. 44th St., New York, NY 10036.

⟨Tips⟩ Finding Out What's Going On

Weekly publications *Time Out* and *Where* provide the most complete entertainment listings, with information on music and dance as well as London's theater scene, including everything from big-budget West End shows to fringe productions. Daily newspapers, notably *The Times* and the *Daily Telegraph*, also provide listings. The arts section of the weekend *Independent* is also a good source.

If you want to take full advantage of London's arts scene, your best bet is to do a bit of research before you leave. To get an idea of what's going on, check out *Time Out*'s World Wide Web page at www.timeout.co.uk. *Time Out* is available at many international newsstands in the U.S. and Canada. In London, it can be picked up almost anywhere.

Another option is **Theatre Direct International** (TDI) (© 800/334-8457, U.S. only), which specializes in London fringe theater tickets, but also has tickets to major productions, including the Royal National Theatre and Barbican. The service allows you to arrive in London with your tickets or have them held for you at the box office.

GALLERY & DISCOUNT TICKETS   Sometimes gallery seats (the cheapest) are sold the day of the performance; head to the box office early in the day and, because these are not reserved seats, return an hour before the performance to queue up. Many theaters offer reduced-price tickets to students on a standby basis. When available, these tickets are sold 30 minutes before curtain. Line up early for popular shows, as standby tickets get snapped up. Of course, you'll need a valid student ID.

The **Society of London Theatre** (© 020/7557-6700) operates the Half-Price Ticket Booth in Leicester Square, where tickets for many shows are available at half price, plus a £2 ($3) service charge. Tickets (limited to four per person) are sold only on the day of performance. You cannot return tickets, and credit cards are not accepted. Hours are daily from 10am to 6pm. We prefer this agency to others who populate Leicester Square. Some might offer you a legitimate discount, but over the years readers have lodged dozens of complaints that their so-called discount ticket turned out to be more expensive than that actually charged at the theater box office. Exercise caution when purchasing tickets at other booths.

MAJOR THEATERS & COMPANIES

Barbican Theatre—Royal Shakespeare Company The Barbican is the London home of the Royal Shakespeare Company, one of the world's finest. The core of its repertory remains the Bard, but it also presents a wide-ranging program in its two theaters. There are three productions in repertory each week in the Barbican Theatre: a 2,000-seat main auditorium with excellent sightlines throughout, thanks to a raked stage. The Pit, a studio space, is where the company's new writing is presented. The RSC performs here and at Stratford-upon-Avon. It is in residence in London during the winter; in the summer, it tours England and abroad. In the Barbican Centre, Silk St., Barbican, EC2Y. ✆ **020/7638-8891**. Barbican Theatre £5–£28 ($7.50–$42); the Pit £7–£22 ($10.50–$33) matinees and evening performances. Box office daily 9am–8pm. Tube: Barbican or Moorgate.

Royal Court Theatre This theater, always a leader in provocative, cutting-edge drama, reopened in February 2000. In the 1950s, it staged the plays of the angry young men, notably John Osborne's then-sensational *Look Back in Anger;* earlier it debuted the plays of George Bernard Shaw. A recent work was *The Beauty Queen of Leenane,* which won a Tony on Broadway. It is home to the English Stage Company. Sloane Sq., SW1. ✆ **020/7565-5000**. Tickets £5–£22.50 ($7.50–$33.75). Box office 10am–6pm. Tube: Sloane Sq.

Royal National Theatre Home to one of the world's greatest stage companies, the Royal National Theatre is three theaters: the Olivier, reminiscent of a Greek amphitheater with its open stage; the more traditional Lyttelton; and the Cottesloe, with its flexible stage and seating. The National presents the finest in world theater, from classic drama to award-winning new plays, including comedies, musicals, and shows for young people. There is a choice of at least six plays at any one time. As an arts center and gathering place, it has an amazing selection of bars, cafes, and restaurants, and offers free foyer music and exhibitions, short early-evening performances, bookshops, backstage tours, riverside walks, and terraces. You can have a three-course meal in Mezzanine, the National's restaurant; enjoy a light meal in the brasserie-style Terrace cafe; or have a snack in one of the coffee bars. South Bank, SE1. ✆ **020/7452-3400**. Tickets £9–£27 ($13.50–$40.50); midweek matinees, Saturday matinees, and previews cost less. Tube: Waterloo, Embankment, or Charing Cross.

Shakespeare's Globe Theatre In May 1997, the new Globe Theatre—a replica of the Elizabethan original, thatched roof and all—staged its first slate of plays (*Henry V* and *A Winter's Tale*) on the site of the 16th-century theater where the Bard originally staged his work.

Productions vary in style and setting; not all are performed in Elizabethan costume. In keeping with the historic setting (when performances took place in the afternoon), the theater is floodlit during evening performances to replicate daylight. Theatergoers sit on wooden benches like those of yore, but now you can rent a cushion. About 500 "groundlings" can stand in the uncovered yard around the stage, as they did in Shakespeare's day. Mark Rylance, the artistic director, wants the experience to be as authentic as possible.

From May to September, the company holds performances Tuesday to Saturday at 3pm and 7pm, and Sunday at 4pm. The schedule is limited in winter, as this is essentially an outdoor theater. Performances last 2½ to 4 hours.

Also in the works is a second theater, the Inigo Jones Theatre, based on the architect's designs from the 1600s, where plays will be staged year-round. For details on the exhibition that tells the story of the painstaking re-creation of the Globe, as well as guided tours of the theatre, see "More Central London Attractions" in chapter 5, "Exploring London." New Globe Walk, Bankside, SE1. © 020/7902-1400. Box office: 020/7401-9919. Tickets £5 ($7.50) for groundlings, £11–£27 ($16.50–$40.50) for gallery seats. Exhibition tickets £7.50 ($11.25); seniors and students £6 ($9); ages 5–15 £5 ($7.50) Tube: Mansion House or Blackfriars.

FRINGE THEATER

Some of the best theater in London is performed on the "fringe"— at the dozens of theaters devoted to alternative plays, revivals, contemporary dramas, and musicals. These shows are usually more adventurous than established West End productions; they are also consistently lower in price. Expect to pay from £6 to £27 ($9–$40.50). Most offer discounted seats to students and seniors.

Fringe theaters are scattered around London. Check the listings in *Time Out* for schedules and show times. Some of the more popular theaters are listed below; call for details on current productions.

Almeida Theatre   Home to the Festival of Contemporary Music (also called the Almeida Opera) from mid-June to mid-July, the Almeida is known for its adventurous staging of new and classic plays. The theater's legendary status is validated by consistently good productions at lower-than-average prices. Among the recent celebrated productions have been *Hamlet* with Ralph Fiennes and *Medea* with Dame Diana Rigg. Performances are usually held

Monday to Saturday. Almeida St., N1. © 020/7359-4404. Tickets £6–£27 ($9–$40.50). Box office Mon–Sat 9:30am–6pm. Tube: Northern Line to Angel or Victoria Line to Highbury & Islington.

The King's Head   London's most famous fringe locale, the King's Head is also the city's oldest pub-theater. Despite its tiny stage, the theater is heavy on musicals; several have gone on to become successful West End productions.

Matinees are held on Saturday and Sunday at 3:30pm. Evening performances from Tuesday to Saturday are at 8pm. 115 Upper St., N1. © 020/7226-1916. Tickets £9–£14 ($13.50–$21). Box office Mon–Sat 10am–8pm; Sat 11am–8pm; Sun 10am–4pm. Tube: Northern Line to Angel.

Young Vic   Young Vic presents classical and modern plays in the round for theatergoers of all ages and backgrounds, but primarily focuses on young adults. Recent productions have included Shakespeare, Ibsen, Arthur Miller, and specially commissioned plays for children. Call for times, as they can fluctuate. 66 The Cut, Waterloo, SE1. © 020/7928-6363. Tickets £18 ($27) adults, £12 ($18) seniors, £9 ($13.50) students and children. Box office Mon–Sat 10am–8pm. Performances Mon–Sat 7 or 7:30pm; matinee Sat 2pm. Tube: Waterloo or Southwark.

2 London's Classical Music & Dance Scene

Currently, London supports five major orchestras—the London Symphony, the Royal Philharmonic, the Philharmonia Orchestra, the BBC Symphony, and the BBC Philharmonic—several choirs, and many smaller chamber groups and historic-instrument ensembles. Look for the London Sinfonietta, the English Chamber Orchestra, and of course, the Academy of St. Martin-in-the-Fields. Performances are in the South Banks Arts Centre and the Barbican.

British Music Information Centre, 10 Stratford Place, W1 (© 020/7499-8567), is the city's resource center for serious music. It's open Monday to Friday, noon to 5pm and provides free telephone and walk-in information on current and upcoming events. Recitals featuring 20th-century British classical compositions cost up to £5 ($7.50) and are offered here weekly, usually on Tuesday and Thursday at 7:30pm; call for day and time. Since capacity is limited to 40, you may want to check early. Take the Tube to Bond Street.

Barbican Centre—London Symphony Orchestra (& more) The largest art and exhibition center in Western Europe, the roomy and comfortable Barbican complex is a perfect setting for music and theater. Barbican Hall is the permanent home address of the London Symphony Orchestra as well as host to visiting orchestras and performers, from classical to jazz, folk, and world music.

In addition to the hall and two theaters, Barbican Centre includes The Barbican Art Gallery, the Concourse Gallery and foyer exhibition spaces; Cinemas One and Two, which show recently released mainstream films and film series; the Barbican Library, a lending library that places a strong emphasis on the arts; the Conservatory, one of London's largest plant houses; and restaurants, cafes, and bars. Silk St., the City, EC2. ℭ 020/7638-8891. www.iso.co.uk. Tickets £6.50–£40 ($9.75–$60). Box office daily 9am–8pm. Tube: Barbican or Moorgate.

English National Opera   Built in 1904 as a variety theater and converted into an opera house in 1968, the London Coliseum is the city's largest theater. One of two national opera companies, the English National Opera performs a range from classics to Gilbert and Sullivan to new and experimental works. All performances are in English. A repertory of 18 to 20 productions is presented 5 or 6 nights a week for 11 months of the year (dark in July). Although balcony seats are cheaper, many visitors seem to prefer the upper circle or dress circle. London Coliseum, St. Martin's Lane, WC2. ℭ 020/ 7632-8300. Tickets £6–£14 ($10.20–$23.80) balcony, £17–£60 ($28.90–$102) upper or dress circle or stalls; about 100 discount balcony tickets sold on the day of performance from 10am. Tube: Charing Cross or Leicester Sq.

Royal Albert Hall   Opened in 1871 and dedicated to the memory of Victoria's consort, Prince Albert, this circular building holds one of the world's most famous auditoriums. With a seating capacity of 5,200, it's a popular place to hear music by stars. Occasional sporting events (especially boxing) figure strongly here, too.

Since 1941, the hall has hosted the BBC Henry Wood Promenade Concerts, known as "The Proms," an annual series that lasts for 8 weeks between mid-July and mid-September. The Proms have been a British tradition since 1895. Although most of the audience occupies reserved seats, true aficionados usually opt for standing room in the orchestra pit, with close-up views of the musicians on stage. Newly commissioned works are often premiered here. The final evening is the most traditional; the rousing favorites "Jerusalem" or "Land of Hope and Glory" echo through the hall. For tickets, call **TicketMaster** (ℭ **020/7344-4444**) directly. Kensington Gore, SW7 2AP. ℭ **020/7589-8212**. Tickets £7.50–£130 ($11.25–$195), depending on the event. Box office daily 9am–9pm. Tube: South Kensington.

Royal Festival Hall In the aftermath of World War II, the principal site of London's music scene shifted to the south bank of the Thames. Three of the most acoustically perfect concert halls in the world were erected between 1951 and 1964. They include Royal Festival Hall, the Queen Elizabeth Hall, and the Purcell Room. They hold more than 1,200 performances a year, including classical music, ballet, jazz, popular music, and dance. Also here is the internationally renowned Hayward Gallery (see chapter 5, "Exploring London").

Royal Festival Hall, which opens daily at 10am, offers an extensive array of things to see and do, including free exhibitions in the foyers and free lunchtime music at 12:30pm. On Friday, Commuter Jazz in the foyer, from 5:15 to 6:45pm, is free. The Poetry Library is open from Tuesday to Sunday from11am to 8pm, and shops display a selection of books, records, and crafts. The Festival Buffet has food at reasonable prices, and bars dot the foyers. The People's Palace offers lunch and dinner with a panoramic view of the River Thames. Reservations, by calling ⓒ 020/7928-9999, are recommended. On the South Bank, SE1. ⓒ **020/7960-4242**. Tickets £5–£50 ($7.50–$75). Box office daily 9am–9pm. Tube: Waterloo or Embankment.

The Royal Opera House—The Royal Ballet & the Royal Opera The Royal Ballet and the Royal Opera are at home again in a magnificently restored theater. Opera and ballet aficionados hardly recognize the renovated place, with its spectacular new public spaces, including the Vilar Floral Hall, a rooftop restaurant, and bars and shops. The northeast corner of one of London's most famous public squares has been transformed, finally realizing Inigo Jones's vision for this colonnaded piazza. Backstage tours are possible daily at 10:30am, 12:30pm, and 2:30pm (not on Sunday or matinee days).

Performances of the Royal Opera are usually sung in the original language with supertitles. The Royal Ballet, which compares with companies such as the Kirov and the Paris Opera Ballet, performs a repertory with a tilt toward the classics, including works by choreographer-directors Sir Frederick Ashton and Sir Kenneth MacMillan. Bow St., Covent Garden, WC2. ⓒ **020/7304-4000**. Tickets £6–£150 ($9–$225). Box office Mon–Sat 10am–8pm. Tube: Covent Garden.

Sadler's Wells Theatre This is a premier venue for dance and opera. It occupies the site of a theater that was built in 1683. In the early 1990s, the turn-of-the-century theater was demolished, and construction began on an innovative new design completed at the end of 1998. The original facade has been retained, but the interior has been completely revamped to create a stylish cutting-edge theater design. The new theater offers both traditional and experimental dance. Rosebery Ave., EC1. ℭ **020/7314-8800**. Tickets £8.50–£60 ($14.45–$102). Performances usually 8pm. Box office Mon–Sat 9am–8:30pm. Tube: Northern Line to Angel.

3 The Club & Music Scene

It's the nature of live music and dance clubs to come and go with alarming speed, or shift violently from one trend to another. *Time Out* is the best way to keep up.

ROCK AND POP

Bagley's Studios   The premises of this place are vast, echoing, a bit grimy, and warehouse-like. Set in the bleak industrial landscape behind King's Cross Station, its interior is transformed 3 nights a week into an animated rave. Its two huge floors are divided into trios of individual rooms, with their own ambience and sound system. Choices will probably include sites devoted to garage, club classics as promoted by AM/FM radio, "banging" (hard house) music, and "bubbly" dance music. If you happen to be in London on a weeknight, various social groups, including lots of East Indian social clubs, rent the place for gatherings, some of which might be open to the public. Saturday night "Freedom" parties are more fun. A crowd in its 20s and early 30s shows up here, and the joint is jumping at 2am. King's Cross Freigh Depot, off York Way, N1. ℭ **020/ 7278-2777**. Cover £10–£20 ($15–$30). Guaranteed openings Fri–Sun 10pm–7am. Otherwise, openings depend on whether a promoter has booked the space. Tube: King's Cross.

Barfly Club   In a dingy residential neighborhood in north London, this traditional-looking pub is distinguished by the roster of rock-and-roll bands that come from throughout the U.K. for bouts of beer and high-energy music. A recorded announcement tells fans—mostly in their 20s—the lineup on any given night, along with instructions on how to reach the place through a warren of narrow streets. You can get virtually anything here—which adds considerably to the sense of fun and adventure. The roster of groups "discovered" here includes Oasis. You'll usually hear three different bands a night. The Monarch, 49 Chalk Farm Rd., NW1 8AN. ℭ **020/7482-4884**. Cover £7–£11 ($11.90–$18.70). Nightly 7pm–2 or 3am, with most musical acts beginning at 8.15pm. Tube: Northern Line to Camden Town or Chalk Farm Station.

The Rock Garden A long-established performance site, The Rock Garden maintains a bar and a stage in the cellar, and a restaurant on the street level. The cellar, known as The Venue, has hosted such acts as Dire Straits, Police, and U2 before their rise to stardom. Today, bands vary widely, from promising up-and-comers to some who'll never be heard from again. These groups appeal to a young crowd from 18 to 35. Simple American-style fare is served in the restaurant. 6–7 The Piazza, Covent Garden, WC2. ✆ **020/7240-3961.** Cover £3–£12 ($4.50–$18); diners enter free. Mon–Thurs 5pm–3am; Fri and Sat 5pm–5am; Sat 5pm–4am; Sun 7pm–midnight. Bus: Any of the night buses that depart from Trafalgar Sq. Tube: Covent Garden.

Shepherd's Bush Empire In an old BBC television theater with great acoustics, this is a major venue for big-name pop and rock stars. Announcements appear in the local press. There's a capacity seating of 2,000, mostly fans in their 20s. The box office is open Monday to Friday 10am to 6pm and Saturday from noon to 6pm. Shepherd's Bush Green, W12. ✆ **020/7771-2000.** Ticket prices vary according to show. Tube: Hammersmith & City Line to Shepherd's Bush or Goldhawk Rd.

JAZZ

100 Club Although less plush and expensive than some jazz clubs, 100 Club is a serious contender. Its cavalcade of bands includes the best British jazz musicians and some of their Yankee brethren. Rock, R&B, and blues are also on tap. Serious devotees of jazz from 20 to 45 show up here. 100 Oxford St., W1. ✆ **020/7636-0933.** Cover Fri £10 ($15), Sat £12 ($18), Sun £8 ($12). Club members get a £1 discount on Sat nights. Mon–Thurs 7:30pm–11:30pm; Fri noon–3pm and 8:30pm–2am; Sat 7:30pm–1am; Sun 7:30–11:30pm. Tube: Tottenham Court Rd. or Oxford Circus.

Ronnie Scott's Club Inquire about jazz in London and people think of Ronnie Scott's, the European vanguard for modern jazz. Only the best English and American combos, often fronted by a top-notch vocalist, are booked here. The programs make for an entire evening of cool jazz. In the heart of Soho, Ronnie Scott's is a 10-minute walk from Piccadilly Circus along Shaftesbury Avenue. In the Main Room, you can watch the show from the bar or sit at a table, from which you can order dinner. The Downstairs Bar is more intimate; among the regulars at your elbow may be some of the world's most talented musicians. This place is so well known that all visiting musicians, along with diehard local music fans, show up here—perhaps even Mick Jagger. On weekends, the separate Upstairs Room has a disco called Club Latino. 47 Frith St., W1.

ℂ **020/7439-0747.** Cover £15–£20 ($22.50–$30) for non-members, £5 ($7.50) for members. Mon–Sat 8:30pm–3am. Tube: Leicester Sq. or Piccadilly Circus.

Vortex Jazz Bar   A bit out of the way, the Vortex is worth the trek, as it books an array of jazz legends as well as new talents. The 20s and 30s crowd drawn here is both cheerful and mellow. Music begins at 9:30pm. 139–141 Stoke Newington Church St., N16. ℂ **020/7254-6516.** Cover £3–£10 ($4.50–$15). Mon–Thurs 10am–11:30pm; Fri–Sat 10am–midnight; Sun 11am–11pm. British Rail: Stoke Newington.

DANCE & ECLECTIC

Nearly all the clubs below cater to a crowd in its 20s or early 30s, with an almost equal mixture of locals and visitors. These clubs hit their groove around 1 to 2am.

Camden Palace   Housed in a former theater built around 1910, Camden Palace draws an over-18 crowd that flocks here in trendy downtown costumes. Energy levels vary according to the night of the week, as does the music, so call in advance to see if that evening's musical program appeals. A live band performs only on Tuesday. There's a restaurant if you get the munchies. 1A Camden High St., NW1. ℂ **020/7387-0428.** Cover varies, but averages Tues £5 ($7.50), Fri–Sat £12–£20 ($18–$30). Tues 10pm–2am; Fri approximately 10pm–6am; Sat approximately 10pm–8am. Tube: Northern Line to Mornington Crescent or Camden Town.

The Cross   In the backwaters of Kings Cross, this club has been hot since 1993. Hipsters come here for private parties thrown by Rough Trade Records or Red Or Dead, or to dance in the space's cozy brick-lined vaults. Call to find out who's performing. The Arches, Kings Cross Goods Yard, York Way, N1. ℂ **020/7837-0828.** Cover £8–£15 ($12–$22.50). Fri and Sat 10pm–6am. Tube: Kings Cross.

Equinox   Built in 1992 on the site of the London Empire, a dance emporium that has witnessed the changing styles of social dancing since the 1700s, the Equinox has established itself as a perennial. It contains nine bars, the largest dance floor in London, and a restaurant modeled after a 1950s American diner. With the exception of rave, virtually every kind of dance music is featured, including dance hall, pop, rock, and Latin. The setting is illuminated with one of Europe's largest lighting rigs, and the crowd is as varied as London itself. Summer visitors can enjoy their theme nights, which are geared to entertaining a worldwide audience. Leicester Sq., WC2. ℂ **020/7437-1446.** Cover £2–£12 ($3–$18) depending on the night of the week. Mon–Thurs 9pm–3am; Fri–Sat 9pm–4am. Tube: Leicester Sq.

Hanover Grand Thursdays are funky and down-and-dirty. Fridays and Saturdays the crowd dresses up in their disco finery, clingy and formfitting or politicized and punk. Dance floors are always crowded, and masses seem to surge back and forth between the two levels. Age and gender is sometimes hard to make out at this cutting-edge club. 6 Hanover St., W1. ℡ 020/7499-7977. Cover £5–£15 ($7.50–$22.50). Tues–Sat 7:30–10pm; Wed 11pm–3:30am; Thurs 11pm–5am; Fri 11pm–4am; and Sat 11pm–4:30am. Tube: Oxford Circus.

Hippodrome Near Leicester Square, the Hippodrome is London's granddaddy of discos, a cavernous place with a great sound system and lights to match. It was Lady Di's favorite in her barhopping days. Tacky and touristy, it's packed on weekends. Corner of Cranbourn St. and Charing Cross Rd., WC2. ℡ 020/7437-4311. Cover £3–£12 ($4.50–$18). Mon–Fri 9pm–3am; Sat 9pm–3:30am. Tube: Leicester Sq.

Limelight Although it opened in 1985, this dance club—located in a former Welsh chapel dating from 1754—has only recently come into its own. The dance floors and bars share space with cool Gothic nooks and crannies. DJs spin the latest house music. 136 Shaftesbury Ave., W1. ℡ 020/7434-0572. Cover £2–£12 ($3–$18). Mon–Thurs 10pm–3am; Fri–Sat 9pm–3:30am. Tube: Leicester Sq.

The Office An eclectic club with a bureaucratic name, one of The Office's most popular nights is Wednesday's "Double Six Club," featuring easy listening and board games from 6pm to 2am. Other nights are more traditional recorded pop, rock, soul, and disco. Ambience wins out over decor. 3–5 Rathbone Place, W1. ℡ 020/7636-1598. Cover £3–£9 ($4.50–$13.50). Mon–Tues noon–11:30pm; Wed–Fri noon–3am; Sat 9:30pm–3am. Tube: Tottenham Court Rd.

Subterania Affordable, unpretentious, and informal, this club changes according to the style of the band performing. Call ahead. The place has a street-level dance floor and a mezzanine-style bar upstairs. The decor is orange, purple, and blue; there are also sofas covered in faux leopard skin. More or less constant is the Friday music card of soul, funk, hip-hop, and swing, and Saturday's house music. Other nights, it's potluck. 12 Acklam Rd., W10. ℡ 020/8960-4590. Cover £5–£10 ($7.50–$15) Mon, Tues, and Thurs 8pm–2am; Wed 9:30pm–2am; Fri–Sat 9:30pm–3am. Tube: Hammersmith & City Line to Ladbroke Grove.

Zoo Bar The owners spent millions outfitting this club in the flashiest and most psychedelic decor in London. If you're looking for a true Euro nightlife experience, replete with gorgeous *au pairs* and trendy Europeans, this is it. Zoo Bar upstairs is a menagerie of mosaic animals beneath a glassed-in ceiling dome. Downstairs, the music is intrusive enough to make conversation futile. Clients range from 18 to 35; androgyny is the look of choice. 13–18 Bear St., WC2. ✆ 020/7839-4188. Cover £4 ($6) after 11pm (Fri and Sat after 9pm). Mon–Sat 4pm–3:30am; Sun 4–10:30pm. Tube: Leicester Sq.

LATIN

Cuba   This Spanish/Cuban bar-restaurant, which has a music club downstairs, features live acts from Cuba, Brazil, Spain, and the rest of Latin America. The crowd is equal parts restaurant diners, after-work drinkers, and dancers. Salsa classes are offered Monday, Tuesday, and Wednesday at 8pm. Classes cost £5 ($7.50). Happy hour is Monday to Saturday noon to 8:30pm. 11 Kensington High St., W8. ✆ 020/7938-4137. Cover £3–£8 ($4.50–$12). Mon–Sat noon–3am; Sun 2–10:30pm. Tube: High St. Kensington.

BLUES

Ain't Nothing But Blues Bar   The club, which bills itself as the only true blues venue in town, features local acts and occasional touring American bands. On weekends prepare to queue. From the Oxford Circus Tube stop, walk south on Regent Street, turn left on Great Marlborough Street, and then make a quick right on Kingly Street. 20 Kingly St., W1. ✆ 020/7287-0514. Cover Fri £3–£5 ($4.50–$7.50); Sat £3–£5 ($4.50–$7.50) free before 9:30pm. Mon–Thurs 6pm–1am; Fri–Sat 6pm–3am; Sun 7:30pm–1am. Tube: Oxford Circus or Piccadilly Circus.

FOLK

Cecil Sharpe House   CSH was the focal point of the folk revival in the 1960s, and it continues to treasure and nurture the style. Here you'll find a whole range of traditional English music and dance. Call to see what's happening. 2 Regent's Park Rd., NW1. ✆ 020/ 7485-2206. Tickets £5–£8 ($5.50–$12). Box office Tues–Fri 9:30am–5:30pm. Tube: Northern Line to Camden Town.

4 Cocktail Bars

Beach Blanket Babylon   Go here if you're looking for a hot singles bar that attracts a crowd in their 20s and 30s. This Portobello joint is very cruisy. The decor is a bit wacky, no doubt designed by an aspiring Salvador Dali, who decided to make it a fairytale grotto (or perhaps a medieval dungeon?). It's close to the Portobello Market. Saturday and Sunday nights are the hot times for bacchanalian revelry. 45 Ledbury Rd., W11. ✆ 020/7229-2907. Tube: Notting Hill Gate.

Fun Fact Members Only: Gambling in London

Long before Monte Carlo, when Las Vegas was a lifeless desert, London was a gambler's town. However, Queen Victoria's reign squelched games of chance to such an extent that no bartender dared to keep a dice cup on the counter. Only in 1960, did gambling return in gaming clubs.

In the West End there are at least 25 gambling clubs, with many more throughout London. Under British law, casinos may not advertise. Hence, if you wish to gamble away your beer money, your best bet is to ask a knowledgeable concierge. You'll be required to become a member and wait 24 hours before you can play at the tables. Games are cash-only and commonly include roulette, blackjack, *Punto Banco,* and baccarat.

Men must wear jackets and ties in all the establishments below; hours for each club are from 2pm to 4am daily.

Some of the popular clubs include **Crockford's,** a 150-year-old club with a large international clientele, located at 30 Curzon St., W1 (© **020/7493-7771;** Tube: Green Park), which offers American roulette, Punto Banco, and blackjack. Another favorite is the **Golden Nugget,** 22–32 Shaftesbury Ave., W1 (© **020/7439-0099;** Tube: Piccadilly Circus), where gamblers play blackjack, *Punto Banco,* and roulette. **Sportsman Casino,** 40 Bryanston St., W1 (© **020/ 7414-0061;** Tube: Tottenham Court Road), features a dice table, American roulette, blackjack, and *Punto Banco.*

The Dorchester Bar   This sophisticated, modern bar is on the lobby level, and you'll find an international clientele, confident of its good taste and privilege. The bartender knows his stuff. The bar serves Italian snacks, lunch, and dinner. A pianist performs every evening after 7pm. In the Dorchester, Park Lane, W1. © 020/7629-8888. Tube: Hyde Park Corner, Marble Arch, or Green Park.

Downstairs at the Phoenix   What's something so old it's new again? This is where Laurence Olivier made his stage debut in 1930, although he couldn't stop giggling even though the play was drama. Live music is featured, but it's the hearty welcome, the good beer, and friendly patrons that make this rediscovered theater bar worth a detour. 1 Phoenix St., WC2. © 020/7836-1077. Tube: Tottencourt Court Rd.

The Latest Rumours   This has emerged as the number one wine bar in the Covent Garden area. Whether it's a Bloody Mary you seek, perhaps a plate of English cuisine, or a reasonably priced bottle of wine, this is one of the most fun joints in town, serving a wide range of drinks, coffees, champagnes, and wines. 33–35 Wellington St., WC2. ✆ 020/7836-0038. Tube: Covent Garden.

Lillie Langtry Bar   Next door to Langtry's Restaurant, this 1920s-style bar epitomizes the elegance of the Edwardian era. Lillie Langtry, the 19th century actress and beauty (and mistress of Edward VII), once lived here. Oscar Wilde—arrested in this bar—is honored on the drinks menu by his favorite libation, the Hock and Seltzer. The Cadogan Cooler seems to be the most popular drink here. An international menu is served in the adjoining restaurant. In the Cadogan Hotel, 75 Sloane St., SW1. ✆ 020/7235-7141. Tube: Sloane Sq. or Knightsbridge.

The Met Bar   Very much the place to be seen, this has become the hottest bar in London. Mix with the elite of the fashion, TV, and the music world. A lot of American celebrities have been seen sipping on a martini, from Demi Moore to Courtney Cox. Despite the caliber of the clientele, the bar has managed to maintain a relaxed and unpretentious atmosphere. In the Metropolitan Hotel, 10 Old Park Lane, W1. ✆ 020/7447-1000. Members only and hotel guests. Tube: Hyde Park Corner.

5 The Gay & Lesbian Scene

The most reliable source of information on gay clubs and activities is the **Lesbian and Gay Switchboard** (✆ 020/7837-7324). The staff runs a 24-hour service for information on gay-friendly places and activities. *Time Out* also carries listings on such clubs.

Admiral Duncan   Gay men and their friends go here to drink and to have a good time and to make a political statement. British tabloids shocked the world in 1999 when they reported this pub had been bombed, with three people dying in the attack. Within six weeks, the pub reopened its doors. We're happy to report it's back in business and better than ever, even attracting non-gays who show up to show their support. 54 Old Compton St., W1. ✆ 020/7437-5300. Tube: Piccadilly Circus.

The Box   Adjacent to one of Covent Garden's best-known junctions, Seven Dials, this Mediterranean-style bar attracts more lesbians than many competitors. In the afternoon, it is primarily a restaurant, serving meal-size salads, club sandwiches, and soups. Food service ends at 5:30pm, after which the place reveals its core: a popular place of rendezvous for London's gay and countercultural crowds. The Box considers itself a "summer bar," throwing open doors and windows to a cluster of outdoor tables that attracts a crowd at the slightest hint of sunshine. 32–34 Monmouth St. (at Seven Dials), WC2. © 020/7240-5828. No cover. Mon–Sat 11am–11pm; Sun 6:30–10:30pm (cafe Mon–Sat 11am–5:30pm, Sun noon–6:30pm). Tube: Leicester Sq.

Candy Bar   This is the most popular lesbian bar in London at the moment. It has an extremely mixed clientele from butch to femme and from young to old. There is a bar and a club downstairs. Design is simple, with bright colors and lots of mirrors upstairs and darker and more flirtatious downstairs. Men are welcome as long as a woman escorts them. 23–24 Bateman St., W1. © 020/7494-4041. Cover £2–£5 ($3–$7.50). Club hours Mon–Thurs 8pm–midnight; Fri–Sat 8pm–2am; Sun 7–11pm. Tube: Tottenham Court Rd.

The Edge   Few bars in London can rival the tolerance, humor, and sexual sophistication found here. The first two floors are done up with accessories that, like an English garden, change with the seasons. Dance music can be found on the high-energy and crowded lower floors, while the upper floors are best if you're looking for conversation. Three menus are featured: a funky daytime menu, a cafe menu, and a late-night menu. Dancers hit the floors around 7:30pm. Clientele ranges from the flamboyantly gay to hetero pubcrawlers out for a night of slumming. 11 Soho Sq., W1. © 020/7439-1313. No cover. Mon–Sat 11am–1am; Sun noon–10:30pm. Tube: Tottenham Court Rd.

First Out   First Out prides itself on being London's first (est. 1986) all-gay coffee shop. Set in a 19th-century building whose wood panels have been painted the colors of the gay liberation rainbow, the bar is not particularly cruisy, and offers an exclusively vegetarian menu. Cappuccino and whiskey are the preferred libations; curry dishes, potted pies in phyllo pastries, and salads are the foods of choice. Don't expect a raucous atmosphere—some clients come here with their grandmothers. Look for the bulletin board with leaflets and business cards of gay and gay-friendly entrepreneurs. 52 St. Giles High St., W1. © 020/7240-8042. No cover. Mon–Sat 10am–11pm; Sun 11am–10:30pm. Tube: Tottenham Court Rd.

Heaven   This club, in the vaulted cellars of Charing Cross Railway Station, is a London landmark. Heaven is one of the biggest and best-established gay venues in Britain. Painted black and reminiscent of an air-raid shelter, the club is divided into at least four areas, connected by a labyrinth of catwalk stairs and hallways. Each has a different activity going on. Heaven also has theme nights, which are frequented at different times by gays, lesbians, or a mostly heterosexual crowd. Thursday, in particular, seems open to anything, but on Saturday it's gay only. Call before you go. The Arches, Villiers and Craven sts., WC2. © 020/7930-2020. Cover £5–£12 ($7.50–$18). Mon, Wed 10:30pm–3am; Fri 10:30pm–6am; Sat 10:30pm–5am. Tube: Charing Cross or Embankment.

Royal Vauxhall Tavern   Originally an 1880s vaudeville pub frequented by London's East End working class, this place has long been a bastion of campy humor and wit. It has been a gay pub since the end of World War II. The tavern received a jolt of fame when, as legend has it, Queen Elizabeth's ceremonial carriage broke down, and the monarch stopped in for a cup of tea. Since then, "Royal" has been gleefully affixed to the name, no doubt suiting the regular queens here. Charington, one of the largest breweries in England, recently acquired this unabashedly gay pub.

Shaped like an amphitheater, the bar has a large stage area and gay themes on weekends. Friday nights are for women only. Saturday is camp night, when the pub overflows with gay men fawning over their favorite cabaret acts. 372 Kennington Lane, SE11. © 020/7737-4043. Cover Thurs–Sun £2–£4 ($3–$6). Thurs–Sat 9pm–2am; Sun 2pm–midnight. Tube: Victoria Line to Vauxhall.

Index

See also Accommodations and Restaurants indexes, below.

ACCOMMODATIONS